Money for Mayhem

MONEY FOR MAYHEM

*Mercenaries, Private Military Companies,
Drones, and the Future of War*

ALESSANDRO ARDUINO

ROWMAN & LITTLEFIELD
Lanham • Boulder • New York • London

Published by Rowman & Littlefield
An imprint of The Rowman & Littlefield Publishing Group, Inc.
4501 Forbes Boulevard, Suite 200, Lanham, Maryland 20706
www.rowman.com

86-90 Paul Street, London EC2A 4NE

British Library Cataloguing in Publication Information available

Library of Congress Cataloging-in-Publication Data available
Names: Arduino, Alessandro, author.
Title: Money for mayhem : mercenaries, private military companies, drones, and the future of war / Alessandro Arduino.
Description: Lanham : Rowman & Littlefield, [2023] | Includes bibliographical references and index.
Identifiers: LCCN 2023014846 (print) | LCCN 2023014847 (ebook) | ISBN 9781538170311 (cloth) | ISBN 9781538170328 (epub)
Subjects: LCSH: Mercenary troops. | Private military companies. | Military art and science—History—21st century.
Classification: LCC UB148 .A73 2023 (print) | LCC UB148 (ebook) | DDC 355.3/54—dc23/eng/20230703
LC record available at https://lccn.loc.gov/2023014846
LC ebook record available at https://lccn.loc.gov/2023014847

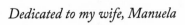

Dedicated to my wife, Manuela

BELLUM SE IPSUM ALET

CONTENTS

FOREWORD

WHEN I WROTE *THE MODERN MERCENARY: PRIVATE ARMIES AND WHAT They Mean for World Order* a decade ago, many thought it hyperbolic bordering on delusional. Not so today. The reemergence of mercenaries and private security actors is a widely accepted phenomenon. It grows each year, and many are worried where it will lead. Alessandro Arduino tells us and picks up the investigation where I left off, explaining the who, what, where, and why of this disturbing trend. As he says, the competition for the monopoly of the state over the use of violence is here, and states are increasingly outsourcing the use of force rather than regulating it. Arduino shows us through extensive field research, explains why it is happening, and highlights implications for the future. Many will find it disturbing, but ignorance is worse.

The privatization of war is returning to international relations in ways people a generation ago thought impossible. Private military contractors are commonly found in conflict zones around the world, and many outclass local militaries and law enforcement. No one truly knows how many billions of dollars slosh around this illicit market. All we know is that business is booming. Today, you can rent former U.S. Special Operations Forces troops, armed drones, and Cybermercs. Since my book, their ranks have swelled, and, as Arduino explains, their operations have grown more brazen: Colombian mercenaries assassinated the president of Haiti, and the world still does not know why. Russia launched expeditionary military operations into Africa and the Middle East for the first time since the 1980s, and their weapon of choice is the Wagner Group. American mercenaries extracted Carlos Ghosn, the disgraced chairman and CEO of Nissan, from house arrest in Tokyo and smuggled him into Beirut, where he remains free. Libya has endured mercenary-on-mercenary combat akin to the European Middle Ages. Private military actors scour war zones in Yemen, Syria, Ukraine, Nagorno-Karabakh, Venezuela, Nigeria, Iraq, Mozambique, Afghanistan, Somalia, Mali, and the Congo region. Arduino takes us on a tour, revealing what they are doing.

Arduino is the world's best expert on China's emerging private security industry. China has the largest domestic private security force in the world, and for years international observers have speculated what might happen should Beijing outsource this firepower. The challenge is that experts who understand the private military industry do not comprehend the complex puzzle of Chinese national security. Arduino does, making him a uniquely important voice, especially as China emerges as a global power. Arduino has lived, studied, and worked in China for twenty-five years. We are lucky to have his singular analyses.

Arduino also shows how privatizing war changes warfare in dangerous ways. The rise of mercenaries is producing a new kind of threat—private war—that threatens to wreak havoc around the globe. It is literally the marketization of war, where military force is bought and sold like any other commodity. It is an ancient form of armed conflict that modern militaries have forgotten how to fight. Should the trend continue, then random billionaires can swipe checks to start, elongate, or end wars. The superrich can become superpowers, and there could be wars without states. This prospect has the potential to upend international relations as we know it, and not enough scholars are thinking about it.

Private security companies and mercenaries are here to stay. Those who think the industry can be safely ignored, regulated, or categorically banned are too late. Even if the world had decent antimercenary laws, who would go into Ukraine and arrest the Wagner Group? The United Nations? NATO? No one. Also, mercenaries can shoot law enforcement dead and literally resist arrest, meaning the private military trend will continue to grow, especially because states are major consumers of their services.

Private security proliferation is generating a mercenary arms race in some corners of the world. As the market for force expands, security becomes a necessary investment and fuels the marketplace in a self-feeding loop. Arduino's field research shows us the new consumers and private security providers. Expect future conflict markets in the usual global hot spots. Generally, it's at the intersection of natural resources, unconstrained political rivalries, monied actors, and weak rule of law. However, introducing an industry vested in conflict into the most conflict-prone places is concerning because it exacerbates war and misery. This is the curse of private warfare; mercenaries do not like to work themselves out of a job. The fourteenth-century Italian writer Franco Sacchetti explains:

> *Two Franciscan monks encounter a mercenary captain near his fortress.*
> *"May God grant you peace," the monks say, their standard greeting.*
> *"And may God take away your alms," replied the mercenary.*
> *Shocked by such insolence, the monks demand explanation.*
> *"Don't you know that I live by war," said the mercenary, "and peace would destroy me? And as I live by war, so you live by alms."*
> *"And so," Sacchetti adds, "he managed his affairs so well that there was little peace in Italy in his times."**

The solution is not ignorance but awareness, and Arduino aptly provides this service. We cannot solve a problem we do not know exists, and not enough people comprehend that the private military world is more dangerous than they assume. But it would be wrong to think of private security organizations as strictly malevolent; they are market actors, not evil ones. The market for force is like fire: it can power a steam engine or burn down the house. The key is knowing what to do with the match. Arduino helps guide the hand.

Sean McFate, PhD
Washington, DC
2023

---

* Franco Sacchetti, *Il Trecentonovelle*, Novella CLXXXI (Torino: Einaudi, 1970), 528–29. For more on this period, see William Caferro, *John Hawkwood: An English Mercenary in Fourteenth-Century Italy* (The Johns Hopkins University Press, 2006).

Chapter One

Private Armies

Introduction

Today's rules-based international order evolved from a world that few would recognize. There were no defined borders, right derived from might, the divine right of kings prevailed, invasions and massacres were justified by religion, and standing armies were small and rare.

With few exceptions, battles were waged by professional combatants who were paid for their services. It was the Age of the Mercenary.

Mercenaries have a long history, appearing in the earliest days of recorded history. A mercenary, also known as a "free lance," a soldier of fortune, or a hired gun, is a private individual, often a soldier, who participates in a military conflict for personal gain. Mercenaries, who are not a part of a nation-state's military, fight for money or other forms of compensation.

The international legal framework on mercenary activities reflects the specific historical context in which it was developed.[1] The term "mercenary" is defined in article 47 of Additional Protocol I to the Geneva Conventions of 1949 as someone who (a) is specially recruited in order to fight in an armed conflict; (b) takes part directly in the hostilities; (c) is promised material compensation in excess of paid combatants in the armed forces of that party; (d) is not a foreign national to the party for whom they fight; (e) is not a member of the armed forces of a party to the conflict; (f) and is not sent by another state on official duty of its armed forces. Subsequently the 1989 UN International Convention against the Recruitment, Use, Financing and Training of Mercenaries[2] addressed the prohibitions on mercenaries but no specific body at the international level is tasked to monitor, oversee, and guide the implementation of the convention. Since the 1960s, the UN General Assembly has passed more than one hundred resolutions criticizing mercenaries.[3] In this respect, the UN definition of "mercenary" in international law has been subject to an increasing scrutiny and debate considering its prescriptive nature. At the regional level, only the Organization of African Unity Convention for the elimination of mercenarism in Africa[4] addresses the "crime of mercenarism."[5]

The continuous evolution of mercenary-related activities that seldom overlap with the private military and security sectors is now crossing the border into cyberspace. Also, according to the Working Group on the Use of Mercenaries as a Means of Violating Human Rights and Impeding the Exercise of the Right of Peoples to Self-Determination ("Working Group on the Use of Mercenaries"), the term *private military and security companies* encompassed corporate entities providing, on a compensatory basis, military and/or security services by physical persons and/or legal entities. Private security companies (PSCs) and private military companies (PMCs) operate in conflict and peacetime situations and are significant providers of military and security products.[6]

The purpose of this book is to examine the changing nature of the privatization of the monopoly on violence outside principles and national regulations proposed by Western governments, with a particular focus on the role of mercenaries and private military and security companies in current armed conflict as well as into the future. Since the wars in Iraq and Afghanistan, the state privatization of its rightful monopoly on violence has been abundantly discussed. There are numerous legal implications in distinguishing between mercenaries and private military and security companies. The issues of PMCs augmenting regular armies' capabilities via training, weapons platform maintenance, and even kinetic action, and PSCs' passive stance guarding infrastructure and people against criminal or terrorist attacks both seemed like settled areas. However, a new breed of mercenaries, quasi-PMCs acting as a state proxy and PSCs rooted in nonmarket economies, just reshuffled the cards in the deck. Chinese private security companies operating in a socialist market, Russian mercenaries spreading from the Middle East to Ukraine, and

Turkish Islamist private military trainers raise compelling questions on the future of the privatization of force.

Included in this analysis is the maturation of unmanned aerial vehicles (UAVs)—drones—that are increasingly a fundamental element of armed forces around the world. Two key elements of this analysis are, first, the degree to which off-the-shelf UAVs are easily weaponized, and second, the structure of the market for UAVs, with particular attention on new market entrants.

Before shifting to the present, it is important to understand the background to today's privatization of the security environment.

In 1648, the roots of the contemporary international order were created by the Peace of Westphalia. For the first time in history, the concept of the "nation-state" became a reality. Borders, passports, sovereignty, and the recognition of a nation's right to its own "internal affairs" formed the foundation of the manner in which nation-states interact with one another to this day.

The concept of the sovereign nation-state spread around the world, but in different ways.

The Berlin Conference (1884–1885), also known as the Congo Conference, chaired by German Chancellor Otto von Bismarck, consisted of thirteen European nations and the United States. The purpose was to codify the colonization of Africa. The product was a map that created fifty countries by arbitrarily drawing lines that were superimposed on more than one thousand indigenous African cultures and regions without their cooperation or representation.

Geography, tribalism, and colonialism played an essential role in the creation of national borders in South America and Asia as well.

With notable exceptions, such as both world wars in Europe, the Korean War, and the Vietnam wars with France and then the United States, armed conflict between nation-states gradually became the exception rather than the rule.

The perception that in the twenty-first century full-scale wars between sovereign nation-states had become a relic of a previous era was widespread. This perception was shattered by the U.S. invasions of Afghanistan and Iraq, the forty-four-day war in Nagorno-Karabakh, as well as Russia's ongoing invasion of Ukraine that began with the annexation of Crimea in 2014, and which notably expanded in 2022.

In addition, violent confrontation between nation-states is being increasingly conducted by proxy forces including nonstate actors.

Of particular interest is the expanding role of mercenaries in national and international disputes. Today's mercenaries, PMCs and PSCs, are the modern reincarnation of a tendency that has its roots in ancient history.

It is not by chance that being a sword for hire has always been called the world's second-oldest profession. The practice of hiring soldiers to secure or to participate in armed aggression has existed since the time of the *Anabasis*. In the *Anabasis*,[7] Xenophon narrates how in 401 BCE Cyrus the Younger had on the payroll a large army of Greek mercenaries that enabled him to overthrow his brother Artaxerxes II and then become emperor of Persia.

Since the dawn of time, mercenary battle groups were able not only to increase the ranks of kings' and emperors' armies but also to provide unique fighting capabilities that required full-time training. The Balearic Islands sling shooters who were contracted by Carthage to fight against Rome during the Punic Wars is a case in point. On the other side of the barricade, the Roman Empire was increasingly under pressure to guarantee a sufficient number of recruits to refill the depleted ranks in the legions. Therefore mercenaries became the quickest way to arm up, especially on the empire's *limes*, the border garrisons. Nevertheless, a short-term solution became a long-term problem, as entire tribes of barbarians were contracted as autonomous militia (*foederati*).

Moving from West to East, during the Byzantine Empire mercenaries provided assault troops. In addition, the majority of the imperial guard ranks (Varangian guard) was composed of Vikings. Another notable example is the Norman Conquest of England, where Flemish mercenaries were the tip of the spear of William the Conqueror's army. Besides the fact that from the Middle Ages mercenaries were frequently associated with the Black Plague, their proliferation grew uninterrupted to a point that during the Italian Renaissance the business of war was considered a minor art form.[8]

Later, during the fragmentation of the Italian peninsula into a multitude of fiefdoms, the *condottieri* were war chiefs who offered the skilled services of their armed men to the highest bidder. The legendary "White Company" was one of the most infamous of the so-called free companies that were "bands of for-profit soldiers who conducted the lion's share of warfare in fourteenth-century Italy. Its troops—a hodgepodge of English, German, Breton, and Hungarian adventurers—were renowned for their skill with the longbow and the lance." In an era when Italy was splintered between warring city-states and medieval lords, the men of the White Company made a killing auctioning their services off to the highest bidder. Between 1363 and 1388, they fought both for and against the Pope, the city of Milan, and the city of Florence, but they were rarely out of the field even during times of peace.[9]

Still in Europe, during the Thirty Years' War, the role of mercenaries reached its zenith also thanks to the demand for firearms specialists. During the same historical period in the Japanese Meiji era, skilled mercenaries such as the Saika Ikki played a significant role in turning battles into victories, offering their harquebuses to the highest bidder.

During the American Revolution, German mercenaries from Hesse-Kassel were to be found on both sides of the battlefield. Later, the term *Hessians* became a generic identifier for German mercenaries that came from other principalities.

Since the idea that national security should only be provided by the state with conscript national armies, the role of money for mayhem in the West started to be relegated to the shadows, but it never disappeared.

From the fifteenth to the nineteenth century, the Ottoman army employed different types of mercenaries defined by their geographical origin or by a peculiar skill ranging from artillery to engineering. Besides the immediate monetary rewards, there was also the right to pillage and plunder a defeated enemy. Mercenaries recruited inside the Ottoman Empire shared tribal affiliations such as the Azabs recruited from the same villages as cheap and expendable groups mostly used as skirmishers during the first attack wave. Other mercenaries were recruited abroad more for their combat prowess than as cannon fodder.

In contemporary China, the negative connotation of the employment of private armies is quite recent. The contempt for the employment of mercenaries can be traced back to the time of warlords from 1911 to 1930, when the power vacuum left by the fall of the Qing imperial dynasty was filled by local rulers and their private armies. The Chinese saying of the "Three Mores" characterizes this period well: More officers than soldiers, more soldiers than guns, more bandits than people.

Officially known as the American Volunteer Group, the "Flying Tigers" consisted of a group of three squadrons of fighter pilots that fought with the Chinese against the Japanese during World War II. While U.S. Army Air Corps pilots earned US$260 per month, the Flying Tiger were paid between US$600 and US$750, with a US$500 bonus for each Japanese aircraft shot down.

After World War II, during the African postcolonial wars, the role of mercenaries and private military companies reappeared with a vengeance. The South African company Executive Outcomes became the paradigm for the provision of highly trained mercenaries profiting from the civil wars in Angola and Sierra Leone. The African continent became the playing field for small but efficient mercenary groups operating advanced hardware and tactics and enabling the local governments to stay in power.

In the 1980s, the fear of mercenaries was related to the megacorporations' globalization trends. Corporations expanded their predatory economic and political influence when the role of the state was progressively in retreat in favor of a privatization of public functions. In this respect the threat posed by mercenaries was linked to the dark side of globalization with global corporations being able to hire their own private army. Nevertheless, the U.S. reliance on contractors since the Yugoslavian war provided an example to defense and security corporations for how the state can reduce its monopoly on violence but remain a strong source of income.

The return of these historical cycles is essential to understanding today's war contractors. It is also necessary to take into consideration that mercenaries are merely a symptom, not the root cause of a conflict. During the evolution of mercenaries from the Greek free lances in Persia to the modern PMC, their importance varied from place to place and time to time, but they were rarely of no significance. Therefore today, as thousands of years ago, nobody is fond of mercenaries, yet everyone has employed them.[10]

Our Business Is Killing, and Business Is Good

The post–Cold War security vacuum is characterized by increasing demand for mercenaries and private military services. The rise of China,

Russia, and Turkey is shaping the market for force, trending away from the corporate path that the United States has traced over the past two decades. The global security architecture is in flux as the United States has been scaling back its military presence, from sheriff of the world to a previous off-shore balancing role.[11] As in prior eras, mercenaries prosper in preserving mayhem and instability. In several instances from Africa to Asia, their actions are again going to be pivotal, igniting conflicts and thus extending their incomes.

Today, the way war is waged is inchoate. Hybrid conflicts from Libya to Syria or from Yemen to the Caucasus are an indication of what is to come. They are a window into the world of heavily armed mercenaries, private intelligence companies that employ skilled hackers, and weaponized UAVs that cannot be seen or detected because they lurk in the shadows but are already present. So-called gray zone activities that fall short of open conflict, from explosive-laden drone incursions to cyberattacks, are supplanting the notion of clashes between large military forces in days of yore, or just provide a convenient *casus belli* if a nation wants to start a war. This trend is summarized in a military patch in the Russian language seized in 2021 during a Belarus police raid against Russian mercenaries: "Our business is killing, and business is good."[12]

Nation-states are outsourcing their monopoly of violence for different reasons: being efficient and economical in the West, to raise necessary manpower in the Persian Gulf States, to protect foreign investments for China, or to hide military forces in plain sight, as in the case of Russia and Turkey. Since Operation Iraqi Freedom in 2003, when the U.S. Army erased Saddam Hussein's Republican Guard divisions from the Iraqi map in a matter of days, China and Russia realized that they had no chance in the event of a direct confrontation with the United States.[13] Therefore both Beijing and Moscow started to develop the ability to deploy a concealed use of force. In this respect, private military contractors and private security companies swiftly have become a decisive component in plausible deniability operations. A conventionally armed private military company, being economic and flexible, is a suitable tool in today's complex and fast-changing global security scenario. Also, Turkey's saber rattling on the global stage featured mercenaries and private military contractors as a core element of Ankara's foreign policy, together with unmanned combat aerial vehicles (UCAVs). An important component in the Chinese, Russian, and Turkish employment of private contractors is motivation compelled by remuneration. Unlike Iran's use of other nonstate actors as proxies, private military and security companies (PMSCs) do not have a politically motivated agenda because money comes first. Compared to Tehran's network of influence that includes nonstate paramilitary actors from Lebanon to Yemen, the PMSCs' commercial incentive allows for closer supervision of their actions compared with ideologically driven entities.

During the past century, the private military industry, which was once dominated by the United States and the United Kingdom,[14] has now reached a real global diffusion with private companies from Kurdistan to South Africa competing for international bids to protect infrastructure or natural resources from Iraq to Libya.[15]

The rise of private military and security firms that operate out of sight, waging wars on behalf of or over the assets of national governments, is already here. The rules of the game have changed, but it is barely noticeable. While the West is still observing conventional warfare doctrines, China, Russia, and Turkey are rewriting the rules of the game by focusing not only on their own strengths but mostly on the perceived weakness of the United States. Nevertheless, shifting from covert operations to a conventional war in Ukraine did not result in the expected outcomes for the Kremlin. The Ukrainian conflict increased the potential for direct confrontation between Russia and NATO, setting the alliance on high alert and giving it a new lease on life. However, mercenaries come to the fore, even in the conventional war between Moscow and Kyiv. Since the early days of the conflict, the threat from the Russian quasi-PMC Wagner Group and Syrian mercenaries willing to fight for Moscow in Ukraine have been used by both sides to muddy the water in the blogosphere.

Unsurprisingly, the global rush for private military companies is rooted in the U.S. outsourcing of what was formerly the state's monopoly on violence.[16] The modern playbook used by China, Russia, and Turkey in the privatization of the security function was written by U.S. contractors during the Iraqi and Afghan conflicts.

Blackwater, the U.S. private military outfit founded by Erik Prince, opened a Pandora's box of modern private warfare.[17] Following the Iraq and Afghan conflicts, the role and the scope of armed contractors have been on the rise. China and Russia are increasing their stake in the game, but they don't play by the rules written in the West. Turkey, a latecomer in the PMCs' sector, is quickly catching up thanks to the combined expansion of its global market share for combat UAVs.[18]

Nevertheless, labeling a Russian quasi-PMC such as the Wagner Group as a "private" company, or a Chinese private security firm that is embedded in a "market economy with Chinese characteristics," is not only confusing, it also casts a negative perception on the entire international stability operation and private security sector. Following the privatization of military functions in Iraq, the private market for force has expanded at a staggering speed. Nevertheless, applying the same label to Russian and Turkish private military companies and even Chinese private security companies is misleading.

Russian contractors from the infamous Wagner Group are good examples of Vladimir Putin's application of Makarov's hybrid warfare doctrine:[19] military and political objectives are achieved with impunity, and nobody is held accountable. Crimea is a case in point. Similarly, Russia and Turkey, in their quest for a return to great power status, utilize PMCs as a cheap tool to achieve their geopolitical ambitions. At the same time, having "private companies" operating abroad allows a system of patronage to funnel cash to the complacent military and government officials' informal elite.[20] Russia and Turkey's return to the table will need two concurring resources: military and economic power. The first, which has been depleted in Russia during the invasion of Ukraine but is on the rise in Turkey, and the second are lacking in both countries. With the Ruble and Turkish Lira in a free fall, Moscow and Ankara are set to increase their use of PMCs as a flexible and inexpensive tool of coercion.

In contrast, China, which is an economic juggernaut with vast but not infinite financial resources, lacks power projection capabilities. Despite the fact that the People's Liberation Army has undergone significant reforms, after President Xi strengthened his grip on power in 2013,[21] China planned to count on a vibrant economy that survived the impact of COVID-19. However, reality had other plans. China lacks battle-tested soldiers.

At the same time, in China as well as in Russia and Turkey, it is a daunting task to map where the private sector starts and the state ends.

While Moscow's and Ankara's PMCs are the tip of the spear of state-sponsored undercover military action, Beijing's private security firms address a security gap in the Chinese global economic expansion spearheaded by the Belt and Road Initiative (BRI). Over the past decade, the United States and Europe have been focused on the benefits of integrating China into the market economy, complacent in the illusion that China "wants to be like us."[22] A similar reasoning was applied to the private security sector, albeit with "Chinese characteristics."[23] It was just a matter of time before they would play by the rules written in the West or even be a small appendix of European and American companies bidding for lucrative security contracts on the New Silk Road. Reality is a cruel mistress as Beijing is choosing its own development path, including PSCs.

Protection and security in the BRI is entrusted to a handful of top Chinese private security firms, among the ten thousand that populate the Chinese internal security market, composed of more than three million operators. Since the end of the Trump administration, the mistrust between Washington and Beijing has led the Chinese state-owned enterprises (SOEs) that operate in the BRI to increasingly rely on Chinese and local security providers.[24] The SOEs avoid, wherever possible, any compromising cooperation with Western security providers.

As China, Russia, and Turkey tinker with their own breed of PMSCs, the rest of the world is taking notice. The Malhama Tactical Group, a "Blackwater of Jihad" outfit, is providing training for profit to Al Qaeda affiliates in Syria and Africa.[25] In this respect, jihadist groups in the Middle East and North Africa (MENA) region have developed new technologies, for example, by reengineering Chinese commercial drones to deliver explosive payloads or for reconnaissance, which have been used in other conflicts including Ukraine.

CHALLENGES IN THE FIELD AND IN CYBERSPACE TO TRACK PRIVATE MILITARY CONTRACTORS

Charting the rise of new private military contractors from Russia and Turkey, as well as Chinese private security expansion, using primary source data, in-person interviews, and field research among operations in conflict zones are daunting tasks. Nevertheless, two factors that are intrinsically related to the business dimension of the private military sector cast some light on this shadowy world.

The first is that proper PMCs and PSCs are still business-driven entities looking for clients; therefore they need to advertise their services and, in most cases, register as a legal business entity. Shell companies in complacent financial paradises can provide some anonymity, but following the money trail is still possible. The second factor is related to a contractor's digital footprint—from social media posts containing war trophies obtained during their deployment to online searches for new gigs during their idle time back home. Both factors provide a trove of information on trends, from age groups to combat skills that contractors are offering or being required to provide by a prospective client.

During the previous decade, the passive security stance taken by Chinese security firms allowed researchers to acquire timely information on their capabilities and international footprint expansion. Recently, the friction between Washington and Beijing has cast deep suspicion on non-Chinese researchers snooping around. A new security law could easily perceive legitimate academic work as foreign intelligence gathering, or even consider it to be a breach of state secrets. Similarly, Russian law is not much different. Security researchers need to register as a foreign agent or risk detention upon their arrival in Russia. At the same time, researching Russian PMCs is not only an academic challenge, but it could morph into a life-threatening task. During 2018, several dedicated Russian journalists and academicians looking at the evolution of the Russian private military sector allegedly committed suicide or ended up in prison on suspicion of high treason.[26] In another case, a documentary production team that was filming the footprint of Russia contractors in Africa was gunned down in an alleged robbery gone wrong.[27]

According to Sorcha MacLeod, a member of the UN Working Group on mercenary activities, the UN is raising awareness on the threats posed by mercenaries.[28] The working group is mandated to monitor and examine the human rights impact of mercenaries, mercenary-related activities, and private military and security companies around the world.

This research is part of what is known as the special procedures of the Human Rights Council.

At the beginning of the new millennium, the working group was established due to the growing concerns about the operations and activities of PMCs in Iraq and Afghanistan. As the role of mercenaries and private military operators evolved during the previous two decades, the scope of the working group expanded in accordance with the risk stemming from unaccountable mercenaries around the globe. At the same time the working group has a dual mandate; on one hand it is related to human rights issues associated with mercenaries' activities, and on the other hand the working group's attention is focused on private military and security companies.

Nevertheless, the constant blurring of lines among mercenaries, private military companies, and private security operators creates dangerous ambiguities and a legal gray area that is prone to abuses. The issue of definitions is very contentious. In this respect, the working group's definition of PMSCs emphasizes the broad nature of services rather than how the companies self-identify. However, as the companies are expanding their services and geographical reach, the definition itself is in constant flux. In the West, the biggest private military security companies are entangled in a complex web of corporate structures that link conglomerates with joint ventures far away from the headquarters in London or Washington. At the same time a significant amount of subcontracting and responsibilities created major issues that stand in the way of a clear-cut definition.

As part of her role with the UN working group on mercenary activities, Sorcha MacLeod was actively involved in the drafting of international standards for the security industry including a proposed UN treaty, the Montreux Document,[29] and the International Code of Conduct for Private Security Providers (ICoC).[30] She has said:

We constantly strive to differentiate between the different types of actors that are covered by our mandate. This, as you can imagine, is very problematic and challenging because different terminologies are used in the public and international domains, so, we see the references to mercenaries, private military contractors, private combatants, foreign fighters. We also see references to private security providers [and to] private military security companies. So there are a lot of different terminologies that are being used.[31]

An important outcome stemming from the working group's research is the specific allegations that concern human rights abuses and international humanitarian law (IHL) violations that are related to mercenaries and the privatization of the state monopoly on violence. For example, in the September 2022 report there is a broader look at the human rights impact of the PMSCs in a variety of different sectors, including the extractive sector, but always with an eye to looking at the wider privatization trends in relation to security.[32]

Similarly, during the Libyan conflict the chair of the UN working group on the use of mercenaries observed that the abuses carried out by mercenaries employed by both warring factions were derailing peace negotiations.[33] According to MacLeod, the ambiguity in the definitions of mercenary and private military operator could be summarized by the Russian Wagner Group, which attracts a variety of different descriptions. While it is commonly referred to as a PMC or a paramilitary group, it also fits the bill for a semistate security force. The group's operations highlight the legal ambiguities inherent in the lack of a formal incorporation. The Wagner Group's pervasive opacity and pervasive ambiguity makes it very difficult to identify applicable laws and regulations as well as to determine from a legal standpoint the real patrons of these organizations, their end game, and the related sources of funding.

Another example is related to the constant flow of reports about the alleged deployment of Russian private military personnel, possibly from the Wagner Group, in the conflict in Libya in support of one of the parties to the conflict, the Libyan National Army. There have been allegations that Wagner personnel were involved in the summary execution of a group of civilians.[34] From the working group's perspective, there are significant challenges in determining who exercised operational command, and who exercised operational control over these individuals. In fact, it is an arduous task to determine what type of compensation the boots on the ground actually received, and what sort of accountability mechanisms, if any, were in place.

In this respect, for states or other stakeholders that have to intervene in an armed conflict or in other high-risk contexts, it is not an easy task to pinpoint where private military contractors cross the opaque and ambiguous line into mercenary activities. At the same time quasi-PMCs are able to refute any involvement in a conflict and therefore avoid their obligations under international law. Therefore the legal limbo where PMCs and mercenaries operate carries significant risks not only involving human rights violations and abuses but also making it problematic to punish the perpetrators.

The challenges that are emerging in contemporary armed conflicts from the action of mercenary-related activities include not only the lack of transparency and accountability but also the fact that mercenaries thrive during conflicts and are another hurdle to overcome in the peace process. The involvement of mercenaries on both sides of the Libyan conflict and their constraint on returning the country to normalcy is a case in point.

Also in some cases, mercenary activities even led to the intensification and prolonging of conflicts, and subsequently resulted in further human rights abuses. It is not a new story as many writers in the past warned against the employment of mercenaries. Machiavelli warns in *The Prince* how treacherous and ineffective it could be to employ soldiers motivated only by the coin as the mercenaries' primary role is to avoid putting themselves at risk, and even switching sides if the tide of battle turns or the opponent pays better.

MacLeod also mentioned that in modern armed conflicts there is a multitude of actors who share some characteristics with mercenaries but do not fall squarely within the very rigid international legal definition. As previously noted, the gray area surrounding mercenarism makes it very challenging to address mercenaries' activities and to report human rights abuses or IHL implications in any sort of coherent manner. In this respect, the increased use of new technologies and development of cybercapabilities in the security domain are only going to complicate the matter. The proliferation of actors involved adds complexity to determining who's involved and to trace back who is responsible for potential human rights and IHL violations.

THE RISE OF PRIVATE ARMIES: A CALL FROM THE PAST?

The rise of private armies encompasses modern soldiers of fortune, private companies that are just a façade for government covert operations, and for-profit outfits that trade the use of force, hacked information, and remote-controlled weapons for a price.

The world is returning to a pre-Napoleonic order in which conflicts are waged by professional outfits and not exclusively by a national army. World War I and World War II are not the norm in defining warfare, but states and national armies persist in using that outdated strategic approach to plan strategies and tactics. For example, Putin's botched armored assault to seize the Ukrainian capital Kyiv in 2022 came down to misjudgments and strategic errors: armored columns moving without coordination with ground troops, scarce airpower, overstretched logistics, and low troop morale. Therefore, the Ukrainian invasion's early failure underlines once more how the use of mercenaries and "little green men" from Syria to Crimea benefitted Russia's return to the global stage instead of an outdated and inefficient return to a full-scale conflict. Even in the tank-on-tank battles in a ravaged Ukraine, there is a role for mercenaries and paramilitary forces. In this respect, the Western narrative against the Wagner Group and Syrian mercenaries is evoking the negative stereotypes related to unaccountable and brutal acts of violence that characterized the soldier of fortune for centuries. Since the first body bags of young conscripts started to arrive back in Russia, Moscow recalled how dead mercenaries and PMCs' contractors do not create social tension. While Putin's invasion of Ukraine is still bent on a World War II strategy characterized by utter disregard for the soldiers' lives, the Russian population's adversity to casualties is related to a shrinking population. Even in the populous China, the effect of the one child policy created a similar aversion to war casualties.

Today the transition to a new security architecture shares several similarities with a type of international ideologically motivated anarchy in which might makes right, but with new tools: killer drones, private intelligence outfits, rent-an-army, and cybermercenaries for hire.

Libya and Syria are a case in point. Several hundred Russian mercenaries with thousands of foreign fighters are changing the way war is fought, which severely complicates efforts to make peace. Using World War I and World War II paradigms for warfare means it is not possible to understand, mitigate, and manage a new crisis. When confronted by an enemy composed of a matrix of mercenaries who are loyal to the highest bidder, hackers conducting their dark art from dispersed but faraway locations, and explosives-laced UAV operators that you only know about after the drone strikes—who do you negotiate with?

In such a world, which is both inchoate while also becoming the norm, there will be no railcar in the Compiègne Forest or a desk on the battleship USS *Missouri* where one side can accept an adversary's capitulation. Even in the Russian invasion of Ukraine the alleged notion of forty thousand mercenaries from Syria[35] and the return of the infamous Wagner Group from the MENA region cast a darker shadow on the conflict.

These are the secretive fighting forces operating all over the globe, hiding in plain sight across some of the most dangerous and unstable regions on the planet. Private warriors are bent on protecting their clients at any cost; not for nationalistic ideologies but for the simple reason that dead clients don't pay.

While their service differentiates in price and capabilities, they all share one common trait: public deniability. Governments or corporations can rescind a contract or even claim that there was no affiliation at all. In 2018, more than a hundred Russian contractors were obliterated in Syria by U.S. artillery and gunship bombardments in a matter of minutes. Nobody raised an eyebrow.

Headquartered in high-rise offices in London, Washington, Dubai, Beijing, and St. Petersburg, the ranks of private military companies are a revolving door from the government and military sector to the lucrative private sector. Even humanitarian organizations consider them a necessary evil to protect their assets and personnel in highly complex environments.[36]

Today's Western military firms are sophisticated multinational corporations in a multibillion-dollar market. But the rise of Russian, Chinese, and Turkish private military firms is going to shift the market for force toward an unexpected direction. At this point, the new direction is unforeseen in the West.

Aside from the human component, the trends in the adoption of unmanned lethal weapons and the future of weapons that can decide autonomously to kill humans are also going to be a component of the private military sector array of services. A pay-per-use UCAV offered to the highest bidder could soon become a deadly reality. Loitering munitions, better known as suicide drones, used by Israel and the Iranian Islamic Revolutionary Guard for remote-controlled assassination are already flooding the weapons market. ISIS's reengineered made-in-China commercial drones used for propaganda operations or advanced artillery spotters complete the picture of what the world will diffusely face in less than a decade.

Evaluating the risk that the private military sector poses to increase the threshold for conflict, the threat to traditional military forces, and the corruption in political circles is essential to gain insight into the rising danger of proxy conflicts in the U.S. rivalry with China, Russia, and Turkey.

Gaining an understanding of the human and political risks that come as part of the market for force will help in differentiating the multiple actors that are too simplistically grouped together under the mercenary label. Also, monitoring today's trajectory in the deployment of contractors by states, corporations, or even terrorist organizations is going to cast some light on what it will mean for the future of warfare.

THE SECOND OLDEST PROFESSION'S HISTORICAL CYCLE

The historical cycle is back to professional soldiers being in the public eye. The employment of free lances never disappeared, it just morphed into the shadows when dying for a flag became more honorable than dying for the coin.

A historical overview of the evolution of "men of war" from Europe to Asia points at the return of mercenaries and endless wars. Since the establishment of the Westphalian order and the birth of modern national armies, the image of the free lances or the *condottieri* has been increasingly negative. As mentioned by Machiavelli, the soldier of fortune does not welcome victory or defeat as both outcomes mean the end of business. Even in today's modern warfare settings characterized by UCAVs and cyberwarfare, from a mercenary's standpoint victory is the harbinger of unemployment and defeat means death or prison time. A common accusation that still finds it raison d'être in future wars is that free lances contribute to a continuous state of insecurity, being unable to support the state's ability to retain a monopoly on the use of force and perpetual uncertainty for the sake of profit. The coup in Sierra Leone promoted by Sandline or the Wagner Group support for the military junta in Mali are a case in point.

During the Iraqi conflicts, the increasing role of private military companies (US$150 billion market) was almost flying below the public media radar, but then the Blackwater Nisour massacre happened. The media outcry generated by the killing of seventeen Iraqi civilians in Nisour Square in Baghdad by the American private military company Blackwater signaled a topical moment on the contemporary public perception of private security contractors.[37] The business model, however, is still there, only the names have been changed. Since the "Blackwater moment" in Iraq, the international media started to portray all of the private military and private security companies to the general public as "guns for hire."

Nevertheless, Blackwater's aggressive tactics in Iraq and Afghanistan have earned critique and scorn; yet, at the same time, they have been praised by the government officials and civilians they were escorting. The United States is still increasing its privatization of the state monopoly of violence. The media describe all the private security sector with the same negative terms such as *soldier of fortune, war dog, licensed to kill,* or *soldier of misfortune,* which deforms reality by creating a dangerous bias.[38] Therefore addressing the legal implications related to the definition of mercenary versus private military contractor and how international organizations contract their security in highly complex regions to the private sector is the essence.

In a nutshell, mercenaries and private military companies are changing the rules of war and peace building. Therefore the growing presence of private military contractors has generated the need for effective public and private participation and reevaluation of existing international law regarding the contractors' oversight, enforcement, and accountability, specifically in armed conflict environments. Any kind of private military outfit is set to profit from chaos and uncertainty. In this regard mercenaries and contractors are still a small cog in the machine of war, and the spread of conflict carries the promise of a prosperous war economy.

As the security requirements increase, the distinction between private security and private military services or even mercenaries gets blurred. On one side of the coin, contracting efficient private security providers is not only going to benefit the multinational companies operating in high-risk environments, but most importantly it should positively affect the local stakeholders. On the flip side, the presence of unaccountable private military and mercenary organizations is a menace for any long-awaited peace process. Several of the accusations directed at Blackwater and the like in Iraq and Afghanistan have now shifted to non-Western PMCs: igniting conflict, increased insecurity and instability, promoting corruption and unaccountability, depleting local financial resources, and hiring talents that could have served in the national armed services. In a nutshell, undermining national sovereignty.

RUSSIA AND TURKEY'S PRIVATE MILITARY RISE AND CHINA'S PRIVATE SECURITY FUNCTION

According to Sean McFate, a veteran, academic, national security strategist, and also a former private military contractor, the post–Cold War security architecture is transitioning into the "Age of Durable Disorder."[39] In McFate's analysis, the future of warfare is going through a profound transformation, and there is a return of nonstate players in waging wars including mercenaries, which some would say is the second-oldest profession.

During the previous two decades, the concept that the twentieth-century age of rule-based order is over is growing. As a matter of fact, the idea of nation-states as the center of gravity of the world order is a very recent concept, as well as fixed state borders and national armies based on conscription.

Discussing the future of warfare with McFate, he mentioned that

mercenaries never disappeared. They started to re-emerge after the Cold War and now they're back in full swing. And we're once again in a world, just like most of world history, in durable disorder with private warfare. Think of private warfare this way: it's like Clausewitz, the military theorist who is the king of conventional war like the Second World War or First World War, meets Adam Smith, the theorist of capitalist economics. And when you blend military strategy with market strategy, that's mercenary warfare. And our four stars [generals] are absolutely not ready.[40]

In this respect China, Russia, and, more recently, Turkey all well understand that the tectonic shift in the security arena requires a new and all-encompassing approach. On the other side of the wall, Western democracies starting with the United States, complacent in its own power status as sole world power, are still considering warfare in a very narrow traditional, Clausewitzian definition.

In McFate's world of durable disorder, nation-states are not going to disappear, but the global environment is changing toward multiple nonstate actors from terrorist organizations to corporations with their own agendas.

McFate's non-state-centric warfare is also echoed by Peter Singer, author of *Corporate Warriors*.[41] Singer defines private military firms as "private business entities that deliver to consumers a wide spectrum of military and security services, once generally assumed to be exclusively inside the public context."

Both views are still rooted in a 1980s vision of megacorporations being more powerful, richer, and effective than nation-states. U.S. President Eisenhower's dictum is still as relevant today as when he spoke it in his 1961 farewell address: "We must guard against the acquisition of unwarranted influence, whether sought or unsought, by the military-industrial complex. The potential for the disastrous rise of misplaced power exists, and will persist."

Since the new millennium ushered in the era of authoritarian states, the role of private military companies with an exclusive market objective has been adopted and morphed by powerful states that do not abide by democratic rules. While Beijing, Moscow, and Ankara profess to practice their own versions of democracy, the West lost its disillusionment with China "becoming one of us," Turkey's early access to the European Union, and Russia being a paper tiger having lost the Cold War.

In this respect, authoritarian states' employment of PMCs is first and foremost linked with political outcomes and secondary with a financial outcome. The difference between the previous Marxist Leninist roots professed by the Soviet Union and the People's Republic of China on security matters is that ideology has taken the back seat. At the same time, in Turkey the call for a return to Neo-Ottoman policies is a powerful historical image in support of President Erdogan's ambitions. In this respect, the image of Janissaries, the Ottoman Empire's top fighters, fits well with modern Turkey's romantic vision of private military contractors.

In effect, Beijing, Moscow, and Ankara are writing their own rules of the game. Russia is promoting PMCs that are closer to a mercenary combat unit than a corporation. China is encouraging local Chinese private security firms to fill the security gap in protecting Chinese foreign investments and personnel working abroad. Turkey is allegedly benefitting from chaos spreading from Libya and Syria to the South Caucasus to recruit and deploy desperate and unemployed Syrians willing to fight for a dime on the dollar.

The problems related to the distinction between fighting for a corporation and fighting for the state as a hired gun or as a contracted soldier of a national army has severe legal ramifications and impacts, from a state's accountability to the recruitment and deployment process. Today's market for force ranges from the centuries-old model of states contracting entire battalions to other national armies, such as today's Pakistani Baloch contractors protecting the king of Bahrain, or former special forces veterans looking at the website shooterjobs.com for a US$150,000 contract in high-risk areas. In this respect, the contemporary debate on the privatization of the state monopoly on violence includes multiple points of view. Examples include the previously mentioned UN working group that takes to the fore the atrocities committed by unaccountable heavily armed men, the International Stability Operations Association (ISOA)[42] that looks at the issue of privatizing the state monopoly of violence from a U.S. lobbyist's point of view, or the International Code of Conduct Association (ICoCA)[43] based in Geneva promoting accountable private security companies. Today, finding the proper set of laws that regulate and differentiate between mercenaries and private military contractors is increasingly a difficult task due to the transition toward a new security architecture. Nevertheless, according to Deborah Avant, a leading researcher on PMCs, "Trying to figure out what it is about them that makes us nervous is probably more important than trying to figure out what to call them."[44]

IN SEARCH OF ORDER: RULES AND REGULATIONS
Looking at an actionable definition to legally frame the difference between mercenaries and private military operators, it is possible to divide the debate into two broad categories: one camp that uses *mercenary*

as a catch-all term, and the other camp that aims to achieve precise legal definitions and categories for the different types of actors, the scope of action, and scenarios in which the private security forces operate.

In an extensive study on mercenaries and norms, Sarah Percy analyzes the moral opprobrium that surrounds the free lances, mentioning that since the mercenaries started their trade, there has been a law against mercenarism. Looking at the current Western literature on soldiers of fortune, Percy denounces that most of the focus is related to the past two centuries looking at the operational perspective without providing a proper theoretical analysis concerning international relations. "However, defining mercenary even loosely is tricky and simple because it is much harder than it at first seems to figure out exactly what separates them from regular soldier or other fighters."[45] According to Percy, two core beliefs from pre-nineteenth-century antimercenary norms are still influencing today's prescriptive definition of a mercenary: the first is that mercenaries are negative actors because they do not fight for a proper cause, and the second is the belief that mercenaries are uncontrolled, thereby undermining the role of the state as the primary holder of the monopoly of the use of force.

Simon Chesterman, a leading scholar in the field of international law applied to PMCs and artificial intelligence (AI), when asked how it is possible to regulate the outsourcing of public security services and limit the use of mercenaries, responded:

In law, definitions are, of course, important. But even more important is interrogating why one wants to define a term and what one is trying to achieve. If I can pick an alternative controversial term, the definition of "terrorist" also provides enormous grist for the mill because there are competing reasons why one is trying to define that term. In terms of a private military security company, you see a similar dynamic that the term "mercenary" was originally intended in the 1980s, at least, to try and define someone who was an illegitimate actor. And the mistake that was made, and this was in the 1989 convention on mercenaryism, was that it is defined by reference to motive—so a mercenary is defined as someone who's fighting outside traditional mil-itary forces and is motivated essentially by private interest.[46]

According to Chesterman, most laws we pay attention to look at whether something is intentional or not, but in the case of mercenaries, it seems more like an attempt to delegitimize a category of actor. The current definition of mercenarism is still anchored to a seventeenth-century attempt to define mercenaries in a negative light as national armies were becoming the norm in Europe. Today's definition is still bent on delegitimizing a category of actor on the basis of their motivation, looking at the negative experience stemming from the postcolonial wars in Africa, as mercenaries facilitated the overthrow of governments on the continent or contested the self-determination movements by means of violence.

In Chesterman's words:

Geoffrey Best, I think, was the military historian who said anyone who was convicted of being a mercenary under that very limited definition should be shot, and then their lawyer should be shot as well because it's such a ridiculous definition, it should be easy for a lawyer to disprove.[47]

However, the legal outcomes and call for transparency that the U.S. military outsourcing generated during the conflicts in Iraq and Afghanistan are a positive step forward in surpassing the self-imposed limitation set in the 1980s. Nevertheless, the shift from a Western-led market for private military and security toward a market with Russian, Turkish, and Chinese characteristics is only going to complicate the matter.

At least in the U.S. context, for contractors who are employed by the U.S. military, there is a sort of accountability under an extension of the U.S. code of military justice.[48]

One of the inherent obstacles in looking to regulate private military companies and even private security companies stemming from Russia, Turkey, and China is also a common problem related to the regulation of any global or transboundary activity. International regulations, more often than not, clash with regional and local laws. Especially when weak governments are unable or not motivated to enforce the law, the presence of unaccountable armed men capable of enforcing their will by means of violence is adding oil to the fire. From the Middle East to Afghanistan, PMCs and PSCs tend to be most actively involved in regions where traditional accountability institutions have broken down, therefore the central role played by national law and order is missing. In this respect, regulators are between a rock and a hard place, and that is why reaching a meaningful enforcement at the international level is such a complex task.

LOOKING TO THE FUTURE

Besides pointing the finger at ongoing risks and threats, the previously mentioned UN working group reports are a valuable tool with which to forecast the trends in the money-for-mayhem sector.

For example, in Europe, as the pressure from refugees escaping from different conflicts is mounting on a daily basis, private security companies are increasingly tasked to operate immigration centers and border management. States are outsourcing other inherent state functions to private actors, namely the control over their borders.

The marketization of border control carried on in the West could be a precursor for China and Turkey while in Russia, especially after the invasion of Ukraine, Russian PMCs and mercenaries will be exclusively devoted to carry on military missions in disguise.

Creating walls managed by private military and security companies calls for new rules and regulation including the management of data and privacy laws. As happened during the conflicts in Afghanistan and Iraq, the official narrative to justify the privatization for the state monopoly on violence and security functions is presented as cost-efficient. The "Statement before the Commission on Wartime Contracting in Iraq and Afghanistan" by the U.S. Government Accountability Office (GAO) and several studies carried out since 2011 beg to differ.[49]

The privatization of border management and the privatization of detention centers is also a prerogative of the West that has not been witnessed in China, Russia, or Turkey. As soon as Beijing and Ankara businessmen realize that the growth of this sector has become a multibillion-dollar business, their approach and internationalization will change, especially in the provision of high-tech-related security services. In this respect, states are increasing their dependence on new technologies to automate and improve immigration and border control. So, for example, high-tech surveillance and detection systems implementations are on the rise; and it implies the collection and storage of a huge volume of biometric data. As in other areas of the security spectrum, new technologies are constantly developed, maintained, and operated by the private sector, becoming an important actor and influencer in the drafting of new immigration and border control policies.

Also, other negative externalities that affect individuals in vulnerable situations stem from the privatization of surveillance and patrolling along migration routes, also carried out by UAVs. Therefore migrants are forced to expand their indirect travel routes, often increasing their exposure to political and criminal violence.

CHAPTER TWO

From Russia with Love

Mercenaries Fit the Bill

THE STAGE

BEFORE PUTIN'S DECISION TO ANNEX CRIMEA AND INVADE UKRAINE, Russia's return to a preeminent seat at the table of global power already appeared to be a difficult task, in part due to an economy in a state of rapid deterioration. Moreover, Putin's gambit of invading Ukraine is casting serious doubt about his future grip on power and the role that Russian mercenaries and private military companies are going to have in the future of Russian warfare. Historically, in the world of money for mayhem, when the funding dries up, the consequences for the sponsors of mercenaries are going to be ugly.

Since the fall of the Berlin Wall, Russia and China have understood that great power competition does not always manifest itself by direct, protracted, and high-intensity wars.[1] In this respect, the fall of Kabul, after twenty years of military presence far from home, represents a harsh wakeup call for Washington. Nevertheless, much of the U.S. strategic debate is still centered on the perceived need to deter and prepare for large-scale, conventional conflicts.[2] Economic sanctions used as a deterrent were not enough to stop Russian tanks from flooding into Ukraine on February 24, 2022.

On the contrary, Moscow and Beijing follow playbooks based on indirect approaches: the Primakov doctrine[3] in Russian, and "unrestricted warfare"[4] and "the three warfares" in Chinese military literature blur the line between war and peace. While accelerating the modernization of the People's Liberation Army, China is not looking any time soon to a kinetic confrontation with the United States, even in the disputed South China Sea. Only crossing well-known red lines, such as Taiwan's territorial independence, could induce Beijing to ponder a full-scale offensive. Similarly, until the invasion of Ukraine, Moscow was bent on an identical path, counting on a long history of proxy warfare that matured during the Cold War. While Russian proxy warfare in the 1970s and 1980s was based on ideological values, today, the Kremlin's playbook has a more pragmatic background. The Kremlin's political agenda is set in high gear toward the recognition of Mother Russia's status as a great power. Therefore PMCs are one of the tools in Russia's hybrid warfare strategy, and it is an efficient tool to achieve precise strategic objectives with a limited expenditure of resources.

During the dissolution of the Soviet Union, informal armed groups began to appear in support of Boris Yeltsin's Russian nationalist interests in security operations across the newly post-Soviet Eurasian space.[5] Still, only during Putin's reign did these groups achieve international status.

Nobody knew Putin's planned endgame for the Ukrainian conflict, but faulty intelligence and hubris created a perfect storm for the Russian Army. As a result, this supposed blitzkrieg became a bloody conflict of attrition, deteriorating the position gained by flexible and cost-effective PMCs on the geopolitical chessboard.

While Russia's penchant for the private military is still on the rise, looking at non-Russian guns for hire from Chechnya to Syria, in the United States the fall of Kabul has generated a new wave of criticism against the privatization of the state's monopoly on force.

In the United States, the first wave of public criticism of contractors was ignited in 2007 by the Nisour Square massacre when Blackwater operators indiscriminately opened fire on Iraqi civilians, killing seventeen bystanders. After the Nisour Square "Bloody Sunday," the American PMC Blackwater generated a media outcry against the employment of private security contractors. The immediate fallout forced Blackwater's CEO Erik Prince to abandon the U.S. government's lucrative contracts.

In light of the United States using private military and private security companies on an unprecedented scale, the wars in Iraq and Afghanistan rapidly become the main market for Western private military contractors. During the Iraq conflict alone, the United States outsourced its monopoly on violence to more private companies than in any previous war, with more contractors than military personnel on the ground.[6] While the number of contractors was staggering, only a minor part was armed and involved in private security services. Since 2008, the presence of U.S. Department of Defense–funded private security contractors peaked in Afghanistan in 2012 at more than twenty-eight thousand individuals and in Iraq in 2009 at more than fifteen thousand individuals.[7]

The second wave of public criticism in the United States followed the dismal withdrawal of the U.S. Army from Afghanistan. Following the Afghan National Army's (ANA) debacle in defending the capital from the Taliban's lightning advance, journalists and academicians rapidly pointed the finger at military logistics and weapon platform maintenance outsourcing as one of the ANA's leading causes of melting like snow in the sun. Intelligence analysts and senior U.S. military officials predicted that the Afghan Army was capable of holding its ground against the Taliban's encircling maneuvering for several years or surviving at least six months in the worst-case scenario.[8] However, in reality the defense of Kabul lasted only eleven days. Following President Joe Biden's call for the Afghan military being able to operate on its own, the total number of all kinds of contractors in Afghanistan dropped by more than half in the last three months from almost 17,000 in April to 7,800 in July and to a few hundred armed contractors during the fall of Kabul in August 2021.[9]

But following the perceived fallacies in military outsourcing in Afghanistan, the fallout on PMCs' responsibilities in the West is yet to be settled. The debate includes the lack of proper oversight in avoiding rampant corruption and lack of transparency. However, the Russian private military sector is developing at full steam ahead as Moscow's top-down approach is devoid of any ethical or humanitarian constraint.

For Russia, the PMCs and mercenaries are a tool to conduct great power politics on the cheap.[10] Russian PMCs operating abroad with no official links to the Kremlin are also an important source of hard currency, gold, or other precious metals for Russia. Ten years of sanctions from the West debilitated the Russian treasury's foreign reserves. The PMCs are paid in cash or by "war barter," precious metals in exchange for security services, which alleviates the negative impact of sanctions. Since the annexation of Crimea, U.S.-led international sanctions on Russia have negatively affected the country's economy and the ability of Russian companies to do business abroad. It is not a surprise that African gold and the possibility of getting paid in hard currency is killing two birds with one stone: financing Moscow's power projection while simultaneously providing precious natural resources to Russia. Following the crippling sanctions imposed after the Russian invasion of Ukraine, the "war barter" offered by the Wagner Group is increasingly essential for Putin's cohort of oligarchs.

According to Molly Dunigan and Ben Connable, senior political scientists at RAND, the Russian leadership and security apparatus have excelled at finding cracks in the edifices of American power in the past decade. While the Wagner Group has been considered the tip of the spear in Russian foreign policy, Dunigan argues that one of Russia's perceived high-end capabilities may be its most exploitable vulnerabilities.[11]

Contrary to other analysts' research on Russian mercenaries, Dunigan portrays the Wagner Group more as a long-term liability than an effective asset for Moscow's power projection. In light of the conflict in Ukraine, one of the options for the United States to raise costs on Russian interference without forcing a direct confrontation is to exploit Russian mercenaries. While it is still debatable where Wagner's efficiency ends and the problems start, Dunigan's prescience on Ukraine's invasion answers a compelling question: Why did the Russian Army perform so poorly during the first thirty days of the botched blitzkrieg? One year before Putin's order to attack, she wrote that the reliance on mercenaries stems from Russia's military's limited capability to project ground power worldwide.

Another report from RAND underlines how Russian strategic airlift is anemic compared to Soviet-era air lift; the Russian military forces, deployments far from Mother Russia borders are particularly challenging for ground forces. Therefore the lack of available military logistics assets affects the Russians' ground force deployment. An example is the need to rely on nonmilitary assets to transport forces and equipment in some scenarios.[12] Also, during the invasion stalemate, the Russian Army's reliance on conscripts showcased several cracks in the perceived armed forces professionalization ranging from the lack of the combined army's proficiency to low morale. Therefore Moscow's necessity to outsource its foreign policy to PMCs with "Russian characteristics" could be considered not exclusively part of strategic calculus but also an unavoidable necessity.

The rise of Russian PMCs, however, must not be perceived as the proverbial card up the Russian Army's sleeve. Russian Army chief Valery Gerasimov has publicly emphasized the importance of developing an overwhelming military superiority over any known and unknown threat instead of preparing for a single type of warfare.[13] The pillaging of the Ukrainian cities of Mariupol and Kharkiv by Russian artillery and rocket barrages seems to contradict Gerasimov's statement as the Russian Army is again using the tactics adopted in Syria and Chechnya, where entire towns were leveled to avoid grinding urban warfare.

THE SCRIPT

Since the time the Soviet Union fell apart, Russia's proxy warfare doctrine has changed. While the U.S. Army was busy training to fight large military forces, Russia chose to compete for power and influence outside conventional battlefields.

Today, Russia cannot count on former Soviet satellite states to provide the proxy forces required for power projection abroad to achieve Moscow's political and economic interests. The presence of several thousand Chechen fighters, sent by Putin's ally Kadyrov, is a pale reminder of the Soviet Union's proxy warfare. The time of Cuban military advisors disguised as tourists in Africa has ended for good. Still, a new group of "touriste'*" is back in Africa where and when Moscow's geopolitical ambitions require support.

Moreover, the root cause of the PMCs' abundance of available contractors may be traced to the dissolution of the Soviet Union. During perestroika's late spark of life under Gorbachev, the Soviet Union unilaterally downsized its armed forces by five hundred thousand soldiers.

---

* *Touriste* is the title of a Russian propaganda movie that portrays heroic Russian contractors supporting the Central African Republic.

Following the Soviet Union's breakup, the Russian military inherited an army based on conscription and a professional officer corps. Since then, the Russian Army has been undergoing a cyclical process of demobilization and efforts to modernize* matched by periods of reformist apathy.[14] Since the previous decade, Russia developed a small number of international PMCs that provide a broad range of services, from the protection of Russian energy companies abroad to antipiracy support on Russian commercial vessels. Nevertheless, they were forced out of sheer necessity to morph into a strategic asset for Mother Russia on the geopolitical chessboard, including Ukraine.

The all-encompassing definition of PMCs applied to the Russian context includes a wide range of nonstate armed actors, from semistate security forces to mercenaries. Also, applying a Western classification to a Russian entity that is based on different values and objectives provides plausible deniability to paramilitary groups such as the Wagner Group, which are essentially the sharp end of Russia's foreign policy. In fact, the use of PMCs is not unique to Putin's Russia. The Russian president appears to have sharpened an old trick used by his predecessors. Armed militias organized at the regional level were quite common during the dissolution of the Soviet Union. Cossack regiments reestablished in Yeltsin's time are a case in point. Under Putin, though, the PMCs have emerged as an essential component of Russian foreign policy. Therefore the Wagner Group is an umbrella term that encompasses quasi-PMCs and mercenaries.

Nevertheless, Moscow operating in the gray areas defined as irregular or hybrid warfare does not mean Russia is giving up regular warfare. Putin's invasion of Ukraine is a case in point. But there is more to the invasion than meets the eye. Besides public deniability, the rise of PMCs in modern Russia offers several benefits, namely a source of income for Putin's cohorts and a safety valve for idle combat veterans craving military action. The grinding war machine in Ukraine solved the latter problem, absorbing all available Russian fighters and even recalling some mercenaries deployed abroad. Moreover, mercenaries and foreign fighters

---

* Since the fall of the Soviet Union, the Russian military has undergone "Grachev's reform," "Rodionov/Baturin's reform," "Sergeev/Kokoshin's reform," "Ivanov-Kvashnin's reform," "Serdyukov-Makarov's reform," and, finally, "Shoygu-Gerasimov's period" (Shamiev).

helped Russians avoid more conscripts' body bags getting back to Russia from the Ukrainian war.

The annexation of Crimea and the military interventions in Syria and Libya showcase how volunteers and private contractors have replaced proxy armies such as the Cubans in the Angolan civil war. Since the beginning of the Ukrainian war, the possibility of recalling the Wagner Group from abroad in conjunction with Syrian mercenaries has been on the table. Nevertheless, the stereotype associated with mercenaries' atrocities has been chiefly used as a propaganda tool on both sides.

THE REHEARSAL

The August 2008 conflict in Georgia, anticipated to be a milk run, ended up to be a difficult task for the Russian Army. The severe shortcomings in Russia's military capabilities made Moscow realize that the modernization of its armed forces was inevitable if the state were to use military power as an effective policy instrument.[15]

Since 2015 the Syrian conflict offered Moscow a testing ground for its military reforms, new matériel, and the use of private military companies.

Prior to the invasion of Ukraine, sending Russian private military contractors abroad was a temporary solution to avoid using heavily armed bodyguards to protect oligarchs roaming Moscow with impunity or, worse, witnessing former Russian special forces veterans recruited by local criminal gangs. Since the dissolution of the Soviet Union, criminal networks moved from segregation toward integration into the state.[16] The availability of demobilized veterans from special forces and intelligence services offered valuable private agents of violence, involved in different degrees of illegal symbiosis with the state.

An example is given by the so-called Chechen syndrome that affected Russian policemen and soldiers coming back to Russia from counterterrorism operations in Chechnya. Since the beginning of the 2000s, Russian academicians, recalling the Vietnam War trauma on American soldiers, used the term *Chechen syndrome* to describe the transposition of war experiences by Chechen veterans in other regions of Russia.[17] Nevertheless, channeling the syndrome's nefarious effects outside the Russian borders via private military means is like applying a small Band-Aid on gangrene.

Another avenue for potential recruitment into the private military life is found among Russian ultranationalist fighters who have returned from the war in the no-man's-land in Donbas and other contested areas in Ukraine. With limited options, given the current decline of the radical far right in Russia, the return of deeply disappointed militants from the Donbas remain potentially dangerous in the event of political destabilization.[18]

THE ACT

The rise of the quasi-PMC Wagner Group has been associated with the so-called Gerasimov doctrine, which is an all-encompassing label for hybrid warfare with Russian characteristics. However, while General Gerasimov has the merit of accelerating the reform of the Russian Army recognizing the role of nonmilitary means to achieve political objectives, it is the Primakov doctrine that constitutes the fundaments of contemporary Russia's strategic return to the Middle East and Africa.

Yevgeny Primakov, an Arabist by training, lived and worked in the Middle East, especially in Syria, as a journalist before becoming head of the KGB and minister of foreign affairs during the Soviet time.[19] The Primakov doctrine considers the Middle East as Russia's soft underbelly.[20] Therefore Russia's military presence in Syria and successively in Libya and Africa has to be seen as a return to the stage and not a new page in Russia's geopolitical playbook. Putin's adoption of Primakov's approach to the Middle East and North Africa is straightforward: ensuring Russia's access to sea lanes of communication and natural resources is crucial for national security and economic survival.

The ubiquitous Wagner Group is the material expression of Russia's extensive theoretical tinkering with hybrid military strategies from Ukraine to Libya. As one of the famous Russian military strategists Generalissimo Aleksandr Suvorov stated, no battle can be won in the study, and theory without practice is dead. Also, it is not by chance that Suvorov is among Gerasimov's favorite readings.

The Wagner Group, a quasi-PMC, is a stern reminder of Moscow's indirect strategy. Since Putin's ascendance to power, the Russian Ministry of Defense operated without independent parliamentary oversight. Therefore individual relationships were more important than the bureau-

34

cratic hierarchy. This allowed Putin's inner circle to operate in the shadows, advancing the cause of private military companies with "Russian characteristics."

Allegedly set up by retired colonel Dimitri Utkin, the link between the group and the GRU, Russia's military intelligence service, and financed by the "highly placed businessman"[21] Yevgeny Prigozhin, the Wagner Group has no official link with the Kremlin nor is it a private army financed by a Russian oligarch. And yet, after many years of activity from Ukraine to the Middle East and Africa, the Wagner Group is still surrounded by speculation. Only fragments of evidence have emerged over its origin and the contractor's involvement in combat operations.

Nevertheless, while the Russian Ministries of Foreign Affairs and Defense deny any relationship with the group, several media outlets reported that Wagner contractors received Russian military decorations,[22] and Prigozhin himself is at home in the Kremlin. Being a cunning businessman with political and social sway, Prigozhin created his own private army. Considering the Kremlin's penchant for military deception, however, Prigozhin could be an actor in the story. He may not necessarily hold the leading role. Instead he likely represents another layer of obfuscation between the Wagner Group and its absolute puppet master.

While the attention on the creation of Russian PMCs gravitates around the figure of General Gerasimov and the Kremlin-linked businessman Prigozhin, there are other prominent Russian figures that might claim the paternity of the Wagner model. According to Sergey Sukhankin, an expert on "war by other means," General Nikolay Makarov, a former head of Russia's general staff, can claim paternity of the strategic development of a new breed of Russian PMCs.

General Makarov adopted the previous experiences of the Soviet Union in the Middle East, Sub-Saharan Africa, and North Africa as building blocks for the theoretical development of private Russian military entities. Gerasimov, however, accelerated Makarov's tinkering into practice.

Also, the evolution of the Russian private military sector includes the actions of numerous actors at different levels of the Russian security spectrum from the general staff to the special forces units and the intelligence sector. At the same time, Putin's elite cohorts benefit economically from the PMCs' spoils of war and do not have any incentive to change the status quo. Direct funding channeled through Putin's entourage is an incentive to keep vague the legal status of the Russian PMCs and to promote the PMCs' expansion toward more lucrative regions.

Yet human rights abuses carried out by armed groups that are not officially recognized by the Kremlin don't mean that international legal actions could not reach Russia. From the Malaysian MH17 airline shootdown over Ukraine[23] to the killing of a Syrian prisoner with a sledgehammer by Wagner,[24] the legal cases against Russian PMCs and related paramilitary organizations are increasing at a dangerous pace for Moscow.

CHAPTER THREE

Russian Gray Is the New Black

THE KREMLIN'S GRAY ZONE PLAYBOOK

ANDREAS KRIEG, AT THE SCHOOL OF SECURITY STUDIES AT KING'S College London, frames the concept of proxy warfare in a broader category that he refers to as "surrogate warfare." Discussing the ongoing proxy war debate with Krieg, he mentioned that the discussion is very much stuck in the twentieth century.

> *It's a debate that comes from the Cold War period mostly—"proxy" refers to the kind of competition whereby one superpower is delegating the burden of warfare to a human surrogate (mostly a state actor; sometimes a non-state actor) for limited wars. . . . Surrogacy is supposed to be more of an umbrella concept which looks beyond proxy warfare, encapsulates proxy warfare also but looks at the wider trend that we see in the technological domain as well and when we look at cyber and artificial intelligence robotics and obviously, looks at how technology, more widely, has been used as a surrogate.*[1]

In this respect, Moscow's surrogate warfare footprint evolved into a post–Cold War setting devoid of any ideological struggle and anchored to cost-efficiency and political risk mitigation. From the Middle East to the African continent, Russia's limited but tactically efficient PMCs footprint enables Moscow to achieve long-term strategic objectives that range from expanding its geopolitical sphere of influence to acquiring natural resources and increasing the arms sales market.

The Russian PMCs' evolution fits into Russia's overall military posture. Conversing with Candace Rondeaux, an expert in decoding the Russian private military security companies, she mentioned that

> *on the surface, the relationship may seem complicated to those who are less familiar with the history of the evolution of the Russian military over the last 30 years. One thing that's important to note is that many analysts have been absent from that conversation for a long time, because the focus of the Middle East has been so drawn to the question of terrorism, ISIS and other groups (like Al-Qaeda) operating in the region.*[2]

Rondeaux traces the evolution of Russian private military contractors to two atypical moments in Russia's recent military history: the collapse of the Soviet Union and President Vladimir Putin's reorganization of the Russian military machine. The so-called Little Green Men presence in Ukraine signals Putin's reorganization of the Russian Army apparatus toward surrogate warfare.

The Crimea annexation's lightning victory represented a success story that Putin was eager to duplicate on a larger scale by deploying flexible small armed units that provide plausible deniability. But it is in the Middle East and Africa that the Russian PMCs started to reach the international media spotlight, and not from a positive angle.

Before the Russian Army's official support of the Assad regime, hundreds of heavily armed Russian personnel surfaced in Syria. On February 7, 2018, not far from Iraq's border in Syria's oil-rich Deir al-Zour Province, more than a hundred Russian mercenaries[3] were obliterated by a combined U.S. attack featuring helicopters and artillery fire. However, not being part of the Russian Army neither ignited any reprisal from Moscow nor escalated the conflict. As the American forces used deconfliction telephone lines to advise the Russian Army command center in Syria to move forces away from a dangerous proximity to an American Army special forces outpost, the Russians responded that they had no control over the fighters.[4] Speculations abound why the Russian Army did not inform the mercenaries and the pro-Assad force of the imminent danger. Guesses range from lack of command-and-control capabilities to a sort of Russian internal payback against Wagner for poaching the most valuable fighters. Nevertheless, the attack is already a textbook case study for plausible deniability. The confrontation between the U.S. Army and Russian armed men did not ignite World War III.

From Syria to Africa, the report on Russian mercenaries' violence on noncombatants, including the beheading of prisoners, kept growing by the day. The UN working group on mercenaries' activities pointed the finger at the Wagner Group as Russian-sponsored mercenaries. As an example, the working group report mentions that the continued recruitment and presence of mercenaries in Libya is impeding "progress in the peace process" and has become an obstacle to upcoming elections.[5]

It is in Syria where the Wagner Group started to showcase its real capabilities. The role of the group in Syria may be divided into four phases that provide a glimpse into the Russian PMCs' future trends to Libya, Sudan, Niger, and the rest of Central and West Africa.

The first phase is related to establishing a beachhead for an incoming Russian official military intervention.

The second phase provides military support to the local regime as a clear statement of Russia's backing without any official involvement. Moscow is sending a message that could not be lost in translation.

The third phase is related to PMCs providing training services while the Russian Army is carrying out air support missions and projecting power in the regime-controlled areas.

The fourth and final phase is disengagement from the conflict after the Russian Army has established a foothold in the region. Once Russia has reached the intended political objective and the military and information battlefields are secured, leaving PMCs in place could create more trouble than benefits for Moscow.

Following centuries of historical experience on mercenaries, it is common knowledge that idle armed mercenaries roaming around a country spell trouble for the contracting authority. In *The Prince*, Machiavelli is adamant in stating that mercenaries are useless and dangerous: "They have no other attraction or reason for keeping the field than a trifle of stipend, which is not sufficient to make them willing to die for you."[6]

Modern troubles stemming from Russian PMCs are related to Moscow's reputational and political costs. The increasing footprint of the Wagner Group in Africa has been met by a rise of sanctions led by the UN, the United States, and Europe. Sixteen European governments, including France, the United Kingdom, Italy, and Germany, mentioned the involvement of the Russian Federation government to provide matériel in support for the deployment of the Wagner Group in Mali and called on Russia to revert to responsible and constructive behavior in the region.[7]

Since 2021, Yevgeniy Prigozhin has been targeted with direct sanctions by the United States, the European Union, and the United Kingdom. The Wagner Group has also been sanctioned by the United States, following accusations of abuses and actions that threaten the peace, security, stability, sovereignty, and territorial integrity of the Central African Republic (CAR). The EU followed shortly with specific sanctions on the group and eleven of its associates on December 13, 2021, for its destabilizing activities in Ukraine, Libya, CAR, and Syria. To add insult to injury, the Chechyan President Kadyrov, prior to sending his fighters to join Putin's invasion of Ukraine, quoted on his Telegram channel that he is claiming the FBI bounty of US$250,000 on Prigozhin's head. Kadyrov noted that he cannot miss out on such a generous reward, while Yevgeny Prigozhin is visiting him in Grozny.[8]

Sanctioning a group that is defined as a private company in a non-liberal market economy is a daunting task. Especially considering that even by Russian standards the practice of private military operations is illegal. Therefore continuing to refer to the Wagner Group as a PMC creates unnecessary confusion in an already murky environment. In "War by Other Means," Sergey Sukhankin defines the Wagner Group as a quasi–private military company. At the same time Kimberly Marten, in "Russia's Use of Semi-State Security Forces: The Case of the Wagner Group," showcases how Wagner does not neatly fit in any previous PMC or mercenary labels. The group's modus operandi is evolving at fast pace and, "while Wagner's leaders have contracted for profit and its members have fought for money, its members believed that they were simultaneously working on behalf of the Russian state."[9]

Considering the Wagner Group as a PMC is a convenient label for the Kremlin as it diverts the focus from Moscow. However, it does not appear that the Group is a registered company. Moreover, even if there was proof of incorporation, it is illegal to operate armed contractors according to Russian law against mercenaries. Subsequently, characterizing the Wagner Group as private obfuscates conveniently a truth that lays in the open: Wagner's chief client is the Russian state. Also, a growing presence of Russian private military and security benefits from the same factors that enable the rise of the Wagner Group: the availability of veterans and the possibility to bargain a way out of the Russian legal system's limitation against operating abroad.

Even Russian Minister of Foreign Affairs Lavrov confirmed reports on Mali contracting the Wagner Group to fight extremism in the Sahel, asserting that it is a business agreement between a state and a private company without Moscow's involvement: "We have nothing to do with this. . . . This activity is carried out on a legal basis and concerns the relationship between the host—this is the legitimate government, recognised by all as a legitimate transitional structure—on the one hand, and those who offer services through foreign specialists to a Russian private military company."[10]

In this respect, the Wagner Group is not alone. In the past two decades, several Russian PMCs registered as off-shore entities, albeit having their headquarters in Moscow and St. Petersburg, worked essentially for Russian state-owned enterprises involved with natural resources exploitation. Other Russian security companies near to the Chinese or even a Western model in the provision of security services lament that the operations carried on by the Wagner Group are damaging their reputation, being perceived as ruthless mercenaries and not as security providers.[11]

This trend offers an interesting historical parallel with the role of Western mercenaries in Africa in the 1980s. Most of the analysis on the privatization of the monopoly of violence during Africa's postcolonial wars is rooted in a few mercenary groups such as the previously mentioned Executive Outcomes (EO). Only a few researchers underlined that at the time several hundred local PSCs operated in the African continent. Nevertheless reporting on EO's exploits was more entertaining. No African private security contractor has been impersonated by Leonardo DiCaprio as happened in *Blood Diamonds*, a 2006 movie showcasing the efficiency of a small group of well-trained and well-equipped mercenaries involved in the illegal diamond trade during the chaos of Sierra Leone's civil war.

Today, the exclusive media focus on the Wagner Group obfuscates the growth of Russian PMCs and their expansion abroad. Contrary to the Chinese PSCs, focused mainly on the Chinese market for security, Russia's private security companies are trying to increase their international client portfolio from Central Asia to the Middle East, particularly the Chinese state-owned companies operating in Belt and Road high-risk areas. In contrast, Russia's quasi-PMCs are devoted to one type of client: Russia's state agencies.

Sukhankin's analysis of the activities of Russian PMCs underscores how from 2019 the Russian private military development has been characterized by two trends. The first trend is related to the expansion of the geographical reach of Russia's private military deployments. As the nature of the conflicts in Ukraine, Syria, and Libya changed, Russian PMCs had to adapt to the new realities or relocate their business elsewhere. An example is related to the Syrian conflict: as soon as the nature of conflict changed with Putin sending in the Russian Army to support Assad, there was no longer any need to operate in the shadows. Therefore the message to the PMCs was loud and clear: Russia no longer needs the active participation of nonstate actors in the area.

Even though Russian PMCs are still present in conflict areas where Russian soldiers are operating, the nature of their activities has adapted into nonmilitary or paramilitary missions including training, close protection for local government officials, and protection of strategic assets such as gold mines or oil fields.

The second trend discussed by Sukhankin is Russia's return to Sub-Saharan Africa. During the Sochi 2019 Russia-Africa Economic Summit,[12] Moscow restructured its involvement in the continent with a long-term strategy that recalled the Soviet Union's former ambitions. According to Sukhankin, even though Russia started active military cooperation with Africa in 2014 and 2015, it was between 2018 and 2019 that Russia marked the growing presence of paramilitaries in Sub-Saharan Africa. In 2018, a vacuum of power in CAR favored the rise of nontraditional Russian presence in the region. From 2019 the Russian PMCs footprint expanded progressively to Mozambique, Sudan, Mali, and Burkina Faso.

From training to active combat operations, the outcomes of the Wagner Group and other Russian PMCs in Africa have not been always positive. Mozambique is a case in point.

In Africa, with the exception of Mozambique counterterrorism operations, Russian paramilitary groups had not played an active part in military hostilities, a task previously accomplished in Syria and Libya. In some respect the presence in Africa is similar to the one played by Soviet military advisors during the Cold War: force multiplier. However, this time ideology has taken a back seat in favor of crude realpolitik and cost-efficiency. Also, Sukhankin concurs with other Russian PMCs watchers, stating that "today Russia's interests are driven by profit seeking, and so they are bereft of this ideological compound that the Soviet Foreign Policy was pivoted towards."[13]

THE LITTLE GREEN MEN EVOLUTION FROM UKRAINE TO SYRIA

Since the annexation of Crimea in 2014, the Russian way of war has been utilizing a wide array of tools defined in the West as hybrid: a traditional combination of conventional and irregular combat operations, support to separatist groups, sponsorship of political protests, economic coercion, cyberoperations, and, in particular, an intense disinformation campaign.[14] In the report "'Little Green Men': A Primer on Modern Russian Unconventional Warfare, Ukraine 2013–2014,"[15] the analysis of the role of Russian special forces as deniable assets is a precursor to the deployment of special forces operators inside the Wagner Group. The report underlines how in the 2014 forced annexation of Crimea, unidentified Russian military personnel occupied strategic positions including airports, media outlets, and other key infrastructure. Armed but without military insignia on their uniforms, the operators, obviously Russian, provided Moscow with a very limited deniability. The Western press labeled the intruders "little green men." Once the key infrastructure was secured, the little green men left the scene, leaving the control to the local separatist forces. Unfortunately, the report was very prescient on the future of the conflict stating that in Crimea, it worked; in eastern Ukraine, it fell short and led to bloodshed.

However, Russian covert intervention in Syria in support of the Assad regime is the real testbed of Russia's meddling with unaccountable and armed small groups operating on foreign soil. From the success story of the little green men in Ukraine, the next step in their deployment far from Russian borders arrived shortly. Yet Moscow's crucial support for the Assad regime's survival needed to be undercover to avoid heavy U.S. sanctions on the Syrian government. At the same time, the pledge of local Syrian sheikhs to grant exploitation rights to recaptured oil fields was an additional financial incentive for Putin. Since then, the Syrian "war barter" model of natural resources as payment for armed support will become the norm for Wagner during the coming years.

Russia's shrinking capacity to support large military operations far from its borders encountered crucial financial support in the MENA region's natural resources exploitation to cover its operations. Therefore Africa's abundance of natural resources was the next logical step.

What immediately differentiated Russian contractors in the Middle East from ragtag local militias and even well-trained mercenaries such as the Serbians who were Muammar Gaddafi's personal praetorians in Libya is the availability of heavy weapons. Focusing on high-quality military equipment and a contractors' age pool over thirty years old differentiates the Wagner footprint from other Russian wannabe PMCs abroad. The operations carried out by non-Wagner Russian contractors are characterized by their outdated Russian military surplus and a younger age base. Even Blackwater, at its peak in the Iraqi conflict, could not display the heavy military equipment that Wagner had at their disposal such as a T72 main battle tank.[16] This kind of "private firepower" was unseen since EO in Africa that deployed the Russian Mil-Hind 24 attack helicopter, a flying tank.[17]

The footprint of heavily armed Russian contractors in Syria did not escape the media's attention, but Moscow was firmly denying any undercover military presence. At the same time, ISIS video propaganda surfaced on the Internet, showcasing identification documents from deceased Russian contractors and even their company IDs. When the actions of the Russian mercenaries in Syria reached the plausible deniability zenith, the choice for Moscow was straightforward: to disavow the entire operation. Just a few weeks before the official involvement of the Russian Army in support of Assad, the FSB detained several Russian contractors at the airport when they returned to Moscow from the frontline. Plausible deniability at its best.

Before Wagner's rise, the discussion over the role of private military companies in Russia was part of an ongoing debate at the Russian parliament, the Duma. In the late 1990s, several Russian special forces operators turned businesspeople pressured Moscow to reform the law in favor of an opening for the private security sector.* Two factions were pressuring the Duma; on one side, the advocates of increased privatization of the Russian state monopoly on violence, and on the other side the military that was mostly against it.

At that time, the increase of piratical activity in West and East Africa, near the Somali coast and the Gulf of Guinea, prompted the need to protect Russia's sea lanes of communication. As a result, companies such as Slavonic and Moran started their African operations under the radar. Compared to the Wagner Group's high visibility, their shrouded operations are justified by two main reasons. The first is the lack of interest in the 1990s for small Russian armed groups along the Red Sea and the Gulf of Guinea. The second is that social media and OSINT† were just at an early stage. Today's social media landscape and the scrutiny of PMCs is different; even the propaganda channels of insurgents and terrorist organizations provide timely reports on the Wagner Group's actions. Also, many selfies posted by Russian contractors populate the Russian social media space on apps such as OK and VK (the Russian version of Facebook) that provide a line of digital breadcrumbs that lead directly to the group's activities.

---

* See appendix II.

† Open-source intelligence (OSINT) refers to any information that can legally be gathered from free, public sources, mostly in cyberspace, about an individual or organization.

For example, Russian guns for hire's social media footprint showcases how most contractors are trained in Russia but are not necessarily ethnic Russian. Many belong to former Russian-speaking post-Soviet countries from Tajikistan to Chechnya. Their online posts include previous deployments in Libya or Syria, promoting their military prowess to get another job overseas.

Even an ebook, written by a Wagner veteran, surfaced for a brief moment online, disappearing shortly after without leaving many digital crumbs. The Wagner veteran claimed to have started his career in Wagner as a simple fighter, becoming several years later the commander of a reconnaissance company. In conversation with Meduza correspondent Liliya Yapparova,[18] the Russian contractor mentioned that he wrote his memoirs in the Russian language after he was severely injured in Palmyra (Syria) and forced to retire. It is still to be proven if the veteran's editorial escapade was an attempt to muddy the waters or just an effort to leave a trace in history instead of an unmarked grave. Marat Gabiullin, the author of the ebook, resurfaced in Paris in 2022, publishing his memoirs using different call signs for his legionnaire brothers including Beethoven instead of Wagner.[19]

Another fragment of information that could shed some light on Wagner's modus operandi is a tactical tablet allegedly belonging to a Russian contractor in Libya. While the BBC confirms that the tablet contains credible information on the group's activity in support of Khalifa Haftar's Libyan National Army's (LNA) fight for power against the Libyan Government of National Accord (GNA), the numerous active measures that surround Russian PMCs' activities raise legitimate doubts from any source of information or better disinformation that surrounds Russian contractors. The role of the Wagner Group in the form of the North African nation of Libya is not dissimilar from the one played in Syria with a high attrition rate and combat support missions. The information retrieved from the tablet includes a detailed map of Ain Zara—a town and oasis in western Libya—that shows drone video footage scouting for GNA positions and several military manuals in the Russian language from drone piloting to mines and explosives.

Therefore it is possible to infer that the Wagner contractors operated independently as a standalone group holding key positions in the frontline defenses providing sniper support, artillery spotting, advanced scouting, or even setting up ambushes and counterattacks.[20]

It is not by chance that the first steps toward a ceasefire between the two warring parties were related to the request to evacuate all mercenaries from Libya. In this respect the Russian Wagner Group seized the media's attention, but at least twenty thousand mercenaries from Syria, Sudan, and Chad joined the fight.[21]

The conditions for a mercenary's pullout is essential in any peace process, and the issue of mercenaries and foreign fighters has long been an obstacle ahead of Libya's stabilization process. Unfortunately Machiavelli's statement is still valid:

Mercenaries and auxiliaries without discipline, unfaithful, valiant before friends, cowardly before enemies; they have neither the fear of God nor fidelity to men, and destruction is deferred only so long as the attack is; for in peace one is robbed by them, and in war by the enemy.

At the time of this writing, the discussion inside Russia is moving toward reforms favoring a legal space of action for local private military companies but no legal recognition of mercenaries. While the Russian Army and the intelligence services are not bent on reforms that will shape the private military sector toward the U.S. mode, a growing number of Russian special forces operators and spooks are finding their way into private security contracting's lucrative business.

The Ukrainian war stalled the Duma discussion on the legalization of private military companies, including the role of Russian armed contractors being able to operate abroad, but it reinforced Putin's need for deniable operations. While the law will not be amended anytime soon, a few state-led companies in the energy sector, such as Rosneft and Gazprom, in 2016 were legally allowed to hire their own armed security[22] and use unmanned aerial vehicles.

Because Russian legal regulations do not allow any Russian PMCs to incorporate and operate in the open, it is improbable that in the near future the Russian private military security sector will evolve outside the close relationship with its unofficial master, the Kremlin. In a post-Putin era, it will not be difficult to foresee Wagner Group splinters that are going to set up shop in Africa and the Middle East with local militias and most importantly local patrons.

Looking at the evolution of the little green men toward today's Russian PMCs, it is possible to provide a prediction on the sector's development. Ideally, classifying the PMCs along a linear spectrum of capabilities and willingness to use violence, it's possible to find Russian PMCs and Chinese PSCs at their extremes. Russia's PMCs are completely different from the Chinese PSCs, not only in terms of capabilities but also in terms of different tasks that they are called on to perform. As a security tool Russian PMCs, as well as the Turkish ones, are the tip of the spear of an armed intervention. Their primary role involves combat operations and upgrading the fighting capabilities of local armies and militias. Moving from the Russian side of the analytical spectrum toward China, the Western PMCs could notably sit in the middle in terms of high capability but less propensity to intervene in kinetic actions while still serving as a force multiplier. In the case of Western PMCs, from Iraq to Afghanistan the preemptive use of force is the exception. At the end of the capability/propensity to violence spectrum sit the Chinese PSCs. Distinguished by their passive stance, the Chinese security service providers are trained to react to a threat and not vice versa.

Both Western and Chinese security companies are registered business entities incorporated in the country of origin (with notable cases of companies having another registered office in complacent fiscal paradises or in areas where the banking sector offers a flexible environment, as is the case for several Chinese PSCs with a Hong Kong subsidiary that allows uncomplicated transactions between US$ and Yuan). In this respect, Russian PMCs are embedded in a murkier legal framework compared to their Western and Chinese counterparts. Russian PMCs do not have legal recognition in Russia, and their legal entity needs to be under a PSC status or just a shell company. The lack of clear legal status in Russia provides an additional layer of obfuscation, but at the same time it hampers the growth of a transparent and accountable private military security sector. Since 2018, the lack of debate at the Duma on the PMCs' law reform indicates that keeping the overall sector in the shadows will allow the Russian PMCs to perform tasks that the Russian Army can't be seen performing.

Interestingly, a 2016 amendment of Russia's military law allows a convenient revolving door from the military to the private sector for short-term paid military service abroad.

Similarly to China, the Russian private security sector is populated by hundreds of PSCs (more than ten thousand in China), but high-level companies that operate abroad are less than a dozen. According to Østensen and Bukkvoll,[23] the Russian PMC sector probably consists of ten to fifteen companies of different sizes and specializations in comparison to a wide array of domestic private security providers. Also the Chinese professional PSCs that are able to operate outside China's borders with high standards are no more than a dozen.

The comparison with China ends here as the Russian PMCs on the international scene not only provide offensive kinetic services that the Chinese are unable and averse to provide, but they also have a closer relationship with the state and the military sector. While the Chinese PSCs abroad are expected to act according to Beijing's requests in case of need, several Russian PMCs have only one client: state agencies. Discussing with Bukkvoll the most relevant Russian PMCs, he mentioned that

> *some of them, such as Wagner or the Ministry of Defence (MoD) proxy Patriot, cater exclusively to the Russian state agencies plus "friends" of those state agencies, be they state or commercial clients. Other companies, for example RSB Group, are more like Western-style companies and actually do offer their services in a commercial market. Some, in turn, appear to be commercial outcrops of military divisions, organised and run by those particular military divisions in order to allow them to "earn on the side" and perhaps allow soldiers from such divisions to operate with plausible deniability. One such example appears to be Shchit (Shield).*[24]

While the presence of Russian PMCs is an early indicator of Russia's geopolitical interests and the possibility of a direct Russian military involvement in the near future, it is also possible to estimate where the Russian PMCs are going to appear next.

In case of a crisis not triggered by Moscow—in the Russian near abroad—Moscow-led military alliances such as the CSTO or Russian peacekeeping forces are going to pave the way. In this case, the presence of private military contractors could spark anti-Russian resentments and be counterproductive. In regions from the Caucasus to Central Asia where the Bear's embrace is seen with a historically deep-rooted suspicion, the presence of Russian contractors could ignite unwanted tension or cause embarrassment for Moscow as happened in Belarus.

In other regions, when Russia's geopolitical and geoeconomic interests are at stake and the local governments are politically isolated, there is a high chance for a Russian PMCs' deployment. In this respect, the African continent's mix of weak states and abundance of natural resources is a magnet for intervention by Russian PMCs.

AFRICA'S RETURN OF MERCENARIES

Since Putin pledged his support to the Assad regime and Russian fighter jets were pouring out of the Khmeimim[25] military airbase in Syria, the Wagner Group promptly relocated its business. Nearby Libya, Sudan, Mozambique, CAR, Mali, the Democratic Republic of Congo (DRC), and Burkina Faso offered lucrative contracts and a landing pad for the return of Mother Russia in Africa. In addition, these countries are blessed with abundant natural resources, from oil and gas to rare earth minerals, and the region holds a strategic position on the great powers' chessboard. Russia is back, but this time the Kremlin's strategy is more rooted in profit seeking than ideology.

Contrary to the lack of attention paid to Russian PMCs roaming the African continent during the 1990s, this time the role of the Wagner Group has been under the microscope from day one. Unfortunately, increased scrutiny from the Russian media and academia on the expanding footprint of the Group in the continent has been accompanied by a series of alleged "suicides" by researchers and robberies gone wrong.

Discussing with Sergey Sukhankin[26] the increasing difficulties to research the evolution of Russian PMCs in Africa, he stated that

first and foremost, it is becoming increasingly hard to find any credible information on this because many Russian journalists—investigative ones—have been silenced. Some of them physically eliminated, as we know what happened in the Central African Republic, some others fell out of windows and the rest were sent to prison.

Considering the so-called private involvement of Wagner-like companies from the Middle East to Africa, the case of Mali is the most emblematic. The government officially called for Wagner's intervention without taking much effort in differentiating between Russia's public or private provision of security services. At the same time the Bamako transitional government requested Denmark to withdraw its ninety-person contingent, based in northern Mali under a European counterterrorism operation, as no permission had been given for the deployment of Danish soldiers.*

The open invitation to the Wagner Group in 2020 was twofold, on one side using the Russian presence as a bargaining chip with the West and on the other side as a quick fix to fill the security vacuum gap left by the drawdown of the French Army. Since president Macron announced the end of France's antiterror Operation Barkhane in Africa's Sahel region in 2021, Russia's unofficial presence in the area has been increasing as well as the number of military coups affecting countries where Russian PMCs started to operate. While president Macron was pushing local states to own greater security and governance responsibilities for themselves,[27] Moscow was more than happy to step in.

Leveraging the Russian presence to gain better deals is also a high-risk gamble for Mali as armed Russian contractors roaming the country create anxieties in neighboring countries from Senegal to Mauritania. Nevertheless, it has not been disputed that since 2013, when French troops entered Mali and were cheered on by the local population, things have changed. Five years after the beginning of the counterterrorism operations against Al Qaeda, ISIS, and other jihadist militants, public opinion in Mali has undoubtedly turned against the presence of troops

---

* "The Danish Foreign Ministry earlier had said Mali's former president, Ibrahim Boubacar Keita, had requested in 2019 that Denmark send troops to join the Takuba effort. But less than a year later, Keita was deposed in a military coup." Jan M. Olsen, "Danish Troops to Leave Mali After Call from Country's Rulers," Associated Press, January 28, 2022, https://abcnews.go.com/International /wireStory/european-force-deeply-regrets-mali-telling-danes-leave-82505179.

from the former colonial power.[28] According to the BBC, some Malian activists claim the French unwillingness to negotiate with the militants is a catalyst itself of the jihadist violence.[29]

It is not by chance that shortly after an increasing Russian presence in Mali, another neighboring country's government, Burkina Faso, collapsed under the pressure of a military coup. The January 2022 coup in Burkina Faso marked the fifth military coup in the past year in West and Central Africa, a region once known as the continent's "coup belt."[30]

Mali is just a tiny piece of a broader geopolitical puzzle that Russia is acquiring in the Sahel and Sub-Saharan Africa. The Syrian playbook, previously tested by the Kremlin during the support of the Assad regime, works like a charm in Africa: returning to the geopolitical scene with limited boots on the ground and in a cost-efficient manner.

From a strategic point of view, Russia still suffers from the inferiority complex of not being considered a superpower since the fall of the Berlin Wall. From an economic point of view, the expansion of PMCs in Africa's natural resource–rich countries offers an important flow of hard currency and precious metals to a cash-strapped country hit not only by a decade of international sanctions but also by weak economic development and dwindling revenues from oil and gas. Another economic imperative for Russia is to secure the sea lines of communication. Both Western Africa and East Africa offer strategic positioning for Russia's maritime ambitions.

Last but not least, from a business perspective the presence of Russian trainers is also set to promote an increase of weapon sales in the region and to promote on a global scale the view of battle-tested new Russian weapons platforms as happened during the Syrian conflict. During the First Gulf War and the Yugoslavian conflicts, the U.S. Army began a revolution in military affairs by battle testing stealth fighters and precision bombs. During the two Iraqi conflicts, sales of the U.S.-made Patriot missile defense system to international customers increased by an order of magnitude. Similarly, the Russian military industry is utilizing Syria as a test field for doctrines and high-tech weapons from land combat drones to air defense systems.[31] While Crimea has been a test bed for new Russian tactics in hybrid warfare, Syria showcased new Russian military hardware. As battle tested is the best marketing slogan for any defense industries, PMCs are the salesmen on the ground.

One year after the rise of Russian contractors in Mali, the U.S. State Department and the European allies enacted targeted measures to prevent Russian contractors from further expanding their presence in the region. Even in this case, the preferred Western weapon of choice to counter Russia, without antagonizing Moscow on the ground, is economic sanctions.

According to a U.S. State Department analysis,[32] a potential deployment of Russia-backed Wagner Group forces in Mali is going to cost US$10 million per month, diverting scarce resource that could have been channeled to improve the local security force's capabilities. The French Minister of Foreign Affairs Jean-Yves Le Drian was less diplomatic than his U.S. counterpart, accusing in an interview the Russia-backed mercenary group of plundering Mali's resources. According to Le Drian, former Russian soldiers, armed by Russia and accompanied by Russian logistics, are using the country's resources in exchange for protecting the junta.[33]

Also, the U.S. and the UN reports provide additional proof of the group's destabilizing activities and human rights abuses from Libya to CAR.

In these places Wagner forces stoked conflict and increased insecurity and instability, causing the deaths of local soldiers and civilians and undermining national sovereignty—all while depleting the national treasury and diverting essential resources that could have been used to build the capabilities of the countries' own armed services.[34]

Furthermore, Bamako's invitation to the Wagner Group is disrupting efforts by the international community to support the fight against terrorism in Mali under the UN's aegis. Since 2020 in Mali, as well as in the neighboring countries, the return of the terrorist threat is on the rise. The volatile security context is characterized by an increase of guerrilla-style attacks by a plethora of old and new actors including Al Qaeda in the Islamic Maghreb (AQIM), Ansar Eddine, Katiba Macina, Jama'at nusrat al-Islam wal Muslimin (JNIM), and Al Mourabitoune.[35]

Nevertheless, the role of twenty thousand international military and police peacekeepers under the United Nations Multidimensional Integrated Stabilization Mission in Mali (MINUSMA) is under debate, with more than two hundred soldiers killed in service.

Already a few years before Mali's open call for Wagner's intervention, the UN working group on mercenaries was presenting a cautionary report on the effects of Russian PMCs in CAR. The UN report denotes alarm at the increased recruitment and use of private military and foreign security contractors by the government of CAR, and their close contacts with UN peacekeepers.[36]

The experts said they were disturbed to learn of the proximity and interoperability between those contractors and the United Nations Multidimensional Integrated Stabilization Mission in the Central African Republic (MINUSCA). In particular, they pointed to coordinated meetings with "Russian advisors," their presence at MINUSCA bases, as well as medical evacuations of wounded "Russian trainers" to MINUSCA bases. This blurring of the lines between civil, military and peacekeeping operations during the hostilities creates confusion about the legitimate targets and increases the risks for widespread human rights and humanitarian law abuses.

While Moscow is still bent on deflecting any allegation of an official involvement in the role of Russian PMCs from Syria to Africa, the Russian disinformation machine is upgrading its game. From a passive stance in deflecting the attention on PMCs via social media disinformation, Russia is shifting to an active stance in the media sphere with action movies portraying the Russian PMCs in a benevolent and humanitarian light. While a landmark legal case has been submitted to Moscow's court of law against Wagner over the torture of a prisoner in Syria, two movies portraying a positive role of Russian contractors in Mozambique and CAR surfaced in Africa and on Russian television channels.

Fake Russian Contractors, Honeypot, and Disinformation for Hire

Following the increased media attention on Kremlin's covert operations in Africa, the Russian disinformation machine sprang into action, casting a dark shadow on MINUSMA's future. Before the Wagner Group's inception, several Russian private military and security companies started to operate abroad, but their number increased overnight when the focus on Wagner began to get traction. Many fake Russian private security companies started to populate the web with requests for contractors and offering security-related services from nonexistent addresses. Not only in Russia is *dezinformatsiya* (disinformation) elevated to the status of an art, but Prigozhin, Wagner's boss, also manages one of the biggest internet troll farms on Russian soil, the Internet Research Agency, accused of meddling with the 2016 American election.

According to Rondeaux,[37] there's a lot of diversionary disinformation about who is doing what, and nobody understands exactly how all this works. In fact, the Wagner Group itself is a "disinformation fiction."

Since 2015, Russia's social networks started to get populated by an increased interest in military companies. MAP PMC, ENOT Corp, Cossacks, and others claimed to be founded by former combatants ready to embrace the adventurous life offered by private military contracting. According to Russian PMCs watchers, all these groups lean more to training centers than private military companies ready to be deployed overseas. From these "PMC empty shells" to virtual PMCs existing only in cyberspace, such as the Turan Group, the step was short.[38]

While the Russian disinformation campaign on PMCs is set to obfuscate the narrative on the real intention and development trajectories of the Wagner Group and similar spinoffs, other countries are utilizing the same disinformation playbook but with a different angle, a honeypot. Bellingcat, an independent international collective of researchers, investigators, and citizen journalists using open-source and social media investigation to probe some of the world's most pressing stories, reported that Ukraine launched a sting operation to lure Russian mercenaries into the open and bring them to trial.

The Bellingcat report, named Wagner-gate,[39] starts with a group of Russian mercenaries arrested in Belarus on the allegation of a plan to interfere with the ongoing election. Initially Russia complained that the alleged mercenaries arrested in proximity to the Minsk airport were part of an American conspiracy to create rifts between Russia and Belarus. In fact the reality was more compelling than fiction. In Wagner-gate the Russian mercenaries are victims of a botched Ukrainian intelligence operation to lure mercenaries that have committed acts of violence in Donbas, in the open. As cyberspace is populated by fake private military outfits, it was not difficult for Ukrainian intelligence to acquire a bankrupt Russian security company and use its name and credentials to build an online honeypot* to attract mercenaries looking for employment. During the interview the contractors themselves were bragging about their past actions in Ukraine, building a legal case against themselves. According to Bellingcat, the final operational scenario aimed to stage an emergency landing on Ukrainian soil of an aircraft carrying the mercenaries from Minsk to Istanbul. Istanbul was a plausible location as it is commonly used as transit hub for a final operational destination in the Middle East. The choice of Minsk was less plausible, but COVID-19 restricted the option of available flights from Moscow and the need to find a second leg of the tour crossing Ukrainian airspace.

Even the authorities in Belarus were unaware of the events unfolding in their country. A local media outlet reported[40] that according to law enforcement agencies, there was a tip on the arrival of more than two hundred militants to destabilize the situation during the election campaign. Thirty-two Russian visitors drew attention to themselves during their stay at a hotel due to their military-style clothing and their behavior in trying too hard not to attract attention. Following the group's arrest by the Minsk OMON police department, the alleged mercenaries were sent back to Russia, compromising the Ukrainian rendition operation.

---

* A cyber honeypot is an online resource intended to mimic likely targets of cyberattacks. In the case of a computer network it can be used to detect attacks or deflect them from a real target. In the case of a web and social media presence it is mainly used to gain data from deceived targets that are willingly submitting their information.

Besides the immediate legal implications of Wagner-gate, the Ukrainian intelligence operation cast some light on the recruitment process used by Russia's PMCs. Similar to other private military contractors from the United States to Nepal or Venezuela, there are large time gaps from the initial contracting period, the deployment period, and the search for a new gig. Aspiring contractors often have to wait several weeks or months and even look for temporary employment while waiting for the go call. One commonality with all the contract business in the privatization of the monopoly of violence is the central role of the fixers or curators. Middlemen, mostly from previous positions in the military or intelligence, provide a necessary link between offer and demand. For example, in Nepal curators have very visible offices in the capital Kathmandu that assemble groups of Gurkhas looking for security jobs abroad, while in the United States websites such as www.shooterjobs.com provide a kind of LinkedIn service to the contractor community. Nevertheless, in the murky world of Russian security contracting, even the FSB had a hard time telling the fake companies apart from the real ones. *Dezinformatsiya* is biting back on its own owner. Even some Russian contractors probing the Ukrainian honeypot reached out to their contacts in Russian intelligence only to get a confirmation that the company they were looking at was legitimate.

Discussing with Eliot Higgins, founder of Bellingcat, on the Ukrainian sting operation it appears that the dark world of Russian private military contracting is all but well structured and organized.

It's the messiness and how it was disorganised—it surprised me more than anything but thinking back on our past research on Russian assassinations and how they mess those up in a way, it shouldn't really be surprising.[41]

Before 2019, the Russian propaganda machine was very careful in dealing with the actions of Russian PMCs abroad, trying to cover and deflect any possible link with the Kremlin. A 2018 law forbids anyone from providing information on those who cooperate with Russian intelligence services abroad. This law could be an effective tool in repressing journalistic investigations of the operation of Russian PMCs. Criminal prosecution of journalists and academics looking at the Russian money for mayhem is a growing concern.*

After 2019, both Putin and the Minister of Foreign Affairs Lavrov openly admitted that the Wagner Group or other PMCs operating as private entities are not contracted by the Russian Federation. As previously mentioned, Russian law bans the use of mercenaries.

In Ukraine and Syria, where the casualties were the most severe among Russian mercenaries including Wagner, Russian investigative journalists tried to assess how many body bags were coming back home as well as wounded contractors or psychologically scarred ones suffering from PTSD. Following an early media outcry,[42] the Russian Ministry of Defense declared the Syrian losses of PMC Wagner a myth and reports of them a mockery.[43]

In Africa one of the common accusations from the United States, the European Union, and Great Britain is that the influx of Russian mercenaries is compromising the ongoing fight against terrorism. As previously mentioned, the accusation plays on different layers. The bottom layer is related to diverting the resources to pay mercenaries instead of training local armed forces in the fight against terrorists and criminal organizations, while the upper layer includes the presence of heavily armed PMCs as an additional obstacle to the ongoing counterterror operation and stabilization operations run by the international coalition.

The accusation did not fall on deaf ears, as the Russian Ministry of Foreign Affairs replied with a tune that has been played in Africa since the time of the Cold War: the accusation of Western neocolonialism.

In Russia the internal propaganda is working at its peak efficiency. Putin's iron fist managed the return of Russia on the international power chessboard, and Moscow's reputation at home has not been scratched even on the surface by the use of PMCs. The near absence of any discussion on PMCs online and in the media has helped to keep most of the internal audience unaware of the problem. At the same time, in the case of body bags coming back home, it's a different reality from the Chechen or Ukrainian conflict. It is not a case of young soldiers that sacrificed their

---

* See appendix II.

life for Mother Russia but someone that chose that kind of job knowing that the possibility of a violent death is part of the job description.

In this respect there is a parallel with China. Both countries witnessed a sharp decline in population. In China it was the one child policy, recently amended, and in Russia several concurring factors mainly related to economics and infrastructure declined. Just a few decades earlier, both national armies did not raise an eyebrow while sending waves of soldiers barely armed against heavy armor. Today Russia's and China's national armies have to take into account the lack of popularity and possible protest stemming from foreign military adventurism. Dying for the motherland is no longer glorious.

The message from the Russian media is that the Russian Federation from Syria to Libya and Africa is winning. According to the Russian propaganda, Putin's iron fist approach to international relations is vindicating the Yeltsin era's embarrassments. Reality differs, and the outcome of Ukraine's invasion will set back Russia's international political and economic stance on the global scene by decades.

Also, it is not only a matter of public opinion control as the average Russian is not even aware of what a PMC is, while the local attention is focused on conscripts getting dragged into the Ukrainian conflict's meat grinder.

From internal propaganda to external information operations, Russia has been quite effective in spreading antineocolonialist propaganda in Africa. An anti-French information campaign in CAR is a case in point, although it is nothing new under the sun as the playbook was written during the Soviet times. A similar playbook is also stemming out from Beijing, but it is not intended to fend off accusations aimed at its growing PSC footprint in Africa. Chinese finger-pointing against Western neocolonialism is aimed at deflecting the U.S.-led critiques of the BRI. Beijing's influence operations focus on countering the Western narrative[44] on the so-called debt trap diplomacy* and not to place a smokescreen on its PSCs' activities in the continent. Yet.

---

* The notion of "debt trap diplomacy" contends that China will use preferential loans to financially entrap economically vulnerable countries as part of a grand strategy to exert political influence.

In Syria, the Russian disinformation machine was already in high gear. According to Sukhankin, Russia's Federal News Agency (FAN) has been rumored to have collaborated with the Wagner Group on the ground. Compared to other local and international media outlets, the FAN agency knows about important events as they happen. In Syria it was not uncommon that after a Russian or Syrian major military operation against ISIS, FAN was the first on the scene to interview the soldiers. Also, FAN had the advantage to cover events, whereas Western agencies are prohibited or unable to operate in order to protect the safety of the reporters. In this respect, the U.S. Army practice to embed journalists in Iraq and Afghanistan has not been lost on Moscow, especially the fact that a single journalist's freedom of expression can cause the fall of a four-star general. *Rolling Stone*'s profile report that brought down General McChrystal is a stern reminder to Moscow to keep a tight leash on its own reporters.[45]

From a disinformation standpoint, the aftermath of the Ukrainian sting operation and failed rendition offers an interesting view on how both sides attempted to spin the narrative by sowing confusion. Multiple conflicting narratives started to populate the web, both from Russian and from Ukrainian sources. The Moscow-affiliated press mentioned a U.S. false flag operation intended to cast doubts in Belarus over Russia's true meddling intentions. The Ukrainian political opposition stated that the sting operation's failure was the result of the Ukrainian president's inner circle.[46]

RUSSIAN ROULETTE: BECOMING A CONTRACTOR

The increased international media scrutiny on the Wagner Group and the Russian propaganda backlash made it problematic to find credible information on the trajectory that Russian PMCs are going to follow in Africa and in the future of war. Crucial information to assess future trends is related to the contractors' age group and capabilities. During the beginning of the Syrian involvement, most of the contractors were highly professional Russian veterans from the special forces. The high rate of attrition in deploying the contractors for offensive operations forced the PMCs to expand the contracting pool to a younger and less experienced wannabe cohort of mercenaries. The hiring conditions in Africa are different as most of the time the missions do not require offensive operations. Therefore a reduced pool of talent could be maintained over time with a lower attrition rate. In this scenario, most of the wounded and casualties are not from direct kinetic action but due to IEDs or guerrilla-style ambushes. Among Western analysts there is still a lingering doubt whether several Russian contractors are still on active military duty or just shifting between the two jobs with a nod from Moscow. In this respect the Russian PMCs share the same doubt with the Chinese PSCs: Where does the state end and the private begin?

Two concurring trends tie today's PMCs with previous soldiers of fortune that have populated the long history of mercenary contracting: time gaps in contracting and the confusion that reigns over the recruitment process.

Russian PMC contractors are rotated in and out of assignments and have to go back home for months waiting for the next contract, forcing them to find other sources of income. Similarly, U.S. contractors coming back from Iraq had the necessity to use their savings while waiting to return to Baghdad. As in the West and China, the market for force in Russia is neither homogenous nor centralized. According to Wagner-gate, while Prigozhin's Wagner Group has been responsible for by far the largest number of government-sponsored overseas operations since 2014 and almost exclusively trusted for combat operations, there are several smaller companies controlled or tolerated by Russia's security services that are able to absorb the offer of Russian contractors. Compared to the United States where the availability of dedicated websites for contractor recruitment are plentiful, Russia has a small online footprint and wannabe mercenaries need to be in the loop in dedicated OK, VK, or even Telegram channels. Salaries are a fraction compared to the American counterpart: around $2,000 per month with bonuses for special forces operators and high-risk deployments. While that kind of money is already a very competitive salary by Russian standards, the road to employment follows a traditional path. An answer to the compelling question of how the contractors looking for a new gig are matched with a possible client comes from a crucial but overlooked role in the shadow business of private military and security industry: the middlemen or curators.

In terms of recruitment, the much discussed and acclaimed role of Mr. Prigozhin as a Richelieu-style gray entity behind the Russian PMC needs to be contextualized in the less studied but very important role of curator in the world of money for mayhem.

Prigozhin is a very wealthy businessman, but not an oligarch. Therefore he did not create an army for himself as happened during the collapse of the Soviet Union with oligarchs setting up their private armies. His personal connection and access to the Kremlin allegedly allows him to operate in the murky worlds of private military and disinformation, but much more as a front person than a kingmaker.

According to Sukhankin, Prigozhin's ability to influence political decisions in Russia is minimal: he's somewhat close to Putin but not as close as other oligarchs or someone from this category, so he is basically a smokescreen.[47]

As a clever businessman Prigozhin was able to spot the privatization of the state monopoly on violence as a good business opportunity, but the strategic and tactic role of PMCs is still rooted in the cogs of the state machine from the Kremlin down to the ministry of foreign affairs, the general staff, and especially the GRU and FSB. Compared to the United States or even to China, the Russian contractors' recruitment system's lack of transparency by design is why the role of middleman must not be discounted.

For years, the Wagner Group denied any official links to the Kremlin. However, in 2023 Prigozhin came out in the open on social media criticizing Russia's top military officials. Mr. Prigozhin's stunning reversal of denying his involvement with the Wagner Group, followed by a bold admission of his pivotal role in the Group's strategic development, is a testament to his callous political ambitions. Since the Wagner Group's open involvement in the Russian invasion of Ukraine, the former catering magnate turned warlord stepped into Russian politics utilizing his media troll factory and mercenaries to undermine the traditional military hierarchy. Nevertheless, without a nod from the Kremlin, it seems unlikely that Prigozhin operated his disinformation network to publicly shame General Shoigu without fear of the Russian Army retaliation. Besides the meteoric rise from "Putin's chef" to ruthless Wagner's boss, Prigozhin is surrounded by mercenaries, meaning that when the pay halts, his army of cybertrolls and guns for hire is gone.

In this respect, Putin's favorite strategy of playing both ends against the middle is in full swing as he tries to deflect blame for the botched invasion of Ukraine to the Russian Army and the human rights abuses to the mercenaries. At the same time, Prigozhin's unpredictable outbursts keep the military on their toes, and when he steps over a redline, the Kremlin is quickly pulling the strings. The order to stop any public criticism of the defense ministry and to cease recruiting convicts to fight in Ukraine is a case in point.

Prigozhin is not alone in his aspirations. Several Russian entrepreneurial/security sector actors are even more ambitious and have a proven track record of causing mayhem around the world. For example, one of the first high-level prisoner swaps in 2022 between Russia and the United States involved Brittney Griner, the basketball star detained in Moscow on drug charges, with Viktor Bout, arguably the world's best-known Russian arms dealer. Bout, who in 2006 inspired the movie *Lord of War*, seized the moment of the collapse of the Soviet Union to source weapons from the stockpiles of the Red Army and sell them to the highest bidder. Since the 1990s, his illegal arms trade has fueled some of the world's gruesome conflicts, particularly in Afghanistan and Somalia.

Prigozhin's rise may have been meteoric, but his fall could be even faster.

CHAPTER FOUR

Mercenaries' Russian Roulette

THE SWORD OF DAMOCLES OVER UKRAINE: THE WAGNER GROUP AND SYRIAN MERCENARIES

SEVERAL MEDIA REPORTS HAVE HIGHLIGHTED THE KREMLIN'S COMMITment to using paramilitary groups, such as Wagner, to carry out attacks to decapitate the Ukrainian leadership.[1] Earlier reports from U.S. and British intelligence hinted that Syrian mercenaries, recruited among pro-Assad forces, were already in Russia at the beginning of the conflict and getting ready to join the battle.[2] Both the Kremlin and Kyiv propaganda used the stereotype of the mercenaries' penchant for violence for their own narrative and agenda.

Two weeks after the invasion of Ukraine, President Vladimir Putin agreed with Russian Defence Minister Sergei Shoigu's proposal for sixteen thousand volunteers in the Middle East to fight alongside Moscow's forces in Donbass.[3] While discussing with Shoigu on Russian television, Putin stressed the fact that the Syrians are volunteering and not getting any monetary compensation, hence cannot be considered mercenaries. The same logic has not been applied by Russia. Russia, which considers foreign fighters on the Ukrainian side to be mercenaries, has declared that the Red Cross convention will not apply if foreign fighters become prisoners.[4]

The sudden U-turn to deploy Russian and Syrian mercenaries and not just regular forces is among the many signs that had led analysts to conclude just a few weeks after the invasion that the Russian lightning war was not working as planned.

65

The Syrian conflict showed how nimble and well-trained combat units motivated by money and not only by the glory of Mother Russia could be a game changer. Ukraine is neither Syria nor Chechnya.

Russia has provided its own cover story—President Vladimir Putin acknowledged sending in troops in order to prevent genocide and to de-Nazify the Ukrainian government—and thus did not need the cover of plausible deniability. In practice, this means Russian special forces teams, especially the ones from the GRU, that formed the earlier Wagner Group core did not need to remove identifying patches from their uniforms, as happened during the "little green men" time in Crimea, or when rotating from Wagner's units in Syria and Libya.

While Wagner's fighters and the allegedly sixteen thousand to forty thousand Syrian mercenaries did not concretize during the first month of war, another breed of imported fighters rushed in to support Russian forces that were bogged down in Ukraine: Chechen veterans led by President Ramzan Kadyrov, a Putin acolyte.[5] The battle-hardened Chechens did not hide their presence in Ukraine either. There is nothing discreet about their posts boasting of the missions they are undertaking on OK and YK, the Russian versions of Facebook. Perhaps this is by design, as telegraphing the presence of Chechens serves as a warning to Ukrainian defenders, given their reputation for brutality. The Chechens are renowned specialists in policing conquered cities. They are known for the cruelty and abuse they administered in Chechnya itself, in the Donbass in 2014 where they intervened, and in Syria where some of their soldiers are still deployed.[6] Albeit the initial figure was overinflated to more than seventy thousand fighters, a more reasonable estimate counts ten thousand Chechens in Ukraine.

Some of the Ukrainians have taken the bait, with troops from the Azov battalion declaring that they would welcome the Muslim attackers with bullets laced with pig's fat.[7]

While the Russian Army is attempting to lay siege to key Ukrainian cities, Russian mercenaries are still a valuable placeholder for Moscow's geopolitical interests in the MENA region.

Wagner and Syrian mercenaries are an efficient way to achieve precise strategic objectives with limited resources.

Ukraine, with its well-trained, though underarmed, defense forces, is well beyond the scope of PMCs. Well before the invasion, Kyiv's intelligence services were bent on preventing Russian mercenaries from expanding their activities from Donbass and infiltrating the major urban areas. Bellingcat's Wagner-gate[8] report on a Ukrainian sting operation is a case in point.

Since Putin started to assemble 190,000 soldiers as an invasion force, Ukrainian intelligence was again alerted to the threat posed by Russian mercenaries. Ten days after the invasion, Ukrainian authorities filled social media with dubious images of ID tags in Russian, Arabic, Persian, and French that allegedly belonged to a Wagner Group of mercenaries in Ukraine.[9] While the Russian invasion force was attempting to envelop Kyiv, Ukraine is at the top in the shadow game being played.

The earlier value of the Wagner Group was the ability to operate in the shadows, not during a full-scale military invasion. At the same time, the role of Syrian mercenaries as an effective component of the Russian invasion is quite unlikely. Ukraine is neither Syria nor Libya. Cultural, climate, and language barriers cast serious doubts on the effectiveness of Syrian fighters. The use of mercenaries in Ukraine only means that Mr. Putin is running out of options, and the number of Russian body bags being sent home is becoming untenable. Wagner recruiting inmates from the Russian prison system is a case in point.

All kinds of mercenaries in support of Russia's invasion could take on the bulk of urban combat operations. Small contractor units are more flexible and independent from the regular chain of command. However, Kyiv is holding its own thus far by maximizing its advantages: a strong willingness to fight for the country, and local knowledge of the territory. When someone fights for the coin and not for the flag, the willingness to risk his own life is drastically reduced.

Nevertheless, the main reason in fostering a pro-Russian mercenary presence is not related to battle efficiency. As previously mentioned, it can limit conscript casualties, which is a potential time bomb for Putin. Also, mercenaries are a convenient scapegoat for the kinds of war crimes Russia is already being accused of. Sean McFate reported in the *Wall Street Journal* that Germany's foreign intelligence service intercepted secret messages confirming Russian mercenaries known as the Wagner Group played a leading role in the massacre in Bucha, Ukraine, mentioning that for those who track the Wagner Group, this was expected.[10]

RUSSIAN PMCs AND THE FUTURE OF WARFARE

Over the course of the past few decades, Russian PMCs proved themselves as a reliable tool for Moscow to achieve well-defined and territorially contained geopolitical ambitions while lining the pockets of the Russian informal elite. The lack of traction in the Duma for legal recognition of the status of Russian PMCs abroad should not be seen as Moscow's will to constrain the sector's growth. On the contrary, being illegal in Russia is not only a useful plausible deniability tool, it also offers leverage. The legal sword of Damocles dangling over the heads of all Russian PMCs operating abroad could be used against them if they deviate from their master's commands and expectations. The discretion that surrounds the Russian PMCs' existence guarantees that informal patronage links could be severed by Moscow in no time should the need arise. Nevertheless, the role played by Russian PMCs is not a one-size-fits-all solution for all of Moscow's security concerns. Therefore the Kremlin's use of PMCs is tailored to specific geographical areas and expected outcomes.

With Russia's near abroad on fire, Russia preferred to deploy peace-keepers instead of contractors. On January 5, 2022, Kazakhstan was on fire. Deadly riots ignited by a sudden spike in liquefied petroleum gas prices spread through the country that was once considered among the most stable of ex-Soviet republics in Central Asia.[11] For the first time since its inception, the Collective Security Treaty Organisation (CSTO), a Russian-led security bloc, sent more than two thousand peacekeepers, following Kazakh president Tokayev's request to stabilize and normalize the situation for a limited period. Previously the CSTO had more often than not preferred to stay on the sidelines when such conflicts erupted—in 2010, during ethnic clashes in Kyrgyzstan, and more recently, during the forty-four-day war between Armenia and Azerbaijan, it refused to do anything. The temporary presence of Russians troops on the ground stoked an old fear in Kazakhstan: Moscow's permanent return to the region.

At the same time, from Syria to Africa the deployment of PMCs is still a preferred tool, preluding a possible Russian official military intervention or being just part of a security package offered to a complacent government. Counterterrorism operations in Mozambique, the support of the regimes in CAR, and Venezuela are cases in point.

The evolution of the Wagner Group started as the tip of the spear of Russian kinetic operations when the Russian Army was not yet officially ready to be seen on the ground. Today the group's money for mayhem business model is gradually compounded by additional services that are a fundamental part of Moscow's hybrid strategy: disinformation and influence campaigns. However, kinetic services and close protection for connivant businesspeople and foreign government officials befriended by Moscow will remain part of the group's core business for the foreseeable future.

According to Rondeaux, an increase in the use of groups similar to Wagner by other countries could escalate the risks globally. Several foreign countries could emulate the Russian modus operandi; PMCs' plausible deniability and flexibility is a temptation even for Western democracies. In this respect, the case of Gurkhas and the French Foreign Legion came to the fore, but there is a fundamental difference. Both are foreign soldiers embedded in a national army and are part of the chain of command. Nevertheless Erik Prince, founder of Blackwater, repeatedly lobbied Capitol Hill during the Trump administration to increase the scope and the role of the U.S. private military sector. One of Prince's main concerns is the preservation of the U.S. private military industry's competitiveness versus the emerging competition from Russian and Chinese private military and security companies. His point of view could not be discounted, especially on China, considering that one of his joint ventures, the FSG in Hong Kong, is regarded as a role model in the ongoing professionalization of the Chinese private security sector. Prince is not alone in the United States in perceiving Russia, China, and Turkey surpassing the American capabilities on the global gray zone chessboard: "That's an effective use of hybrid capability and until the United States gets smarter and more synched to respond to those things, that model of foreign policy will, I think, continue to be exploited by [Russian President Vladimir] Putin and the Chinese Communist Party."[12]

What is already known is that Russia's behavior in using private military resources differs from China's, but there is a possibility of convergence of interests. While a very improbable convergence of PMC interests between Russia and the United States could only spell disaster, it cannot be totally denied in the murky world of money for mayhem.

Tracking the evolution of the Russian PMCs' expansion abroad also provides a deeper understanding of Russia's international behavior and trajectory. Afghanistan, the Caucasus, and Central Asia's fragile stability are new alleys for Russia's PMCs' development while the Russian army is bogged down in a bloody stalemate in Ukraine.

At the time of the Taliban retaking power in Kabul, there was a brief spark of speculation on possible Russian and Chinese private security companies' involvement in Afghanistan. The political and economic interests for both states and contractors is there, but with different objectives. Both Moscow and Beijing are looking to increase their intelligence data collection in order to have an early operational plan for any kind of conflict that could cross the Afghan borders and spill into Central Asia. At the same time, the Chinese PSCs have a direct economic interest in protecting Chinese investments that Wang Yi promised to the Taliban during the meeting in Tianjin with Mullah Baradar. Russian PMCs lack the Chinese economic incentive and the memory of the Soviet-Afghan war is still vivid in the minds of the Afghans.

Compounding the ghastly history of Soviet involvement in Afghanistan with the Afghan tribal mentality that despises any foreign presence in their territories makes it quite unlikely that Russia's PMC footprint will expand in the region. Similarly, during the violent crisis that erupted in Kazakhstan, the Russian army intervened by deploying three thousand troops and tanks in key strategic areas under the aegis of the CSTO and not as a private entity. In the near abroad, where Russia needs to stabilize the situation, there is no need for deniable operations. While a Turkish private military presence in Central Asia is not on the table, the possibility of the presence of Turkish PMCs in Afghanistan cannot be totally dismissed.

At the same time, Moscow's deployment of PMCs far abroad or where the Kremlin needs a spearhead to ignite a full military escalation means that the role of the private military contractors is set to rise.

Russia's evolving use of PMCs is stained by several unsuccessful operations from Syria to Mozambique. Nevertheless, the positive outcomes that surround the involvement of PMCs far outweigh the negative consequences for the Kremlin. Moreover, having the Russian Minister of Foreign Affairs acknowledge that the private Russian security service providers are not under Moscow's control confirms that they are here to stay.

Discounting the contractor's loss of lives that did not encounter public opposition in Russia, the international sanctions specifically designed to cripple the use of Russian mercenaries had a limited impact, compared to the overwhelming sanctions that hit Russia after the invasion of Ukraine.

Also, the media uproar on the human rights abuses carried out by the Russian Wagner Group and similar outfits do not create severe drags on Moscow's willingness to change the course on mercenaries' expansion.

In this respect, Moscow's reputation has not been affected as happened with the U.S. involvement in Iraq following the Blackwater Bloody Sunday massacre in Nisour Square. Nevertheless, for the Russian security firms looking to expand abroad, it is getting harder for their client pool to avoid being perceived like a bloodthirsty Wagner Group spinoff. In this respect, the machismo and the Spetsnaz romantic view surrounding the Russian PMCs' ethos is well received by authoritarian governments looking for a quick fix to their security apparatus and power projection, mainly against internal opposition. This trend in Moscow's calculations does not imply that a new breed of Russian PMCs will increasingly supplant the role of the Russian Army. Also, when the limited use of PMCs will face a more vigorous opposition from the international community or when increasing acts of violence on the civilian population are going to backfire, Moscow can pull the plug without batting an eye. During the earlier stages of the Russian PMCs' involvement in Syria, the FSB had already had a dress rehearsal for the arrest of Russian contractors coming back home from the frontline.

From the Kremlin elite that economically benefits from the status quo, the incentive for an evolution of the Russian PMCs is minimal. Considering PMCs an efficient cash cow that can be milked without incurring international sanctions, the cohort of actors that benefit from preserving this illegal model is predictably going to oppose the sector's recognition and legalization. From the Russian military-industrial complex, the evolution of PMCs, as is happening in China, could lean toward a high-tech evolutionary model. Chinese PSCs are becoming ambassadors of China's crowd management technologies, such as facial recognition. Similar to the high-tech security solutions that the Chinese PSCs are offering along the BRI, the Russian PMCs are already promoting the sale of Russian military equipment and providing training for local armies.

Nevertheless, compared to China's application of AI to facial recognition and population control advancement and to the Israeli and U.S. race for autonomous combat drones, Russia's military development is still centered on the human factor. Humans in the loop is still part of the Russian military doctrine that influences the development of the PMCs sector toward a more traditional evolutionary pattern. The lack of a Russian-made UCAV presence in the Ukrainian conflict pales in comparison to what the Ukrainian Army did with a few dozen Turkish TB-2 combat drones.

The world of money for mayhem is fast changing and prone to abrupt disowning by the contracting governments and the withdrawal of political protection from home. Nevertheless, the PMC experiment has been successful, and the lesson the Kremlin is learning is that when the private military machine is not broken, there is no need to fix it. According to Østensen and Bukkvoll:[13] "Although Russian PMCs are not always cheap nor necessarily always successful, there is little to suggest that the Kremlin should stop using them."

As Turkey imitates the Russian model more closely than the Chinese, the risk of a global PMC race is real. In this respect, monitoring, regulating, and coordinating the PMCs' role will be a serious concern and a priority for the time to come. The Russian PMCs have already witnessed overlapping capabilities with influence operations. While the strategic objective remains the same, adding cyberwarfare capabilities and influence operations to the available tools on the client's menu is a natural evolutionary step.

In a nutshell, Russian PMCs are here to stay, which has severe implications for both the global order and the international security system. In this respect, the Wagner Group's presence in Ukraine is not a game changer but a psychological weapon allowing brutality at a minimal political cost.

There is a venerable saying that the military constantly prepares to fight the previous conflict. Today, the expanded use of mercenaries and contractors merely compounds the transformational influence of UAVs and cyberattacks on modern warfare.

Following Russia, Turkey's presence in the PMC market clearly illustrates that the barriers to entry are remarkably low. Two factors strongly suggest that mercenaries returned to the scene as a commodity. First, mercenaries and contractors are, in economic terms, perfect substitutes. A Syrian mercenary is more or less identical to one from other countries ravaged by decades of war. Second, the cost of a commodity is established by supply. Russian and Turkey's entry into the privatization of the monopoly on violence increases supply, which in turn tends to stabilize or even reduce the cost of engaging contractors. In this respect, China is on the sidelines with PSCs, mainly composed of unarmed Chinese personnel.

Nevertheless, lower cost and greater supply indicate that contractors and mercenaries are returning as a permanent feature of the system of international security. There is currently no reasonable way to inhibit the creation of new mercenaries. Therefore an essential question that must be examined is whether within this relatively new system there is a way to regulate the market of money for mayhem in any meaningful way.

CHAPTER FIVE

Private Security with Chinese Characteristics

No More Local Guards, Not Yet Wolf Warriors

WOLF WARRIORS?

A CONVOY ESCORTING CHINESE WORKERS ESCAPING FROM A VIOLENT attack is crossing an unnamed African country ravaged by war. Abruptly the convoy is surrounded in a no-man's-land by tanks and heavily armed soldiers. All hopes are lost when the tanks' main guns start to zero in on the civilian convoy. Suddenly a Chinese flag appears on the top of the convoy's leading truck, and the soldiers' commander shouts: "They are Chinese! Stop!"

The end of the Chinese patriotic blockbuster *Wolf Warrior 2** well summarizes Beijing's preoccupations and wishful thinking over its private security sector: Chinese infrastructures and personnel are increasingly under attack, and Chinese contractors are nothing less than a contemporary Rambo. While the first statement holds true, the second has a long way to go.

The Chinese private security companies operating far from China's borders are considered a latecomer in the privatization of the state's

---

* *Zhanlang II (Wolf Warrior 2)*: China's deadliest special forces operative settles into a quiet life on the sea. When sadistic mercenaries begin targeting nearby civilians, he must leave his newfound peace behind and return to his duties as a soldier and protector. https://www.imdb.com/title/tt7131870/.

monopoly on violence.[1] Besides a late start, the security necessities demanded by the BRI's global reach accelerated the professionalization of the Chinese private security industry. On the contrary, the Chinese internal market for security services has been dwindling due to several concomitant factors: the shift from cash to online transactions, the automatization of guarding functions, and the government enforcement of welfare payment regulations.

The adoption of digital wallets from superapps like Alipay and Weixin (WeChat Pay)* as well as the Digital Yuan have drastically reduced cash transactions[2] and the need for armored transports in China. At the same time, China's Ministry of Public Security began to reform its intelligence structures in the early 2000s to reestablish information dominance over an increasingly fluid, connected, and technologically sophisticated society.[3] Therefore facial recognition software, ubiquitous AI controlling in real time millions of citizens via networked surveillance (such as CCTV), and bulk data collection have drastically reduced the need of boots on the ground in the surveillance loop.

Suddenly, the gold rush ignited by China's "going out" policy and the investment bonanza that characterized the early years of the BRI provided a new stream of revenue for the cash-strapped Chinese private security industry.

The BRI reflects China's ascendance in the global arena, economically, politically, and strategically. Considered President Xi's flagship foreign policy initiative, the BRI is centered on developing connectivity infrastructures to promote trade† and development.[4] Since 2005, well before the beginning of BRI, the value of China's overseas investment

---

* Alipay has perhaps surpassed WeChat Pay in active users. Alipay reached 1.2 billion monthly users in 2019 and WeChat Pay surpassed one billion users in 2018.

† The Ministry of Commerce shows that China's nonfinancial overseas direct investment (ODI) into BRI countries expanded by 13.8 percent year on year to US$7.4 billion in the first five months of 2021, accounting for 17.2 percent of the total. Total ODI rose by 2.6 percent to US$43.3 billion from the same period in 2020. Specifically, outbound investment into information transmission service sectors continued to grow strongly and increased by 49.4 percent. Construction-related investment has slowed, however, owing to difficulties in making country visits. The contract value of construction projects decreased by 1 percent to US$46.5 billion across BRI countries in the first half of 2021, accounting for 56.2 percent of the total. Economist Intelligence Unit, Belt and Road Quarterly Q2, 2021, https://www.eiu.com/n/belt-and-road-quarterly-q2-2021/.

and construction combined reached US$2.2 trillion.⁵ Therefore the need
to support China's SOEs that are investing in complex environments has
expanded the Chinese market for security services on the global scale. In
this respect, the main difference among Chinese PSCs and their Russian
and Turkish counterparts is that the Chinese PSCs provide passive security services, mainly to Chinese clients.

During 2013 state visits to Kazakhstan and Indonesia, President Xi
charted his vision for the so-called Silk Road Economic Belt (SREB) and
Maritime Silk Road of the Twenty-First Century (MSR) as the new Silk
Road with China at its center. The SREB land connection links Central
Asia with Europe, and the MSR links ASEAN with Africa and the EU
via sea lanes of communications. Both land and sea connections cross
highly complex environments that require specific risk-management
solutions. Therefore the Chinese private security sector fills a security gap,
in protecting Chinese infrastructure and citizens, until Beijing is confident and able to depart from its decades-old principle of noninterference⁶
and have a stable military presence outside its own national borders.⁷

While Chinese noninterference (interchangeably used with non-
intervention) is a constant feature of China's foreign policy, there is a
long-standing debate in China on the necessity of keeping the principle alive. The debate reflects the new place that China reached in the
contemporary world order and the contradictions between maintaining
a low profile in international affairs and projecting an assertive image
as an alternative to the Western-based order. As usual, Beijing is opting
for a pragmatic approach: slowly departing from noninterference when
a specific opportunity arises. In the "New Era of International Relations
Not Defined by the U.S.,"⁸ the increasing complex and fluid environment
benefits Beijing's privatization of the monopoly of security service abroad.

During the past decade, Beijing's ability to project its image as a
developing country, and pretending not to be a former colonial power,
was no longer able to protect Chinese citizens and investments abroad
against political and criminal violence. Recalling the wishful thinking
of *Wolf Warrior 2*, the main character just needs to show the Chinese
national red flag during a battle to prevent any attack on the Chinese
workers. An identical mindset is shared by the majority of Chinese

companies' managers who believe that calling the Chinese embassy will suffice to solve any crisis, even kidnappings and armed aggression. The mantra propagated by the state media in China that everyone along the BRI loves China is facing a harsh reality check from Eurasia to Africa. Unfortunately, *Wolf Warrior 2*'s wishful thinking has not gone unnoticed at the Chinese embassy in Kyiv. Following the Russian invasion of Ukraine on February 24, 2022, the Chinese embassy advised Chinese nationals living in Ukraine to display the Chinese flag on their cars if they have to go outside. Two days later, a U-turn on WeChat, the Chinese messaging app: "Don't highlight your identity or display identifying symbols," the embassy recommended in the post.[9]

CHINESE PSCs' EVOLUTION: THE THIRD PHASE

In light of the development of China's security requirements, the Chinese PSCs' evolution could be framed into three distinctive phases.

The first phase is related to the 1993[*] law that allows, in a very restrictive way, the licensing of private security companies in Mainland China. The regulation is part of premier Deng Xiaoping's broader policy of China "opening up" to the West, allowing a limited privatization of the state security function. The first state-owned security company was established in 1984, which was the starting point of modern security services in China. For more than a decade only state-owned security companies were allowed to operate in a market that reached up to three thousand state-owned companies at its peak. From the 1993 security industry opening to the private sector, there are more than ten thousand PSCs with several million security personnel. At the same time, the state-owned security companies decreased from three thousand down to less than one thousand.

According to the 1993 regulations, only former military and police personnel could apply to the relevant authorities for a license and register a private security company. Also, the same law states that private security officers cannot carry weapons. Future amendments of the law expanded

---

* See appendix III.

the sector's reach, but the earlier limitations are still shaping the evolution of the PSCs with Chinese characteristics.

In 2019 a new law amended some of the earlier limits including the PSCs' option to provide armed escort services while transporting cash and valuable goods, and being a former public security officer is no longer an essential requirement to apply for a license. Nevertheless, the Chinese PSCs' evolutionary trends are still following the path set in the 1990s. Most of the several thousand Chinese PSCs based in Mainland China are still founded and directed by former security officers and the core personnel is recruited from the People's Liberation Army (PLA), People's Armed Police (PAP), and the police force. At the same time, the detailed law on PSCs operating in China clashes with the lack of a precise set of rules and regulations for the PSCs willing to operate abroad. The ongoing legal vacuum leaves the entire sector open to competition from semilegal Chinese PSCs that set up shop abroad without the proper licensing at home. For example, in 2018 five Chinese nationals traveling to Kenya on a tourist visa ended up in prison while trying to set up an unlicensed private security company.[10]

For many decades, China's reticence on global security governance was a function of its long-term strategy of keeping a low profile in foreign policy and focusing all efforts on the pursuit of economic development. Deng Xiaoping's desire to open China to the rest of the world also created an ambiguity that promoted a Western illusion for decades: the impression that China wanted to emulate the Western development model, including the liberal market and democratic values. There was a widespread tendency to underestimate China's potential or to assume that, as it developed economically, the emergence of a middle class would call for political transformation toward a Western democratic model.[11] Also, this misconception shaped the perception that the Chinese PSCs were set to follow the path traced by their U.S. or European counterparts. Reality differs.

The second phase of the Chinese PSCs' progression started in 2013 with the launch of President Xi's BRI. Beijing has witnessed firsthand how the sole reliance on economic development and the principle of noninterference could not completely shield Chinese workers and infrastructures from criminal and political violence. As such, security is an increasingly important priority, especially for Chinese companies operating in politically volatile areas. Compared to private military companies, the Chinese PSCs are tasked with a passive role including assets protection from riots, theft, kidnapping for ransom, terrorism, or even maritime piracy.[12] Therefore the necessity to protect Chinese personnel and infrastructures along the BRI and China's maintaining the decades-old principle of noninterference created a profitable business opportunity for the Chinese PSCs to follow their local clients abroad.

While China is still promoting the concept that its transition to a great power will be peaceful, the ongoing alteration of the geopolitical equilibrium in the Indo Pacific is increasing anxieties on Beijing's potential to disrupt the U.S.-led global order. President Xi's "China's Dream" marks a shift from keeping a low profile in international relations.[13] Therefore Beijing's reassertion of its historical standing as a great power casts doubt in the international arena on the PSCs' expansions' real intentions. While the PSCs' operations abroad are focused on protecting Chinese interests, Beijing's pursuit of greater recognition is casting reasonable qualms on possible PSCs' hidden agendas, particularly with reference to intelligence gathering.

The third, ongoing, phase is related to the impact of COVID-19 and the increasing friction with the United States. The pandemic accelerated the Chinese security sector consolidation, reducing the mid-size Chinese PSCs' avenues for profit and forcing mergers, hostile acquisitions, or even bankruptcy among hundreds of security companies. At the same time, COVID-19 not only created a huge business disruption overseas, but it also added additional services that the PSCs had to perform at no additional cost. The pandemic forced the private security personnel in Mainland China to enforce protective mask wearing and safe distancing policy requirements without creating an additional source of revenue at home. Prior to the pandemic, the Chinese security sector was already witnessing a consolidation among the ten thousand companies operating in Mainland China. The drivers were essentially related to the central government's enforcing of the welfare payment as well as anticorruption policies. Previously, most of the small and medium PSCs were able to offer underpriced services, avoiding paying their officers the mandatory welfare tax. Also, Beijing's strong grip on anticorruption enforcing,[14] even in remote provinces far from the capital, leveled the playing field, enabling legitimate PSCs to compete against illegal encroaching business practices. Last but not least, the automatization of several security functions via facial recognition and AI applied to crowd control drastically reduced the volume of necessary security guards. At the same time, most Chinese small and medium security companies were not able to acquire the new hardware nor attract the necessary talents to manage the IT security platforms.

For at least two years since the beginning of the pandemic, the limitations on international travel constrained new deals and also reduced the scale of ongoing BRI projects that have been delayed or even canceled. Proper security solutions were the first to be hacked down by the Chinese SOEs' cost-reduction programs. Unfortunately, with some notable exceptions in the Chinese natural oil and gas sector and ICT, the Chinese SOEs and private companies investing abroad still consider security services as a minor appendix to the overall investment project and an unnecessary cost. A proper security solution carries a steep price, but most of the time the company managers headquartered in their glass towers in Beijing or Shenzhen prefer the cheapest solution available.

Many security company managers still lament the sector's race to the bottom in terms of prices versus capabilities and a common reactive stance: increasing security only after the kidnapping or killing of Chinese workers is hurting the company's brand reputation.[15] At the same time the race to the bottom trend with PSCs providing cheap and substandard services is affecting the industry's overseas services. The numbers of horror stories of Chinese DIY security companies' mishaps are staggering.[16] These DIY "mom and pop" security companies are more soldiers of misfortune than soldiers of fortune. The lack of professionalism of these newcomers includes laughable close protection security details, also referred to as bodyguards, being unable to follow their high-value client at the airport because they forgot to apply for a visa. On the same path a Chinese PSC hiring Chinese language students specialized in Arabic to work as interpreters in Pakistan and Afghanistan, where the main languages spoken are Urdu, Pashto, and Dari.

Also, the pandemic severely limited the in-person meetings and the under-the-table corruption that surround the expansion of small semilegal Chinese PSCs abroad. A manager, working for a prominent Chinese PSC, mentioned that a lot of small to medium Chinese PSCs that are used to maintaining their international client portfolio by bribing their way out of problems are in dire need of face-to-face meetings: "Giving red envelopes* to smooth new deals and acquiring local licenses and permits is not going to be easy on Zoom."[17]

Another driver of change is related to civil-military fusion (CMF) in shaping the role of the Chinese PSCs overseas and the increasing competition with the United States. Under Xi Jinping's leadership, China's growing military prowess and ongoing reform of the PLA goes along with the already mentioned shift from the noninterference principle. Since Xi Jinping asserted a strong grip on the party-state-military power relations, the recalibration of the PLA roles and missions has drawn a wide attention abroad.

Strangely, the evolution of the private security companies with Chinese characters did not receive the same consideration. Although China's CMF strategy includes objectives to develop and acquire advanced dual-use technology for military purposes and deepen reform of the national defense science and technology industries, its broader purpose is to strengthen all of China's instruments of national power by "fusing" aspects of its economic, military, and social governance.[18] Unfortunately, the examination of the relations between the Chinese Communist Party, the national security apparatus, and the private security sector is limited at best. According to Richard Bitzinger and James Char,[19] the PLA enhancements in operational capabilities, both in terms of its hardware and its "heartware"—the human elements of its development such as operational culture and doctrine—has been triggered by profound realization of its previous limitations vis-à-vis the U.S. advanced military operations of the previous century. Similarly, the private security sector has been conscious of its own limitations compared to the Western and Russian counterparts, but legal and financial limitations are still hampering the sector's much-needed reforms.

---

* A red envelope is a gift of money inserted into an ornate red pocket of paper, given on some important occasions, such as Chinese New Year. The term is also used as an allusion to a bribe.

A fourth phase could stem out in a future not too far from the three factors established during the Xi presidency: the ongoing preferential role of SOEs as driver for a market economy with Chinese characteristics, the acceleration of civil-military integration toward civil-military fusion, and an increase of violent attacks against Chinese individuals and infrastructure overseas. The phase four seeds have been already planted. An example is given by the fall of Kabul to the Taliban; the international terrorist organizations no longer considered Beijing a secondary target, mentioned Raffaello Pantucci, a counterterrorism expert:[20]

> *Groups like al Qaeda and the Islamic State were so focused on targeting the United States, the West more generally, or their local adversaries that they rarely raised their weapons toward China.*

Therefore a call for professionalization of the PSCs' capabilities to protect Chinese interests abroad has already begun. It remains to be seen whether China will succeed in promoting its agenda, and what the implications of the Chinese PSCs' evolution could be. The impact of efficient Chinese PSCs that are able to communicate with the Chinese military and public security forces overseas is not easy to assess; however, the strategic and security implications will be profound.

CHINESE PSCs: WHAT IS NEXT?

The Chinese PSCs' expansion in Africa and the Middle East shows how the Chinese private security industry evolves, and looking at two leading companies could present some insights to understand the overall sector.

In this respect, the Chinese PSCs' footprint in Africa is still limited to unarmed guards who patrol buildings, parking lots, and factories. Although China shares a long-term tradition of investing and cooperating with African countries, the investments spearheaded by the Chinese SOEs and their security needs contracted to the Chinese PSCs are a new phenomenon. The ongoing demand for private security differs considerably from the demand of mercenaries in Africa's postcolonial wars. Unfortunately, the presence of Russian contractors in the region is muddying the waters. While there is a certain ambiguity in grouping the Chinese PSCs in Africa with the Russian contractors and calling both mercenaries, the difference abounds. An example of the different approach to security threats happened on November 25, 2019, when three Chinese miners were kidnapped at gunpoint in the Nigerian state of Osun.[21] Nearly a month before, five Russian private military contractors and twenty local soldiers were killed in Mozambique during an ambush by militants allied with the Islamic State.[22] Both incidents reveal that protecting assets from criminal and political violence is a common task for both the Chinese PSCs and the Russian PMCs. The first group guard Chinese economic interests, while the second is actively involved in increasing the combat capabilities of governments that are integral to Russia's realpolitik in Africa. In this respect the presence of Russian heavily armed contractors overshadows the media attention to and overall interest in Chinese contractors operating inside gated compounds.

However, Chinese security companies operating proficiently at an international level are still a tiny fraction of the overall Chinese PSCs' footprint. Nevertheless, their experiences, even the negative ones, are an essential milestone for the ongoing reform of the Chinese National Standard for security services that is supposed to close the legal gaps in the provision of Chinese security services outside China's borders. Probably, the Chinese PSCs will still be limited by Chinese law from carrying weapons. Nevertheless, carrying weapons is not a key issue for professional services in most Chinese PSCs' global operations. Armed guards can be hired locally or in the international market for force. In this respect, what can be perceived as a limitation could be a blessing in disguise, helping the Chinese PSCs' security sector to develop alternative solutions from surveillance technologies solutions and automated crisis management as an alternative to the use of lethal force.

According to Huaxin Zhongan Security Group[23] (HXZA) director Liu Qing,[24] the companies operating in the Chinese private security sector aiming to achieve international standards are more the exception than the norm. That is why HXZA, considered a leading PSC in China, is trying to elevate itself above the average Chinese PSCs by acquiring international recognition and certification. The company is a certified member of ICoCA* and achieved the certifications of ISO 28007, ISO 18788, and PSC-1 to operate internationally in complex environments such as the maritime domain. Although HXZA is one of the main international maritime security service providers in China, the company's main revenue is still anchored to the Mainland. Nevertheless, the interest in internationally recognized certifications is part of the company's long-term plan to expand its services outside the pool of Chinese clients. Again, something outside the usual Chinese PSCs' thinking box. The Chinese domestic market is quite secure and does not require the complexities that the ICoC operating environment requires. Nevertheless, there are many parts of the ICoC that can benefit the Chinese private security sector professionalization before the PSCs will follow their clients outside the country.

Another leading Chinese security company that is closer to the government is the Haiwei[25] group. In several African countries where the security threat is limited, such as Tanzania to Ethiopia, Haiwei ensures the protection of Chinese construction and logistic companies, their core clients along the BRI. Knowing its own limits, Haiwei is not prone to jump into complex environments, but the African fast-changing security landscape is already proving to be severe challenges in the Ethiopian civil war.

The Chinese government's future attempts to regulate overseas operations of Chinese PSCs will probably focus on the compliance with Chinese and local laws, avoiding any kind of negative spillover that can compromise the BRI win-win narrative. Almost the entire group of Chinese security managers interviewed agrees that Chinese armed security contractors are a double-edged sword that may not necessarily result in Chinese PSCs being more competitive than Western PSCs.[26] Nevertheless, the allure of a "Blackwater model" is still palpable among the Chinese security practitioners that have a former military background and the overall machismo that surrounds security services.

One of the main problems stemming from Chinese operations abroad, and not only in the security sectors, is the obsession of relying exclusively on Chinese employees. Only a few Chinese PSCs understand

---

* See appendix III.

the need to have local personnel employed not only as boots on the ground but also in management. Being able to speak the local language and know the local culture and legal requirements is a necessary step to set up a proper business. Even fewer Chinese PSCs among the already small group that works with local security officials are inclined to hire third-country nationals to provide high-end security functions. High prices and communication difficulties are just two of the several problems in hiring foreign talents. Even a few cases of long-term contracts for Western foreign managers are negatively affected by the ongoing U.S.-China competition. Russian private security contractors are still an option, but the aforementioned language problem and the reputations of the Wagner Group in Africa and the Russian Army following the invasion of Ukraine are not going to facilitate any business soon.

Still, Chinese top companies from HXZA to Haiwei already realized that in the security industry military or police experience is important but needs to be integrated with a wide array of capabilities including retired diplomats, insurance experts, medical professionals, salesmen, and data analysts.

BLACKWATER WITH CHINESE CHARACTERISTICS

Contrary to the past, the trajectory of Chinese PSCs is set on a limited cooperation with Western security companies, but one exception is still making waves in the private security arena: Frontier Services Group (FSG).

In 2014, FSG, incorporated in Bermuda and headquartered in Hong Kong with an office in Beijing, was founded as an "advanced logistic" company by Erik Prince, the creator of Blackwater. FSG's footprint lies in protecting Chinese interests outside China that span from the Middle East to Africa and Southeast Asia. The position of the FSG toward the BRI is straightforward: the BRI is a win-win plan, not a neocolonial tool.[27] Having CITIC, a Chinese financial juggernaut, as majority shareholder, FSG oversees security for several Chinese projects along the BRI.

In 2016 FSG and Prince got back into the authorities' spotlights following an investigative report from Intercept that pointed the finger at an alleged FSG attempt "to sell defence services in Libya and other countries in Africa has widened to a probe of allegations that Prince received assistance from Chinese intelligence to set up an account for his Libya operations through the Bank of China."[28] An FBI investigation followed shortly because Libya, which has been ravaged by a civil war, is under UN arms embargo.[29]

The year 2017 is when FSG officially shifted from logistics service to security service, something that its Chinese counterpart was looking at from the beginning. The acquisition of a training center in Beijing to nurture future private security contractors was the first step toward a larger training camp in the autonomous province of Xinjiang. The plan was never taken to a conclusion due to an increase in the international condemnation of the treatment of the local Uyghur minority. Also, Prince officially mentioned that he was not aware of the program.

In April 2021, Mr. Prince resigned as executive director and deputy chairman of the company.[30] FSG is currently headed by Li Xiaopeng, and the company chairman is Chang Zhenming, representing CITIC, which is the majority stakeholder. The role of Li in FSG is not by chance as he previously controlled one of the leading Chinese PSCs, Dewei (DeWe) International Security Limited, which was acquired by FSG in 2021.[31] According to the FSG website, the main business lines of Dewei and its subsidiaries are security services and health care rescue services, provided for overseas Chinese-funded enterprises including public security consulting, public security training, overseas on-site public security management, and public security technology protection. Since then, FSG's business has progressively expanded from Africa to ASEAN, a region less affected by the negative effect of the COVID-19 pandemic on the economy and still a profitable avenue for the expansion of the BRI. While the connectivity infrastructure investment drive spearheaded by the BRI is still the main client for Chinese PSCs in the region, the Chinese interest in acquiring long-term leases for naval bases are raising some eyebrows in the U.S. intelligence community. FSG already has several clients in Cambodia and Laos, considered two countries in the ASEAN community closer to Beijing. The client portfolio ranges from protecting Chinese bank branches to Siam Reap International Airport and the construction sites of the high-speed railway that is connecting the Laotian capital Vientiane to China.[32] In the 2021 interim report

FSG underlines how, "owing to [the] COVID-19 pandemic, the Group did not render any new activities in any sanctioned country or to any sanctioned company or sanctioned individual which might expose to any of the sanction risks." Nevertheless, the business model seems to pay off as the company reported a positive revenue from contracts with customers for the first quarter of 2021.[33]

Besides the fact that the machismo that surrounds the Blackwater narrative is still present in some parts of the Chinese private security community, the fact that the presence of Mr. Prince in FSG is shrinking proves that the Chinese's "third way" to protect China's interests abroad is on its way.

CHAPTER SIX

Defending the BRI from Africa
to the Middle East

THE AFRICA-CHINA RELATIONSHIP THROUGH THE PRISM OF THE PRIVATE SECURITY SECTOR

OVER THE PAST FEW YEARS, AFRICA HAS WITNESSED AN INCREASING presence of private military companies and mercenaries, ranging from the ubiquitous Russian Wagner Group to the South African Dyck Advisory Group (DAG).[1] In addition, Chinese private security actors are expanding their footprint in the continent, while still maintaining their usual passive stance. As is happening from Central Asia to South America, the evolution of the BRI in the African continent has generated a demand for security services. It has also promoted a fertile business environment for the diffusion of Chinese PSCs.[2] In this respect, the African continent is riddled with a wide range of conflicts that involve state and nonstate actors. Political fragility, jihadist militias' expansion, religious tensions, tribal rivalries, settler/herder confrontations, unequal distribution of water resources, and natural disasters linked with climate change are a constant source of anxiety for China.[3]

The November 2022 kidnapping of five Chinese nationals near a mine in southeast DRC and the March 2023 killing of nine Chinese miners in CAR are cases in point.[4]

In light of the growth in China's geoeconomics needs, several African countries are fundamental for China's economic development. This explains why the security sector in Africa involves a multidimensional approach from Beijing:

- Security guarantees from local governments.
- Active participation in UN peacekeeping missions.
- Expansion of the Chinese private security sector.

While the decades-old principle of noninterference is slowly evolving toward selective engagement, Beijing is still determined to avoid direct confrontations such as sending the PLA to guarantee the security of Chinese investments in foreign counties. However, Beijing is maintaining a "balanced vagueness"[5] in dealing with the evolving crisis, which means betting on both sides of the problem.

China is still going to abide by its core principle of noninterference in internal affairs based on the international order centered on the United Nations and underpinned by international law until Beijing is ready to get involved in the foreign security quagmire. For the moment, however, high-risk areas from Sahel to Western Africa are not a priority for Beijing. Therefore contracting private security companies for guarding duties is partially filling the security gaps without the need for official Chinese boots on the ground.

Considering the ongoing and future crisis, risk assessment and mitigation within African countries participating in the BRI requires a wide range of security services, including maritime protection against pirates.

One of the worst attacks on Chinese energy interests in Africa happened in Ethiopia. In 2007, the independence movement Ogaden National Liberation Front (ONLF) targeted a Chinese-run gas field to insert a wedge in the cooperation between the Addis Ababa regime and Beijing. The attack claimed the lives of seventy-four workers, of which nine were Chinese nationals. In an ONLF communiqué, the rebels cautioned that all foreign energy companies will be targeted if they deprive the Ogaden people of their resources. Also supporting the Ethiopian central government in denying the Ogaden right to self-determination was another point of contention against China's presence in the region.[6]

Similarly in Sudan, the Darfur Justice and Equality Movement,[7] an armed group opposed to the central government in Khartoum, targeted Chinese workers in order to constrain the government's relationship with China. Since South Sudan declared its independence, threats to Chinese workers have become the norm. In 2012, forty-seven Chinese employees of China's state-owned Power Construction Corp. were attacked by a rebel group and twenty-nine were held hostage.[8] Following the previously mentioned kidnapping of five Chinese miners in DRC, the Chinese Enterprises Association invited FSG's security company in DRC to conduct an online security training for seventy-three Chinese companies based in the region.[9]

The shocking attack on a Chinese gold mine in the Central African Republic in March 2023, where nine Chinese nationals were killed and two others were wounded without any culprit being brought to justice, may have involved mercenaries. The motive of the attack on the Chinese-managed gold mine remains unclear as no militant organization has laid claim to the assault, nor did the attackers steal valuables and equipment or try to kidnap Chinese workers for ransom.

Therefore the security situation in the region is complicated not only by weak states not being able to protect China's interests but also by the expansion of Russian mercenaries that provide training services for the local military or even take part in the conflict. The precarious security situation and the vulnerability of Chinese workers in the region underscore Beijing's challenges when a new security actor, the Wagner Group, operates in the same area but with opposite interests. China's BRI necessitates stability to prosper, while the Wagner Group thrives in chaos.

Therefore the presence of unaccountable mercenaries, whose local actions may not align with Moscow's instructions, could cause tension in the newly formed "no-limits" Sino-Russian relationship.[10] Compared to other regions where Chinese PSCs are operating, the African private security dimension is characterized by several anomalies.[11]

First, the African continent still carries the stigma associated with mercenary actions that occurred during postcolonial conflicts. Second, well before the launch of the BRI and Beijing's endorsement for PSCs to go abroad, several Chinese companies operating in Africa, in sectors ranging from natural resources extraction to small businesses, set up their own private armed militias.[12] Third, while the Chinese PSCs' footprint is limited to a handful of countries, the so-called coup belt in Central and West Africa is witnessing the return of mercenaries, including the rapid expansion of the Russian Wagner Group.

While East Africa is home to the first Chinese overseas military base and Djibouti represents Beijing's concrete response to a changing international security environment, Chinese companies operating in Southern and Eastern Africa are betting their security on Chinese PSCs. In order to evaluate the role of the Chinese PSCs in the region, it is essential to consider the interactions between China's military and maritime engagement in the African continent as well as the role of the Chinese blue helmet peacekeeping missions.[13]

The first military base outside China in Djibouti as well as the expansion of Chinese PSCs overseas are two sides of the same "latent power." According to Sun Degang, China cultivates latent power for economic interests in the Middle East and Africa while downplaying the military dimension of its growing global power. Even the first Chinese military base overseas in Djibouti reflects China's risk aversion, pragmatism, low-key behavior, and emphasis on the security-economy nexus.[14] Therefore China's strategic footprint in regions far from its shores is rooted in avoiding conflict as much as possible, while Chinese PSCs operating abroad need to defuse and mitigate risk and not create confrontations with local stakeholders.

More often than not, the message from Beijing, to avoid any local trouble that can backfire on China, is not reaching the PSCs operating in Africa. Especially the small Chinese PSCs that are just the last component of a lengthy subcontracting process did not get the memo. The case of illegal miners shot in a Chinese-owned mine in Zambia[15] is a case in point.

Nevertheless, the presence of Chinese investments in Africa, especially in the mining sector, predates the BRI. These investments were driven by the private sector more than by SOEs. During that time, and even now, in several areas in Africa, small private Chinese firms and groups of small businesses contract local armed militias or even arm themselves for protection. Several times, this DIY modus operandi has ended in tragedy.

Since the expansion of President Xi's flagship foreign policy initiative, SOEs are increasing their presence in the African continent, and their security requirements are demanding professionalism and adherence to the Chinese regulations. As recently as 2015, the Chinese Ministry of Defence's white paper on military strategy elucidated the requirement to be able to protect its own citizens abroad while simultaneously securing the sea lines of communication and the land routes essential to the country's energy and trade security. In 2018 the Chinese government implemented a comprehensive set of regulations to address the security necessities of Chinese companies operating overseas: the Security Management Guidelines for Overseas Chinese-Funded Companies, Institutions and Personnel. The guidelines not only codify the training requirements, security assessments, and risk mitigation procedures, they also address issues such as information sharing.

In the African development-security nexus, it is compelling to consider the interactions between China's military and the expanding presence of Chinese PSCs. Considering that Chinese PSCs are a latecomer in the African security sector, however, the process of integrating security, conflict resolution, and economic development is still plagued by major shortcomings and unintended consequences. At present, China's PSCs are still evolving from local security enterprises operating in low-risk environments in Mainland China to international companies able to maneuver independently in complex environments. Several Chinese PSCs are already extending feelers in the continent to establish profitable business partnerships, especially in Djibouti, Egypt, Ethiopia, South Africa, and Tanzania.

Also in Africa, the security contracting race for the cheapest option still plagues the overall Chinese security sector's internationalization process. Nevertheless, a new wave of Chinese PSCs has found a profitable niche market that requires advanced security services and not just guarding a warehouse's CCTV. These services include the protection of Chinese businessmen and diplomats against kidnapping or the protection of Chinese commercial vessels transiting through high-risk waters, just to name a few. In this context, a small number of Chinese PSCs, out of more than several thousand companies based in China, are showcasing the required capabilities. Nevertheless, the evolution of the Chinese private security footprint in Africa's complex security environment offers precious insight into the future of Chinese PSCs as a whole.

Therefore local best practices and lessons that Beijing can extract from Cape to Cairo are not only of paramount importance for the Chinese-African cooperation mechanism but also for the evolution of the entire Chinese private security sector.

NOT JUST PROTECTING OIL: CHINA'S MIDDLE EAST SECURITY QUAGMIRE

Over the past decade, China has become the largest foreign investor and trading partner with the Middle East. Almost 40 percent of China's energy imports come from the Gulf Cooperation Council alone, with the largest portion from the Kingdom of Saudi Arabia. In addition, oil imports from Iran and Iraq are set to increase due to increasingly warm diplomatic relations and economic cooperation. It is not by accident that at the end of 2021 Chinese Foreign Affairs Minister Wang Yi visited the region extensively, and in January 2022, foreign ministers of seven Middle East countries visited China, including members of the Gulf Council Cooperation (GCC) like Bahrain, Saudi Arabia, Kuwait, and Oman. In addition, Turkey is growing its economic and technological cooperation with China. In a time when the United States seeks to reduce its strategic footprint in the Middle East, China is increasing its presence in the region.[16] At the same time, the outbreak of war in Ukraine accelerated this regional dynamic, as most Middle Eastern countries are performing a balancing act between Washington and Beijing, with differing degrees of engagement. However, becoming the region's economic and technological juggernaut is not going to shield Beijing from becoming entangled in the Middle East's many conflicts.[17]

In this respect China is not eager at all to replace the security provider role that the United States has played for many decades in the Middle East. For many years Chinese academicians have warned Beijing to avoid getting entangled in the Middle East quagmire; nevertheless the Chinese military footprint in the region is growing from weapons sales and also its naval presence. While China is still recognized as an unwilling security provider, the role that the PSCs are going to play in the Middle East, as is happening in Africa, is set to increase in scope and requirements. At the same time China plays an enviable position in the MENA region, being simultaneously able to enjoy good relations with Israel, the Gulf monarchies, and Iran. Also, by forging Saudi Arabia–Iran rapprochement based on the message that economic development goes hand in hand with security stabilization, China strengthened its image as an alternative to the West in the Global South.

The new security dynamics ignited by the United States repositioning its forces in the Middle East is forcing the Chinese government to take a more active stance in the security arena, whether the government is prepared to do so or not. Chinese SOEs and especially those related to the energy sector, however, require proficient risk management, which forces the Chinese private security sector to evolve. Similar to what is happening in Africa, China has grown increasingly anxious about the security situation in the Middle East. Guaranteeing the country necessary energy security, open sea lines of communication, and the development of its BRI, an ongoing war in Yemen and a never-ending dispute on a nuclear Iran calls for a delicate balancing act.

As mentioned on the Chinese security footprint in Africa, contracting private security companies for guarding duties partially fills the security gaps without the immediate necessity of PLA overseas operation. At the same time, the growing Chinese security presence in the Middle East is a serious concern for the United States and its allies. At the time of writing, Beijing is adamant that there is no plan for additional military bases after Djibouti and Tajikistan. Still, the United States is pointing the finger at possible international ports that can have a military and civilian dual use or are just a hidden military base as happened in the United Arab Emirates (UAE). A report by the *Wall Street Journal* hinted at suspicious construction work inside a container terminal built and operated by a Chinese shipping corporation in the Emirates' port city of Khalifa. The report indicated that U.S. intelligence agencies found evidence of construction work on what they believed was a secret Chinese military facility in the UAE.[18]

Nevertheless, well before the BRI inroad in the Middle East, the first Chinese PSCs adventuring outside China had set foot in Iraq and Sudan, protecting Chinese SOEs operating in natural resources extraction and trade. From the late 1990s, most of the Chinese PSC operations in the Middle East were tasked with the same security objective: shielding Chinese engineers against kidnapping for ransom and the Chinese-built infrastructure against attacks from militants or criminal organizations.[19]

Since 2011, when the Arab Spring elevated the region's insecurity by a notch, Beijing was between a rock and a hard place. Starting to place boots on the ground was against the principle of noninterference that would get China stuck in the Middle East quagmire. At the same time, the light boots on the ground presence granted by the PSCs became a viable placeholder. Also, in the Middle East, Beijing's security stance is "shifting away from harvesting economic benefits while avoiding political entanglements . . . albeit in a cautious way."[20]

Following the fragmentation of power in Iraq, the collapse of the Muammar Ghaddafi regime in Libya, the blockade in Qatar, and the ongoing civil unrest in Syria, the Chinese private security sector needs to cope with a fast-moving security environment. From basic guarding services involving checking workers' identities and protecting equipment from looting, the Chinese PSCs in the Middle East are now called on to provide advanced security services including anti- and countersurveillance tasks and antidrone protection. Since 2013, with the increase in infrastructure investments spearheaded by the BRI, Beijing has aimed to link the MENA region with the Chinese trade corridors along the China-Pakistan Economic Corridor (CPEC), Central Asia, and the Mediterranean basin. In addition, China's increasing foreign direct investments in the Middle Eastern economies and a more significant presence along the Red Sea and the Western Indian Ocean sea routes have amplified the threat spectrum to China.

EXPANDING CHINA'S SECURITY FOOTPRINT IN THE MIDDLE EAST

While the African continent witnessed firsthand the return of mercenaries in the postcolonial wars, the Middle East was the first region to experience the rise of PMCs, starting with Iraq.[21] As the Iraq war has been an eye-opener for Beijing to modernize the PLA, the Chinese private security sector also took the hint from the Blackwater model to look for new business opportunities abroad.

The deployment of professional Chinese PSCs in the Middle East is a perfect fit with Beijing's policy to avoid projecting power abroad and specifically to avoid getting dragged into the quagmire of the Middle East's shifting security sands.[22]

While China still lags behind the United States as the leading security provider in the MENA region and elsewhere on the African continent, it is the regional economic juggernaut. In 2018 the MENA region ranked as the second-largest recipient of investment and Chinese construction projects worldwide after Europe, and the trend is growing.[*]

Nevertheless, security remains one of the most difficult challenges. Beijing's development-security nexus is further complicated by a growing presence of more than one million Chinese expatriates in the MENA region, ranging from construction workers to businesspeople, students, and even religious pilgrims to Saudi Arabia and Iran.

In China's Arab Policy Paper (2016), Beijing outlined the blueprint for economic and cultural development with Arab states and enhanced connectivity with the rest of the BRI. In the white paper, only a paragraph is dedicated to security cooperation: "Jointly enhance the capability to cope with non-traditional security threats, support the international community's efforts to combat piracy, continue to send warships to the Gulf of Aden and waters off Somalia to maintain international maritime security, and conduct cyber security cooperation."[23]

As previously mentioned, the Chinese companies' approach to risk management varies from company to company, but the SOEs in the natural resources exploitation business are better funded and better equipped in terms of management to request and pay for the needed security services.

While China's defense cooperation in the Middle East is still very limited compared to the United States and Russia, the military cooperation trend in the region is growing and the Chinese PSCs are positioned as "brand ambassador" for Chinese high-tech security products. According to the Stockholm International Peace Research Institute (SIPRI), China provided only 5 percent of arms transfers to the MENA region between 2014 and 2018, compared to the United States (54 percent) and Russia (9.6 percent).[24] However, Chinese military hardware sales and transfers in the region are niche sectors involving combat-armed and

---

[*] Afshin Molavi, "China's Global Investments Are Declining Everywhere Except for One Region," *Foreign Policy*, May 16, 2019, https://foreignpolicy.com/2019/05/16/chinas-global-investments-are-declining-everywhere-except-for-one-region/, last accessed August 25, 2020.

scouting drones and missiles. An example is the transfer of an armed drone production line to the Kingdom of Saudi Arabia.

China's energy requirements are entangled in a wider and more complex security dynamic in the Middle East.

The "three sisters"—China National Petroleum Corporation (CNPC), Sinopec Group, and China National Offshore Oil Corporation (CNOOC)—reached a high level of risk management and mitigation capabilities well before the other Chinese SOEs. In December 2019, a fourth player was added with China Oil & Gas Piping Network Corporation* (COGPC),[25] established to manage all Chinese gas pipelines.

In this respect, multinational companies, especially involved with natural resources exploitation, are used to operating in high-risk environments, and the Chinese state energy giants do not differ from their international peers. From the Middle East to Africa, attacks on Chinese oil facilities have cost the lives of local and Chinese workers. Therefore it is likely that China's energy sector SOEs have learned how to cope with security risk the hard way.[26]

Half of China's energy security depends on the Middle East. In 2019, Iraq became China's third-highest source of crude oil imports, after Saudi Arabia and Russia, with a value of $23.7 billion.† Since the beginning of 2018, Iraqi crude supplies have plugged the gap generated by Saudi Arabia's planned output reduction until the Saudi-led OPEC+ dispute with Russia in early 2020 and by U.S. sanctions on Iranian crude exports. Following the impact of COVID-19 on oil prices and the drastic cut in oil exports by at least 15 percent in June 2020 to meet the OPEC+ planned reduction, oil exports from Baghdad have become more important for China.‡ During February 2020, Iraq boosted oil sales to China, reaching 1.32 million barrels per day (mbd), in part thanks to the increased productivity from the Kurd-

---

* Zhen Xin, "China's Oil Giants Spin Off Pipeline Assets," *China Daily*, July 25, 2020, http://www.chinadaily.com.cn/a/202007/25/WS5f1b8f8ba31083481725bffc.html.

† Daniel Workman, "Top 15 Crude Oil Suppliers to China," *World's Top Exports*, July 11, 2020, http://www.worldstopexports.com/top-15-crude-oil-suppliers-to-china/.

‡ "Crude exports to China from northern Iraq, via the Turkish port of Ceyhan, also saw a significant rise in May. Shipments to China made up 44 percent of overall exports of around 400,000 bpd last month, according to data from TankerTrackers.com." In Noam Raydan, "Demand and Storage Cause Notable Shifts in Iraq's Oil Flow to India, China," *Forbes*, June 12, 2020, https://www.forbes.com/sites/noamraydan/2020/06/12/demand-and-storage-cause-notable-shifts-in-iraqs-oil-flow-to-india china/#31f1333d2c78, last accessed July 19, 2020.

ish region.* The defeat of ISIS in Iraq has enabled a fragile stabilization, but the energy assets are still a preferred target by politically motivated actors whose objective is to destabilize the fragile Iraqi political and economic situation due to the strategic importance for Iraqi state revenues.

Most of the Chinese oil field concessions in Iraq are in the relatively safer southern part of the country. However, the expansion of the Chinese SOEs is moving toward exploration blocks in the less safe northeast. While the projects provide good prospects for new sources of oil and gas, they also call for additional security measures. Similarly in war-ravaged Yemen, before a complete pullout of Chinese workers in 2010, two Chinese engineers were abducted not only for monetary gains but also as a bargaining chip to lure China into the looming civil war.

Well before the BRI, when the countries that attract Chinese investments were not able to protect Beijing's interests and personnel, Chinese SOEs employed an established multinational private security provider. An example is Control Risk, a U.K.-headquartered security company that protected Chinese oil fields in Iraq.

Since 2015, the Chinese market for private security in energy evolved from the cooperation with international security companies to Chinese PSCs carrying the bulk of security responsibilities and managing local armed militias.

DEFENDING US$63 BILLION: CHINESE PSCs IN PAKISTAN

On a dry and dusty morning in the port city of Karachi, a woman in local dress loitered as a white van approached. As the vehicle arrived, an explosion rocked the area, and flames consumed the van. The gruesome scene was captured by CCTV near Karachi University. It recorded the assassination of three Chinese teachers and a Pakistani driver by a suicide bomber from the Baloch Liberation Army.[27]

The victims were not Chinese security or diplomatic personnel. But being staff of the university's Confucius Institute made them high-value targets for a politically motivated assassination nonetheless.

---

* Anthony Di Paola, "Iraq Boost Monthly Oil Sales to China by a Third Despite Virus," *Bloomberg*, March 2, 2020, https://www.bloomberg.com/news/articles/2020-03-03/surge-in-iraq-oil-sales-to -china-boosts-gulf-exports-amid-virus, last accessed July 18, 2020.

The US$63 billion China-Pakistan Economic Corridor (CPEC), considered one of the most ambitious projects in Beijing's BRI, has been hit by numerous terrorist attacks, and Pakistani security has been trying for more than a decade to halt separatist militant attacks on Chinese workers. The attack on the Confucius Institute personnel represents an escalation. As Chinese diplomats and businesspeople living in the region step up their security protection, teachers are a soft target, meaning their security is mainly left to the local police.

The April 26, 2022, attack could thus mark the tipping point in Beijing's plan to accelerate the professionalization of Chinese PSCs to provide protection for the BRI. Beijing's caution in deploying the PLA overseas has seen Chinese PSCs evolve to become a tool to defend Beijing's interests abroad.

According to Bensy Teo, marketing director for China Cityguard Security Service Group (CCSSG), a PSC based in Shanghai, Beijing will definitely emphasize having more security for any Chinese investments in Pakistan. A recent government note to Chinese enterprises investing overseas mentions the need to engage Chinese PSCs cooperating with local private security outfits.[28]

CCSSG, which has been in Pakistan for almost nine years, is headquartered in Lahore. It works with a local PSC mainly staffed by former Pakistani military personnel. The company's operations in Pakistan reflect the challenges for Chinese PSCs, not only in Pakistan but also in other highly complex environments: having an exhaustive understanding of the region, and carrying out due diligence on prospective security partners.

With respect to the latter, which is seen as vital to Chinese PSCs working abroad, Beijing still prohibits private contractors from carrying weapons while overseas, so they must partner with local ones for kinetic functions where Chinese companies are falling short.

CCSSG's Mr. Teo warned:

Some of these Chinese PSCs that operate abroad with less professional expertise fail to consider the overall situation in which an attack occurs, without looking at proper planning in terms of escape, evacuation, and prevention. For example, a Chinese company may have an office within a building and have guards stationed in their office, but they fail to evaluate the quality of the security company that is managing the entire building.[29]

These shortcomings mean that Beijing will have to reconsider its outsourcing of overseas security provision to PSCs. In addition to the lack of quality, the manpower pool is shrinking. China's reliance on automation for security functions, from facial recognition software to AI, means there are fewer people with the talents required. Those that are available are getting increasingly expensive to hire.

Another factor that will tame Beijing's lust for PSCs to defend its interests abroad is its own National Cybersecurity Law.* The law will alarm host countries: it means China's regulations will conflict with their own in terms of privacy, Big Data cross-border flows, and ultimately in the use of AI for facial recognition and population control. This is likely to make working with Chinese PSCs less than an attractive option.

Despite all this, China is pressing ahead. Chinese PSCs are still looking at possible partners from Pakistan to the Middle East, and especially in central Africa. It seems that in China, the negative press that Russia's Wagner Group has received from Syria to Ukraine has been lost in translation.

With Chinese overseas—particularly in Pakistan and Africa—increasingly becoming the target of violence, Beijing will have to bite the bullet when it comes to looking after the well-being of its citizens abroad. Whether it will discard its playbook on PSCs or the PLA remains to be seen. However it decides, the moves to come will have important repercussions starting with Pakistan's high-risk areas.

DEFENDING CHINA'S NEAR ABROAD: CENTRAL ASIA

Moving from South Asia to Central Asia, Niva Yau, an expert on China's western peripheral diplomacy including Central Asia and Afghanistan, mapped the presence of Chinese PSCs in Kazakhstan, Kyrgyzstan, and Uzbekistan. Discussing with Yau the Chinese PSCs' footprint in the region, she mentioned that the level of presence is different in each of the three

---

* See appendix III.

countries, mainly due to local legal restrictions.[30] The first Chinese PSC that set up shop in Central Asia was Xinjiang Shamo Tewei in Kazakhstan. Since 2013, the company provided close protection security services for Chinese engineers working in the extraction industry, a common occurrence not only in the region but also in Africa and the Middle East. In Kyrgyzstan, the Chinese PSC Zhongjun Junhong provides a more sophisticated service compared to their peers including political risk assessments and training.[31] The striking difference from the usual Chinese PSCs operating abroad is that the company has a local weapon license granted by authorities.

Yau mentioned:

The local private security sector is quite large in both Kazakhstan and Kyrgyzstan for different reasons. For Kazakhstan, because there's a lot of money; for Kyrgyzstan because there's a weak state and a lot of political instability. Chinese PSCs here set up joint ventures with Kyrgyz local private security, whereas in Kazakhstan the local Kazakh private security companies, they have a large labour union group. They lobby in the Kazakh parliament to resist Chinese entry into the Kazakh market because they already have good relationships with the Russian private security companies.[32]

Central Asia is a highly complex environment, especially in Kyrgyzstan and Tajikistan where economic and political fragility are compounded with the negative spillover from the neighboring Islamic Emirate of Afghanistan. Some of the contracting between Chinese SOEs and Chinese PSCs operating in Central Asia is on public tenders published online on Chinese government websites, but the subcontracting process with local partners is marred by difficulties and a total lack of transparency. It does not come as a surprise in countries where the corruption index still ranks among the highest in the world.[33]

Therefore Chinese companies' cooperation with local private security counterparts is negatively affected by lack of professionalization and endemic corruption.

On the positive side, Chinese PSCs in Central Asia provide a best-practice model for other Chinese PSCs adventuring abroad. That is close collaboration with the Chinese embassy. Considering that the region shares long borders with China and is also the birthplace of the BRI, being the cradle of the ancient Silk Road, the Chinese government has taken several important steps to promote the coordination between the various stakeholders abroad. Such coordination mechanisms include the embassy pushing to establish security management guidelines.

This trend is part of the 2018 document "Security Management Guidelines for Overseas Chinese-Funded Companies, Institutions and Personnel,"* but the implementation of the 170-page guidelines that Chinese companies operating abroad should abide by is still neither widely adopted nor enforced along the BRI. A core element presented in the document and already mentioned as a possible growing activity for the Chinese PSCs operating overseas is the newly established mechanism called the "Belt and Road National Security Intelligence System."† The report is not shy to openly advocate the data collection role that the Chinese private security sector is called on to perform while outside the Chinese borders. As mentioned in the previous chapters, the regulation mentions explicitly that the new security mechanism aims to make intelligence gathering more transparent across different ministries concerning foreign affairs. Chinese PSCs are expected to report to Chinese embassies.

The recommendations presented in the guidelines, which have been published under the aegis of the Chinese Ministry of Trade and not the Ministry of Foreign Affairs or the Ministry of State Security, are strategic in faraway regions where China lacks the proper data-gathering and assessment capabilities. In the near abroad, however, Beijing has already in place well-established bilateral and multilateral security cooperation agreements.

For example, in Central Asia the joint intelligence gathering efforts in preventing the "three evils of extremism, separatism, and terrorism" falls under the purview of the Shanghai Cooperation Organization (SCO). Therefore Chinese PSCs in the region are required to add more granular

---

* See appendix III.
† See appendix III.

data but not be a part of government-to-government collaborations. In a nutshell, it is very detailed data about local criminal groups or local political risks analysis that could enable Beijing and the SOEs to make proper assessment in case of long-term investments.

At the same time some Chinese DIY PSCs, as happened in Africa, tried to exploit legal loopholes to overcome local restrictions on foreign PSCs. For example, in Kazakhstan the legal restriction is not only related to the ban on foreign contractors to carry weapons as happens in other parts of Central Asia, but the entire foreign private security sector is not allowed to operate in the country. Therefore, in Kazakhstan, allegedly some Chinese PSCs are incorporated as "logistics services," something not far from FSG's early playbook in Africa, or the security contracts are signed and enforced in Beijing with the close protection detail following the Chinese workers abroad under a business visa.

Contrary to China, Russia has a different PSC footprint in Central Asia, and it is the case of real PSCs and not paramilitary groups like the Wagner Group. In case of trouble in the region Moscow doesn't need little green men or the Wagner Group, it can send CSTO troops as happened in 2021.

Until Tokayev became president of Kazakhstan, there were Russian PSCs in Kazakhstan cooperating with the Kazakh private security companies. Discussing with Yau, she mentioned that

the Kazakhs are okay with it; they're okay with working with the Russians in Kazakhstan because the Russians actually also let the Kazakh private security companies work in Russia so there's a good collaboration there. This is not the same for China—we don't see Kazakh PSCs in China for example; this will be quite unthinkable.[34]

On January 3, 2022, Chinese president Xi Jinping exchanged celebratory messages with Kazakhstan's recently elected President Kassym-Jomart Tokayev and the country's founding father, Nursultan Nazarbayev, to mark the thirtieth anniversary of diplomatic ties between the two countries.[35]

Just two days later, Kazakhstan was on fire. Deadly riots ignited by a sudden spike in liquefied petroleum gas prices are continuing across what was once considered among the most stable of ex-Soviet republics in Central Asia, and the repercussions may extend beyond its borders. However, the eruption of popular protest in small rural areas that suddenly engulfed the two most populous cities in the country is nothing new. Not only in Kazakhstan but all over the region, a long-term unrest could spell economic disaster as landlocked countries of Central Asia are a linchpin of the BRI, which is already reeling from the COVID-19 pandemic. This would cast serious doubt on the viability of the BRI's land connections and energy supply routes, which link Turkmenistan's gas and Kazakhstan's oil reserves to China via its westernmost province of Xinjiang. At the time of writing there is no report of Chinese or Russian PSC involvement during the riots or as an early warning system as all the countries bordering Kazakhstan were caught by surprise.

Worse, the crisis in Kazakhstan could have generated a domino effect that ensnares other less stable countries in the region, such as Tajikistan and Kyrgyzstan.

The situation in Kyrgyzstan doesn't differ much from certain regions in Africa where the combination of weak government, criminal groups, and profitable mining activities run by Chinese companies create a volatile environment prone to violence. One difference with Africa is set in the expansion of the Chinese private security sector toward new technologies. While in Africa and the Middle East it is already happening, in Central Asia it is not the case. The SCO and other bilateral security cooperation structures between China and the Central Asian countries include high-tech surveillance technology for military and civilian use aimed at border control and population surveillance in urban areas, with the top Chinese companies from Huawei to Hikvision already operating in the region without the need of Chinese PSCs being their ambassadors.

CHAPTER SEVEN

How China Sees Its
Own Private Security Sector

ACADEMIC DISCOURSE

IN CHINA, THE ACADEMIC DISCOURSE AROUND THE CHINESE PRIVATE security sector differs substantially from the international perception of China's PSCs. In the West, English- and French-language articles and academic papers offer a broad interpretation of Chinese PSCs, from trained mercenaries to incompetent guardians. On the contrary, in China, the academic discourse is centered on the implications of the need to protect the BRI and the necessary evolution of new laws and norms that regulate the private security sector.

Since 2015, the Chinese academic view of PSCs reflects Beijing's growing concerns over the deterioration of the BRI's security.

In November 2015, a large-scale hostage-taking incident occurred at the Radisson Blu Hotel in Bamako, the capital of Mali. The terrorist attack ended up with the tragic toll of nineteen lives. Three Chinese top executives from China's state-owned Railway Construction Co., Ltd. were among the victims. Just after the attack, President Xi stressed the importance of strengthening overseas security to ensure the safety of Chinese citizens.

On March 5, 2017, Premier Li Keqiang pointed out in his government's report to the Fifth Session of the Twelfth National People's Congress the need to accelerate the improvement of overseas rights protection mechanisms and capacity building as a helpful supplement and a virtual extension of the construction of the national overseas security system.

According to Pei and Wang,[1] in the era of globalization, the expansion of Chinese overseas interests has become a national interest. Therefore providing security services is a new trend in safeguarding overseas interests.

During the implementation of the BRI, China's overseas interests increased in complexity and risk.

The overall discourse on the privatization of China's overseas interests' protection is mostly focused on three areas: Pakistan, Africa, and the maritime domain. However, from a legal standpoint, the academic analysis can be summarized in four trends: legal issues for Chinese security companies' conduct of overseas armed security business, legal regulation of Chinese private security companies' maritime armed escort, the government-company coordination model of Chinese overseas interests' protection, and the private security model of Chinese overseas citizens' protection.

Discussing with Zhou Zhanggui, a Chinese academic specialized in private security, he mentioned that

> *if we look at the views of Chinese academic circles and international scholars on the professional development of private security industry in China . . . it is mainly in laws and policies, international standards, talent training and co-operation methods overseas direct operation, direct investment or M&A. The Chinese and Western context of "private" is different. In China, it refers to the social market-oriented security service industry. Actors in the field of market-oriented security services are still divided into "state-owned" and "private"; private security companies mainly undertake the auxiliary social service function of public security departments. Due to the above factors, the business characteristics of Chinese private security companies are as follows: first, the main market is the domestic market inside China; second, the main business is not a high-risk business; third, for private security companies that went overseas, in general, most Chinese PSCs do not have enough capacity of performing business in overseas high-risk or complex areas. . . . This is different from the international private security industry, from the Western perspective.[2]*

An extract from the *Journal of Fujian Police College*[3] well summarizes the Chinese view on its own private security industry:

Risks and the ever-expanding overseas security market have provided significant opportunities for (Chinese) private security companies to "go global." Private security companies "going out" are also faced with insufficient support from (China's) policies and regulations, and there is a big difference with foreign advanced security companies. The country should strengthen top-level design, introduce third-party institutions, . . . strengthen internal management, and provide the world with security solutions with Chinese characteristics.

As the BRI accelerates the Chinese "going-out" strategy, the amount of Chinese capital and the number of enterprises and workers increased their footprint in overseas markets. As China has entered what President Xi termed the New Era, security necessities that Beijing has to face in protecting Chinese nationals abroad have become increasingly prominent. The majority of Chinese researchers concurs that effectively safeguarding overseas Chinese citizens' legitimate rights and interests is a significant challenge.[4] According to the National Bureau of Statistics, since 2000 the number of Chinese residents abroad has exceeded ten million people, and it has been increasing at a high speed of 18.5 percent per year. However, the government's security capacity building has not kept the same speed as the Chinese migrations.[5] It is a shared opinion among Chinese academicians that the central government needs to promote the marketization of the security function, making it possible to let private security companies be a main cog in the overseas security management machine. Streamlining government functions and developing an efficient private security market follows the Western modus operandi supporting the private security sector, not the Russian model. Nevertheless, from a Chinese standpoint, the maximization of the private function needs to serve a public good, not just provide an individual benefit.

While being discounted in the Western narrative, China's requirement to protect the growing Chinese overseas community is abundantly debated. According to Cui Shoujun,[6] the overseas Chinese are an external extension and integral part of the Chinese nation and the overseas Chinese communities are the main organizational form of overseas Chinese. His view is quite common in China: "The overseas Chinese communities serve not only as an important force for safeguarding the rights and interests of overseas Chinese but also as an important strategic resource for implementing the Belt and Road initiative."

Since the start of President Xi's New Era, the consolidation of the overseas Chinese community has not escaped the attention of many governments, especially in the United States.[7]

In light of a worsening security environment along the BRI and considering the increasing imbalance in the security demand/offer, the Chinese communities living abroad are perceived to be part of the solution and not the problem.

Only recently, the overseas Chinese are regarded as a supplementary asset to the official security forces in China. The overseas Chinese communities' support of the security function is rooted in their local knowledge of the political and legal environment as well as being acquainted with the public opinion and social conditions of the countries in which they live. Moreover, the overseas Chinese networks, based on long-standing connections with local politicians and the business community, provide a fertile ground to leverage a local security function to support the incoming Chinese PSCs. Therefore Cui suggests that the overseas Chinese communities' priorities in the BRI security system should be focused on building a "Major Overseas Chinese Affairs" (大侨务) working environment, strengthening the self-building of overseas Chinese communities and their collaboration with enterprises, improving the service platform of "Overseas Chinese Help Centre" (华助中心), and promoting an overseas joint protection mechanism.

In the maritime domain, the legal discourse is related to the threats to national sovereignty stemming from unregulated foreign private security companies and the requirement to provide safety along the naval chokepoints. According to Liu and Xing,[8] to match the private security companies' growth in the maritime sector and protect China's overseas interests, the Chinese government should encourage strategic cooperation with Southeast Asian private security companies. The Chinese PSCs' involvement in maritime security governance in Southeast Asia, with particular reference to the Malacca Strait and Indonesia's Belawan port, is an essential part of much-needed Chinese PSC reforms. Also, the focus on straits and ports is an integral part of the expanding role of the private security sector. As the regulation that delves into the local private security operations in Southeast Asia is considered murkier and affected by complex relations with local governments, the Chinese researchers' advice is that China should further tap the potential of local maritime private security companies and pay attention to different practices and relationships with local officials. In a nutshell, the Chinese private security industry should seize the opportunity to improve their business and enhance innovation and awareness of the regional security environment.

At the same time, a common talking point among Chinese academicians and analysts is the present necessity for the Chinese private security sector to cut the umbilical cord with the Chinese central and provincial governments.

Chinese PSCs need to exert their own initiative and move out of the government dependence's comfort zone. This drastic change is necessary to promote the internationalization process of the Chinese PSCs. Improving competitiveness and business capabilities is achieved by strengthening the partnerships with foreign private security companies and learning from their best practices. At the same time, the cooperation with local companies, not only in the maritime domain but in the overall private security arena, could solve two main operational problems: providing local armed security or small weapons leasing and improving the relationship with the local government. If addressed correctly, both issues will not ignite friction with local stakeholders and avoid crisis scenarios involving Chinese contractors discharging their weapons. Shooting at alleged pirates could carry for Beijing a high price to pay. In this respect the lesson learned by Italy in terms of state responsibility during the shooting of Indian fishermen mistaken for pirates did not go unnoticed in Zhongnanhai.[9]

CHINESE EXPERTS CALL FOR THE PRIVATE SECURITY SECTOR REFORMS

According to Yan Su's analysis of private military security companies in the perspective of international law,[10] the most compelling issue in studying private military and security companies is not its concept but its business model. According to international law, PMSCs are not to be considered mercenaries. Nevertheless, the inherently governmental functions are not clearly defined in international law, and states should further clarify their connotation in rules development.

In this respect, during the development of the BRI, Su mentions that China should participate effectively in constructing the rules of international law for private military security companies and develop an overseas security service system that fits the BRI's requirements. Also, most Chinese academic papers that analyze the demand for overseas security address a veiled critique of the government-centered overseas security mechanism. Overreliance on consular protection and the insufficient support of local governments has already been proven to be a risky bet.*

The traditional way of safeguarding overseas interests, rooted in diplomatic agreements and cooperation with the host government, will not protect Chinese infrastructure and personnel where the local government is weak or could profit from insecurity. In this respect, the Chinese academic community regards the Chinese PSCs as an effective option to avoid political friction with the local governments, especially in countries that have experienced colonial rule and military conflicts. Moreover, instead of private security contractors, a military presence could generate concerns among the population that remembers the not-too-distant colonial rule. Nevertheless, Chinese researchers forget that in many countries, like in Africa, the memory of bloodthirsty mercenaries is still very alive, and foreign contractors could still be perceived as a hostile force.

Another critique from the Chinese side is related to the fact that from the perspective of international humanitarian law, many international scholars group private military security companies indiscriminately with mercenaries in addressing the potential risk of human rights violations. An example is given by the classification of the Russian Wagner Group as a private military company. Labeling Wagner as "private" is one major obstacle to addressing the reform needed by the private military and security sector. Without a precise classification, it will be challenging to provide an efficient law and proper enforcement.

While ambiguities in the murky world of money for mayhem suit both Russian and Turkish models, the Chinese process of private security sector internationalization is going to suffer from a lack of proper regu-

---

* See appendix III.

lations. Nevertheless, the Chinese academic discourse is more centered on the conceptual analysis of Western private military security companies than the Eurasian counterparts under the Russian and Turkish leashes.

Interestingly, Chinese legal scholars address the problems stemming from the Blackwater model in Iraq and Afghanistan and the inherent criticism drawn by the U.S. government contracting models and not the Russian one in Africa or the Middle East. At the same time, Chinese international relations scholars are more interested in the efficiency rooted in the Blackwater model and what lessons can be applied to promote the evolution of Chinese PSCs. Again, the Russian PMCs are not much in the picture.

From a legal standpoint, Chinese scholars are adamant that the military functions are inherent to the government and should not be outsourced. Also, the Chinese PSC sector doesn't need to follow the same path traced in the United States or Russia. At the same time, the security discourse is centered on the necessity to face the contradiction between various nontraditional security threats and the decline of military personnel.[11] In this respect, the contradiction underlined by Chinese scholars is rooted in the attitude of some Western countries, such as the United States and the United Kingdom, that have outsourced a large number of military functions, and such outsourcing is likely to result in massive human rights violations. Therefore the suggestion is that the policy development of the Chinese private security sector has to follow the Chinese central government guidelines that adhere to the UN Convention on the obligations of the contracting parties and the responsibility not to delegate to PMCs "inherent" governmental functions.*

The UN Convention's provisions recognize the legality of private military security companies as a whole; if the scope of business crosses into inherent governmental functions, the activity of the private military contractors may fall under the purview of mercenaries violating human rights and humanitarian law.[12]

---

* According to the draft United Nations Convention Article 4 (Responsibility of the State for the Supervision of Private Military and Security Companies), paragraph 3, any Contracting State neither delegate nor outsource inherent government functions to private military and security companies; Article 9 (prohibition of delegation of and/or outsourcing inherent government functions) states that parties should define and limit private military and security services.

Since the fall of the Berlin Wall, the number of minor conflicts has been growing. Therefore the growing uncertainty and a massive influx of Chinese workers worldwide create a perfect storm for Chinese consular services. In areas considered safe for China, the consular activities are already stretched to the maximum. At the same time, in a complex environment, the Chinese Ministry of Foreign Affairs cannot guarantee the safety of expat workers. The problem is related to a staffing shortage and how consular protection is structured. The embassies' and consulates' security function is mainly set on a passive stance, meaning intervening after the crisis has erupted. Lacking active means to effectively protect workers when an attack occurs signifies that embassies and consulates need to rely on the host country's capabilities and willingness to resolve the crisis.

Since the beginning of the new millennium, the military option to evacuate many Chinese nationals stuck in local turmoil has increased. Nevertheless, Beijing does not take the opportunity lightly to send military personnel abroad, even for a rescue mission, as the option is entangled by high political costs in case something goes wrong. From a Chinese perspective, the increasing number of Chinese citizens living, working, and traveling abroad has imposed an obligation on the state to protect them. Also, since President Xi promoted the BRI's "going-out policy," there is an expectation among Chinese citizens that the central government will protect them while abroad. Just two decades earlier, there was not much confidence among overseas Chinese on the state's support in case of crisis, but the perception is changing, and expectations are rising.

The Chinese leadership used to assume that, in most cases, other foreign powers would evacuate Chinese citizens along with their own from situations of unrest abroad. But things have changed over the past decades, and Beijing has introduced new policies and capabilities that have generated new hopes among the Chinese population. As China wants to be recognized internationally as a responsible rising power, providing security abroad is a new imperative.[13] While the country's capabilities to project power and influence abroad are expanding, the protection of overseas Chinese is also generating anxiety in other countries. In light of a Chinese high private security footprint, there is a growing perception that protecting overseas Chinese and the BRI projects is an excuse to strengthen China's assertiveness in world affairs.

Table 7.1. Number of Chinese overseas citizens evacuated during political and natural crises from 2010 to 2023

2010 Kyrgyzstan, ethnic conflict	(1,299)
2011 Libya, political conflict	(35,860)
2011 Egypt, political conflict	(1,800)
2014 Libya, political conflict	(1,177)
2015 Yemen, political conflict	(571)
2015 Nepal, earthquake	(5,685)
2016 Israel, fire	(159)
2016 Great New Zealand, earthquake	(125)
2016 Japan, blizzard	(500)
2017 Indonesia, volcanic eruption	(2,700)
2022 Ukraine, war	(6,000)
2023 Sudan, political conflict	(1,300)

Sources: www.globaltimes.cn; https://www.migrationpolicy.org/article/china
-development-transformed-migration; https://www.sipri.org/sites/default/files/files
/PP/SIPRIPP41.pdf.

In this respect, most Chinese researchers agree that international and Chinese PSCs bring many advantages, including operational flexibility, reaching remote locations, understanding the local risks in case of a crisis, and carrying a low political sensitivity. As the PLA's capability to project force and protect Chinese citizens overseas continues to grow along with the so-called noncombatant evacuation operations (NEO), Beijing is also increasing its eagerness to upgrade its citizens' protection policy.

As China's global influence expands, unexpected friction could arise when the policy of overseas citizen protection is applied to situations that are clashing with local necessities. At the same time, a common opinion is that PSCs are a piece of the broad security puzzle but not a complete solution by itself, as PSCs are a valuable supplement to protect China's overseas interests.

As the BRI is expanding in developing countries, flashpoints can quickly stem from ethnic and religious conflicts, terrorist attacks, or areas of friction between significant powers. Therefore the numbers of large-scale hostage-taking incidents and the killing of Chinese workers are on the rise.

Summarizing the view of Chinese academics, the operational requirements that the entire Chinese private security sector needs to undergo include improved security risk assessment and risk prevention capabilities and standardized operating procedures in communicating with the Chinese military and the United Nations peacekeeping forces if locally available. Price is also an essential factor driving the expansion of the Chinese private security sector abroad. Although Western security companies are considered to be in the high range of professional service provision, their price tag is well above the Chinese companies' willingness to pay. Also, another advantage that goes hand in hand with the Chinese contractors speaking the same language as their client is that Chinese SOEs perceive a Chinese PSC to preserve the company's business operations. Also, the sector's expansion during the past decade represents a pool of resources that even the Chinese embassies and consulates could tap. Several Chinese diplomatic structures contract Chinese PSCs to manage their security services ranging from being a security manager for local armed contractors to providing security training for the Chinese citizens living in the area.

A near-future trend in the evolution of the PSCs' footprint abroad is related to the Chinese government's reliance on private security companies to maintain the safety of overseas property and personnel safety. This trend encompasses another tendency: Chinese PSCs' internationalization via the acquisition of foreign security companies. The past decade has witnessed a trend in purchasing international enterprises and assets to integrate local resources. For example, acquiring international operational licenses, armed guards, and a local client portfolio put the Chinese PSCs on a fast track in achieving a globally prominent position.

Also, several researchers are not shy in mentioning that private security companies can collect information on the economic and social development environment and security threat sources of the host country.

Walking on Thin Ice: Private Security or Mercenaries?

From Chinese legal scholars' point of view to the international relations practitioners, the message is straightforward:[14] the Chinese extraterritorial service of private security companies has gotten rid of mercenaries' negative influence and needs to abide by the rule of law. Yet the lack of certainty of international conventions put China between a rock and a hard place: Beijing's absence of control on the PSCs' global action and the lack of clear and enforceable international regulation could hamper China's interests and reputation.

While the Chinese private security industry is still in dire need of obtaining security guarantees from Beijing, monitoring the evolution of the legal frameworks and the legitimacy of foreign private security firms' extraterritorial services will help China consolidate the nonmilitary role of its private security industry. Also, learning from the experience and lessons, including the adverse outcomes of the United States and the United Kingdom, will improve the Chinese PSCs' licensing system and establish monitoring, complaint, jurisdiction, and remedial mechanisms to respond systematically to prevent and mitigate a crisis.

Summarizing the Chinese researchers' critiques of the current status of the private security sector in China and the much-needed reforms, the areas that need urgent development are related to the insufficient policy planning and legal support for private security companies. The discourse can be condensed in four key points. First, from the perspective of domestic law, the regulations are evolving in a stable manner being anchored in the 2009 main legislation on private security companies, while the establishment and qualifications of security companies operating abroad is still in a legal limbo. While the legislative norm for enterprises to conduct overseas business is improving by the day in terms of financial requirements, human resources management, and state support, the security framework has seriously lagged behind.

The second critique related to the overall BRI is the lack of "one-stop shop" to acquire all the necessary operational information as many ministries and government departments have their own say on the matter. From the Ministry of Foreign Affairs to public security there is an overlapping of administrative regulations on the overseas business expansion of private security companies. While Beijing is clear that in the face of increasingly severe overseas security challenges there is a compelling need to protect China's overseas interests, how to build a regulatory framework is still mired in uncertainty.

The third critique is related to the expertise gap with international Western security companies and the negative perception that the private security industry is receiving from the Russian Wagner model. In this respect the call from academia is related to improving not only the Chinese personnel capabilities, as Chinese retired military personnel generally do not have the experience to deal with sudden crises in foreign lands and are generally unable to communicate in English or local languages, but they also lack the risk prevention and risk management competencies. The Chinese PSCs need to nurture talent that is able to communicate and cooperate with foreign law enforcement agencies, engage in overseas security operations, and manage outsourced resources.

With regard to the fourth point, the researchers agree that the private security company operating abroad must strictly abide by the laws of the host country and relevant international legal norms and "tell the story of the Belt and Road well, spread the voice of China, and leave a good reputation in the host country to gain the recognition of the local people."[15] Also, the industry should actively develop overseas security products that are anchored in China's fast technology product development and production.

Zhou Zhanggui accurately captured the Chinese academic discourse on the risks and opportunities that the Chinese PSCs will face:

There is an urgent need to improve the overseas regulatory cooperation mechanism. In order to promote the effective supervision of overseas Chinese private security service enterprises, avoid violating international law and the laws and policies of the host country and having a negative impact on the rights and interests and human rights of local communities, strengthening international co-operation in overseas supervision of Chinese PSCs is the premise. We should promote the transformation of the supervision mode of China's overseas PSCs, effectively connect with the international "multi governance" supervision mode and carry out active dialogue with the United Nations, the International Committee of Red Cross, the ICoCA and other institutions.[16]

CHAPTER EIGHT

The Evolution of a
New Chinese Security Actor

HIGH-TECH SECURITY: FROM CCTV TO AI

DISCUSSING WITH LIU QING, MANAGER AT HUAXIN ZHONGHAN (HXZA), the *Wolf Warrior* movie, he mentioned that the movie

> *was very popular in China. But it's just a movie. It is misrepresenting the security business and we also try to educate the public that Chinese PSCs are trying to compete with western counterparts in know-how and intellectual aspects not in use of force. In reality, sophisticated PSCs serve clients as managers of risks and enablers of business in complex environments, this is the model we are working on.*[1]

Not only are some SOEs a bad judge of risk but also several Chinese private companies are often unwilling to spend money on qualified security services. Other Chinese companies understand well the risks that they face but are unable to afford a proper security solution. Low security budgets in China are still a product of several interconnected issues ranging from a safe environment at home and lack of proper education on threats to the risks of working with low-quality security service providers outside China. It is only a matter of time for the sector to mature but, as happened with the insurance sector in China, mistakes could be costly. Chinese insurance companies learned the lesson and are paying for premium security services especially when hiring PSCs to protect vessels against pirates. The trend in antipiracy professionalization could soon spread to the entire Chinese security sector abroad. According to HXZA management, the company is mostly well known abroad for the maritime security business, but it accounts for only around 7 percent of the turnover. In addition to the international operations in South Asia and Africa, the company provides manned guarding and technology with over twenty-two thousand employees in China guarding banks, airports, universities, and other such locations across the country.[2] Regarding crisis management, it is also important to remember that for medium to big Chinese PSCs the internal market is also a vital component of their revenue stream.

During the past decade as the maritime security industry witnessed a period of consolidation, the Chinese sector followed the same path. In this respect the main Chinese security providers expanded their business model from security operations on vessels to integrating solutions including port management and port construction companies, a core pillar of the Chinese BRI, and even more a vital point of friction between Beijing and Washington.

As other companies are following their Chinese clients' expansion in the overseas market, the Middle East and Latin America are taking the next logical step to provide static security, executive protection, CCTV operators, static site security, training, risk assessment, K&R response, and security technology integration.

The Chinese private security companies that are called to protect assets and personnel from the Middle East to Africa, if properly trained and managed, will enable the Chinese SOEs to penetrate new markets previously considered inaccessible due to security concerns. The right mix of country risk analysis and crisis management provided by an experienced Chinese private security company is not only going to benefit the Chinese interest in the BRI but also the local stakeholders.

As mentioned earlier, the Chinese private security market is still poisoned by aggressive low-cost bidding practices from companies that offer substandard security contractors, barely trained to open a gate. Nevertheless, several complex and fast-changing security environments from Africa to Central Asia are providing a natural selection in the professionalization of the Chinese private security sector, especially toward high-tech security solutions.

The Digital Silk Road expansion along the BRI is promoting "digitization with Chinese characteristics." Beijing's Digital Silk Road aims to place China at the core of the fourth industrial revolution, which encompasses digital security, e-services, and smart cities integration, and includes everything from underwater fiber-optic cables to the Beidou satellite navigation system.

In light of the worsening U.S.-China strategic rivalry, Beijing is increasing its strategic presence in the MENA region not only to preserve its energy security but also to assert its rise in the digital realm. While many countries are trying to thread the eye of the needle by balancing the use of Chinese tech against American efforts to block the use of such systems, Chinese PSCs are spearheading Beijing's "digital will."

But it is in the smart cities sector where the rubber meets the road when it comes to a possible future collision of interests between China, the United States, and regional actors. Smart cities will require the integration of Chinese sensors, Big Data analytical software, and narrow AIs—those tasked with completing specific tasks—and this has broader national security implications.

For example, in this sector Chinese PSCs are moving from providing a basic guarding service at the entrance of a building to a comprehensive set of high-tech solutions including semiautonomous patrol robots that roam a building in search of suspicious objects like abandoned bags or detect uncommon behaviors among bystanders. This is essentially an evolved robot vacuum cleaner with sensors coupled with narrow AI. The very simple act to patrol a building lobby by a security robot creates an avalanche of privacy issues starting with the use of the collected video feed and biometrics data of the bystanders, just to name a few. In this respect, the borders between national security and civilian infrastructure are progressively blurred due to technologies' dual-use implications and the strategic role that access to Big Data is playing in the AI race. China's own ambition to become a "cyber great power," and what that means when it comes to data access, is fueling suspicion of Chinese PSCs operating high-tech equipment abroad.

While in regions like the Middle East, China's role as security provider is still a matter of debate and foresight, the region's digitalization with Chinese characteristics is proceeding at full speed. From 5G, to cybersecurity, e-services, and Big Data analytics, China's digital inroad in the Middle East is here to stay.[3] Therefore the operational space that is offered to Chinese PSCs adventuring abroad is increasing by the day.

Chinese security companies that are moving away from low-balling bids are looking to offer additional services to their clients, integrating high-tech solutions that are already available at home. Today the Chinese private security sector has preferential access to competitively priced and high-quality AI-enabled facial recognition and surveillance drones that are denied entry into the U.S. market. Access to this equipment could not only reduce the operational costs but also create a competitive edge versus Western private security competitors that cannot acquire the same technology due to restrictive regulations at home.

Moreover, the use of CCTV and Big Data analysis are going to shift the private security sector posture from a pure passive/reactive stance toward a more active one. Predictive analysis and a higher degree of preventive solutions is going to enable risk prevention with limited or no use of violence.

Nevertheless, the Chinese National Cybersecurity Law* is going to make life for Chinese PSCs going abroad quite difficult, especially in countries that have their own approach to national security in the cybersphere. Even countries that rely on the Digital Silk Road by acquiring Chinese hardware for the communications network are taking into consideration these implications. The growing gathering and processing of large amounts of personal data to track and identify individuals poses new challenges for Chinese PSCs using that kind of data overseas, and the doubt that sensitive information is finding its way to Beijing is still lingering in the air. Each state understands technology is far from neutral and the ongoing algorithm weaponization is already having long-lasting impact on the development of smart cities and society altogether. Rich Gulf monarchies in the Middle East that have the chance to balance their exposure to Chinese technologies from other countries, especially in Africa, have two choices: embracing the Digital Silk Road or no access to new technologies.

---

* See appendix III.

While most of the Chinese PSCs operating abroad state that they are not directly using weapons, hiring local armed security forces, or providing guns in very specific situations such as vessels escort in pirate-infested waters, promoting in the long run an integration with the host country's security sector needs to take cybersecurity and Big Data protection to the fore. While PSCs' crossing the proverbial red line on data security could create friction between Beijing and the local partners, the recovery and repatriation of Chinese fugitives and assets abroad is still a red line that the Chinese PSCs are well aware not to cross.

ASSET RECOVERY CROSSING A RED LINE?

No hiding place overseas for fugitive officials, reports the *China Daily* in an article on the arrest of Dai Xuemin, former manager of a state-owned trust and investment company in Shanghai.[4] Dai, a most-wanted fugitive, who has been apprehended after fourteen years on the run overseas, faces charges of embezzling 11 million yuan (US$1.8 million), according to the Communist Party of China Central Commission for Discipline Inspection (CCDI). Since 2014 the Chinese leadership started to implement structural reforms in both domestic and foreign policies focusing on addressing notable domestic security challenges such as the fight against corruption, and a tightening of internal (antiterror) measures.[5]

From 2014 to the end of 2016, during the height of the hunt for corrupt officials that have escaped the country, the CCDI reported that 2,500 Chinese citizens who escaped overseas to avoid criminal charges have been repatriated. The hunt carried out under the slogan "Catching the Tigers and Flies" well reflects Beijing's ongoing commitment to crack down on corruption by bringing to justice both high-ranking executives (tigers) and low-ranking officials (flies).[6]

A decade ago, the anticorruption campaign moved from China to overseas in an attempt to repatriate Chinese fugitives and the money stolen over years of corrupt malpractices. Since 2018, following the global economic crisis, stricter rules on money transfer overseas have reduced the problem. The amount of embezzled money stashed abroad is estimated to be in the range of billions of US$.

Beijing's hunt for corrupt officials is supported by Interpol and national police forces that cooperate with China in finding and repatriating stolen assets. Nevertheless, due to the high number of cases, Beijing is increasingly informally calling on Chinese PSCs with international connections to locate the fugitives. This time the experience of the Chinese former police officers that transited to the private security sector was valuable as this job required police skills and not military training. In this respect the Chinese PSCs' local knowledge and network of fixers and informers are a precious asset to Beijing in obtaining timely reports and finding the right person. Nevertheless, once the alleged criminal is located the Chinese PSCs know that further steps in the direction of a capture and repatriation to China of Chinese individuals in foreign countries is going to cross more than one red line.

INTERNATIONALIZATION AND COMPLIANCE
The BRI's win-win promise of economic trade investment coupled with China's foreign policy of noninterference is already showing cracks in the armor due to the growing insecurity of Chinese workers.

Therefore the Chinese security sector's call for professionalization is not only going to benefit the Chinese SOEs that contract efficient private security providers but will also enable closer cooperation with the local government's security forces, international insurance companies, and most importantly local stakeholders. In this respect, the adoption of international standards and clear guidelines that safeguard local communities are not to be considered an unnecessary cost but the pillar for a long-term shared prosperity. In order to prevent tragedies as happened with Blackwater or the Wagner Group's act of violence against civilians and their subsequent backlash on the United States and Russia, Chinese academicians are calling for a screening mechanism that will allow select firms with the appropriate capabilities to operate in high-risk environments overseas.

China is actively trying to stay away from security crises and religious and sectarian rivalries that are beleaguering countries from Africa to the Caucasus. Unfortunately, playing the third world developing country card is no longer in today's China's deck.

The Arab Spring was a wakeup call for Beijing with the evacuation of thirty-six thousand Chinese workers in Libya during the civil war as a case in point. Beijing cannot separate economic issues from security issues.[7]

Engaging with a voluntary code of conduct such as ICoC and obtaining the relevant certification to comply with their human rights, due diligence, and risk-reducing guidelines is one road to professionalization that could also benefit local stakeholders. Therefore the professionalization of the Chinese security industry could help it mature and give more Chinese companies the confidence to operate in unstable and violent environments.

On the other side of the coin, the presence of unaccountable private security and military companies or even mercenaries with loose government affiliations and the total lack of transparency and accountability are going to generate negative ripple effects involving not only the contracting company but also the local population. Moscow's footprint in the MENA region to Ukraine is a case in point.

Zhou Zhanggui mentioned that

> *China will not follow the model of Russian security companies or American security companies subjectively and objectively. On the whole, China is willing to participate in international affairs under the multilateral framework of the United Nations and abide by universally recognised international regulations. China is one of the 17 countries that first initiated and signed the Montreux document and has always not supported all forms of mercenary behaviours. In recent years, the "Blackwater" model of the US and the "Wagner Group" model of Russia have been criticised by many parties on many platforms, such as the United Nations mercenary working group and the United Nations Human Rights Council. I don't think mercenaries are among the security service options considered by China. . . . China will not follow the "Blackwater" or "Wagner" model. . . . In the future the main service objects of China's overseas security services are the safety and security of overseas Chinese personnel and Chinese-funded projects.*

As mentioned earlier, the female suicide bomber that killed three Chinese teachers in Pakistan represents an escalation of violence against Chinese citizens abroad. Beijing's BRI infrastructure and personnel are increasingly under attack, and security requirements are accelerating the professionalization of the Chinese private security industry. In this respect the analysis of the evolution of the Chinese PSCs' "third way" cannot be done using Western parameters nor Russian ones. While the Western private military and security sector is still a beacon in terms of professionalization for the Chinese PSCs, Beijing is set on its own way to develop the private security industry at home and abroad. It seems clear that Beijing is cherry-picking from foreign companies what it values in terms of crisis management capabilities, but it is not emulating the Western development model, including its core values. For example, former Israeli military, intelligence, and cybersecurity experts are welcome in China, not only as companies but more often as individuals, as they offer a practical approach to training and augmenting Chinese private security companies without preaching any foreign ethical principle.[8]

While the decades-old principle of noninterference is slowly evolving toward selective engagements, the approach to international crises, including the Russian invasion of Ukraine and the return of the Taliban in Kabul, is showcasing how Beijing is maintaining a "balanced vagueness" in dealing with the evolving crisis, meaning betting on both sides of the problem.

In this respect China is not in a hurry to fill the previous role of the United States as the world's sheriff, and Beijing's passive stance to any kind of crisis is first and foremost linked to avoiding getting swamped in the Afghan cemetery of empires or the Middle East quagmire. However, the Chinese military footprint is growing in terms of weapons sales and while China is still recognized as an unwilling security provider, the role of PSCs as a security gap filler is expanding.

As President Xi's Belt and Road expansion is still considered the main driver in China's foreign policy, there are rising expectations among the Chinese population that the central government will protect them while abroad and in cyberspace.

As soon as the Chinese PSCs move out of the government's comfort zone, market competitiveness and business capabilities are going to be an asset on Beijing's global chessboard, but at the same time the increasing scope of action could create some headaches for the Chinese Ministry of Foreign Affairs. The red lines that Chinese PSCs are going to deal with in the coming years are essentially four: being indiscriminately associated with mercenaries due to the potential risk of human rights violations, being considered a foreign agent in collecting data that could have implications for the hosting country's national security, enabling local corrupt malpractices, and crossing legal lines while attempting to recover Chinese assets abroad. In a nutshell, making Beijing lose face.

CHAPTER NINE

Turkey's New Janissaries?

NEO-OTTOMANISM AND DEEP STATE

China may be a Johnny come lately to the world of private security, but Turkish companies are the newest kids on the private military block. Unlike China, but like Russia, Turkish privatization of the state's monopoly on violence produced companies whose future depends on the country's leader. And, like Russia's Wagner Group, they were baptized by fire in conflicts in the Middle East and Africa.

As the Russian Wagner Group's future is closely linked with Putin's survival after the Ukrainian invasion gambit, the Turkish private military and security sector, spearheaded by SADAT International Defense Consultancy, is closely linked with Turkey's strongman, President Recep Tayyip Erdogan. While Putin looks at a new Russia[1] rooted in Eurasianism,[2] Erdogan embodies the same political logic of zero-sum competition but for global Islamic leadership. Today, Turkey's competition against Saudi Arabia and Iran for the control of the region has a new component that ranges from Muslim mercenaries to incorporated companies that provide money for mayhem.

While the attention is polarized on Russia, there is a surprising unawareness that there is a new player in the market for hired guns: Turkish contractors. In this respect Turkish PMCs are allegedly linked with recruiting mercenaries in conflict areas where they operate from Syria to Libya, disrupting the thus far sweet deal the incumbents have enjoyed. While Turkish PMCs are a relative newcomer, Turkey counts on hundreds of years of experience in dealing with money for mayhem.

What is new is the fact that Turkey under President Erdogan's assertive international policy is going to offer not only an army for rent but
also an air force for hire with the ubiquitous Turkish UCAVs. Baykar
took the world of combat UAVs by storm; Turkish PMCs could replicate
the same success taking the West, China, and Russia by surprise.

Since a decade ago, many Middle Eastern and North African states
witnessed the collapse of a centralized authority, providing a fertile ground
for foreign-sponsored actors ranging from irregular militias, proxy military formations, and mercenaries as power projection assets. According to
Ömer Taspinar, a security expert on Turkey in the Middle East, "At peace
with Turkey's Muslim heritage and multiple identities, neo-Ottomanism is
also much more ambitious and idealistic than Kemalism in projecting Turkey as a regional superpower."[3] Following the 2011 Arab Spring, Turkey
seized the moment to expand its influence in the region.

A notable example is Turkey's military assertiveness in Syria, which
reflects the country's transformation from its former policy of looking to
the West into a resurgent power in a new age of geopolitical competition.[4]
Similar to Putin's narrative based on the unique character of the Russian
civilization, rooted in Slavic Orthodox communitarian traditions, Erdogan's neo-Ottomanism is looking at a new place for Turkey on the geopolitical chessboard. James Dorsey, an expert in Middle East affairs, warns:
"Amid speculations about a reduced US military commitment to security
in the Middle East, Turkey has spotlighted the region's ability to act as a
disruptive force if its interests are neglected."[5]

While Turkish police training is well respected and appreciated in
high-risk areas such as Mogadishu International Airport in Somalia, Turkish PMCs are expanding their presence abroad accordingly.

As happened in Moscow and Beijing, Ankara saw the opportunity
presented by the contractors during the U.S. wars in Iraq and Afghanistan. Nevertheless, the conflict in Syria and Libya offered Ankara a fertile
ground to recruit and deploy non-Turkish mercenaries the same way the
Ottoman Empire was used: from cannon fodder to professional soldiers
of fortune. Today, Turkey's PMCs are another tool in the expanding arsenal of President Erdogan's assertive Neo-Ottoman vision of the world.
The unique characteristic of SADAT Defense and the other Turkish

PMCs is the possibility of combining the offer of boots on the ground with the famous Turkish UCAVs. It is quite probable that a combination of an "army for hire" with an "off-the-shelf air force" will provide Ankara with a profitable export asset for political and economic gains. Turkish drones from the Middle East to Ukraine have shown how limited funds can offer effective off-the-shelf airpower. Combining both options of private soldiers and private armed drones could provide Ankara with an edge to contain the Russian PMCs' expansion in the same areas that Erdogan is looking at, from Tripoli to Mogadishu.

Mercenaries and soldiers for hire are not a piece of news in Turkey. The Ottoman Army's centuries-old history is a reminder of how money for mayhem works. Looking at Ottoman history, the image of janissaries is the first to come to mind while looking at foreign professionals specializing in waging war. Yet the comparison of the contemporary Turkish PMCs to the Ottoman Empire's janissaries is beguiling but misleading. Since the fifteenth century, the Ottoman Army increasingly relied on different types of mercenaries from various regions with varying fighting capabilities and unique skills.

Today the janissaries are considered a kind of *ante litteram* foreign special forces at the service of the sultan, but labeling them mercenaries is as misleading as marking the Russian Wagner Group as a private company. Since the late fourteenth century, the janissary corps was built on young Christians, sent as tribute from the Balkan provinces, who converted to Islam then enlisted in the Ottoman Army, but not as a mercenary force.

From the fifteenth to the nineteenth century, the Ottoman Army used different types of mercenaries defined by their geographical origin or the task they were paid to accomplish. Besides the immediate monetary rewards, which seldom were just the right to pillage and plunder a defeated enemy, their final goal was to move from an auxiliary position to being part of the Ottoman Army's ranks.[6] Basically, moving from a temporary job to the safety of an employee for life with a guaranteed pension. Similarly, today's contractors have the same compelling problem to secure a continuous stream of gigs as their time in between deployment in war zones is not conducive to any financial gain. In the course of the history of the Ottoman Army, it was not uncommon for the mercenaries to exceed the numbers in the standing army. For example, the number of contractors supporting the U.S.-led war efforts in Iraq and Afghanistan reached almost a ratio of 1.5 contractors for each U.S. soldier deployed. Today's trend is not far from what was happening just a few centuries ago.

Since the fall of the Berlin Wall, the growing integration of contractors across the spectrum of military bases abroad has prompted some analysts to remark that the U.S. military cannot function without these contractors.[7] That was the case in the Ottoman Army, not only in numerical terms but also by force of specialization. An example is related to the Okaban, a kind of combat engineer corps that was tasked with building roads and bridges and the related logistic support when the Ottoman Army was on the move.[8] Similarly, the famed and feared Ottoman artillery counted on Hungarian and other European specialists' siege expertise.

Other Turkish mercenaries shared tribal affiliations such as the Azabs recruited from the same villages as cheap and expendable groups that had "the honor" to be the first assault force during a battle. In a time of peace, they were mainly tasked with patrolling the borders and fighting bandits. Similarly, the Pandors, Christian mercenaries, were paid to protect border garrisons from Serbia to Bosnia and Bulgaria. As the advent of firearms determined more remarkable changes in the Ottoman Army structure, several mercenaries' units, such as the Sekban, became famous for their skill in firearms. Other auxiliary units were composed of Cerehors mercenaries from the southern province of the empire, well known for their combat skill, who were tasked as standing units in defense of the newly conquered territories.[9] This was like contemporary Peruvian or Nepalese contractors defending fixed emplacements in the Baghdad green zone on behalf of the U.S. coalition forces.

While national armies were becoming the norm in Europe, in the late seventeenth century, the Ottoman Army counted on even bigger mercenary companies recruited in bulk. Their captains were responsible for the men's equipment and daily necessities. In the seventeenth century in Turkey, the discussion of the utility of mercenaries, especially the (in) famous Anatolian free companies, witnessed the same debate on the role of mercenaries present in Machiavelli's *The Prince* or, more recently, in the 2020 report from the U.S. GAO on the efficiency of contractors in Afghanistan.[10] The writings mentioned earlier arrived at the same conclusion as the Ottoman chronicles: mercenaries are useless during battle and are also a financial menace to the empire's stability. The GAO wording on the role of contractors during Afghanistan's reconstruction echoes the one in the Ottoman chronicles: "Shows systemic internal control weaknesses that increased the risk of waste, fraud, and abuse."

Even in the Ottoman chronicles, which considered mercenaries a backbone of the empire's security apparatus, it is possible to see mercenaries labeled as an evil force. Nevertheless, a necessary evil. Another parallel drawn from the Ottoman chronicles into the contemporary use of soldiers of fortune in modern warfare is how to deal with disbanded mercenaries' units once the conflict has reached its conclusion.

For example, at the end of long military campaigns paid by the Ottoman coin, entire companies specializing in the use of firearms were suddenly unemployed. While some became bandits, others tried their luck abroad, fighting as musketeers or in the artillery corps for the Indian Mughal Empire. The ongoing discussion centered on the allegedly thousands of foreign mercenaries supporting the Russian Army in Ukraine is not far from the ongoing debate. The question of what will happen to them or even the Russian Wagner Group contractors once the war is over is not dissimilar to the one asked in the Ottoman chronicles.

As discussed in the previous chapters, after the Peace of Westphalia, mercenaries were perceived more as a threat than an asset. At the same time the ratio of mercenaries in the Ottoman Army surpassed the number of standing units, reaching almost 75 percent of the total. In 1860 during the Abdulhamid era, the distrust for Ottoman generals and the push for the army's modernization with the support of Prussian weapons and training reduced the role of local mercenaries in favor of foreign specialists drastically.[11]

In modern times, Turkey's irregular warfare capabilities became a pillar of national policy. Since the 1950 multiparty election and the loss of the Turkish Armed Forces' direct connection with the government in power, the Turkish term *derin devlet* (Deep State) turned out to be of everyday use in the lexicon of Turkey's politics. Kemalist supporters of the Deep State, mainly from the ranks of the armed forces, conducted covert operations against what Ataturk defined as internal enemies, left-wing sympathizers, Kurdish independentists, and Islamists. According to Yanarocak and Spyer,[12] President Erdogan's political party, the Islamist AKP, a former adversary of the Deep State, inherited the modus operandi of the Deep State in dealing with its own internal and external adversaries. The new breed of Turkey's security defense companies are not modern janissaries, but if President Erdogan's expansion of Turkey's interests abroad is going to proceed with the same speed since 2016, their role is going to acquire similar fame.

A New Private Military Force Stemming from Purges and Demobilization

Looking at the trend of the military reforms from Beijing to Moscow and finally Ankara, it is possible to draw a similar inchoate pattern and the unique role that private security and military companies are carving in states where the notion of "private" is anything but straightforward.

Chinese president Xi Jinping's reform of the PLA started with the purge of numerous generals and the drastic demobilization of thousands of uniformed men. While the official narrative is rooted in the modernization of an army that will fight and win the wars of the future, the immediate objective is to shape a balance of power within the PLA to avoid any potential challenge to the party's authority from within the military ranks.[13] Therefore controlling the gun on behalf of the party is nothing new under the sun in Zhongnanhai.

Similarly, Xi's Russian counterpart Vladimir Putin's reform of the Russian Federation's armed forces was a basket full of sticks but no carrots. The purge of generals not in line with the Kremlin was followed by the establishment of a force under Putin's direct control, the Russian National Guard. Formed in 2016, the paramilitary force combined several previous internal security forces under a unified structure that reports directly to Putin without interference from the army or the intelligence circles. Equally, with regard to Xi's political drive to reform the PLA, the Russian National Guard counterbalances the influence and threat of a revitalized Russian Armed Forces, having roughly the same staffing levels as the military's ground forces and the ability to assume direct command of military units in a crisis.[14] In both countries, private security and military companies found their own specific niche filling a gap in providing security services. In China, protecting the BRI where the PLA could not operate, and in Russia as the tip of the spear in hybrid operations. Ankara's evolving security environment does not differ much from the other two authoritarian counterparts, and the evolution of PMCs with Turkish characters will follow the same pattern.

Turkish president Erdogan's army reform plan started brutally following a coup attempt that almost forced him out of his own country. After the July 15, 2016, coup attempt, Turkey's highly professional army shifted from being a traditional pillar of nationalism and secularism established by Mustafa Kemal Atatürk and a sizable NATO partner into a tool of Erdogan's expansionist foreign policy.[*] In light of the military purges in the aftermath of the July 15 coup attempt, the Turkish Armed Forces (Türk Silahlı Kuvvetleri or TSK) have been adversely affected, ranging from combat strength to the availability of experienced commanding officers.[15] That's when a new breed of Turkish private military companies came to the fore.

As happened with the Wagner Group in Russia, using the PMC label is also a convenient and efficient way in Turkey to develop a government-aligned paramilitary structure. SADAT International Defense Consultancy is where the rubber meets the road in growing Turkey's private military industry. The company, founded by retired Brigadier General Adnan Tanriverdi, being ideologically driven on the same path as Erdogan's Islamist government, is also at the center of an ongoing debate in the West regarding its role as a shadow operator for Turkey's nonofficial maneuvers. General Tanriverdi's forced retirement from the TSK due to his declared political Islamic tendencies is a fact, but SADAT's footprint in Syria, Libya, Nagorno-Karabakh, and Qatar is yet to be acknowledged by Ankara.

Suat Cubukcu,[16] American University and Orion Policy Institute terrorism expert, divides Erdogan's paramilitary structure into three layers: the first layer is composed of pseudo-military groups that function

---

[*] In a classified military dispatch seen by Reuters, 149 military envoys posted to the alliance's headquarters and command centers in Germany, Belgium, the Netherlands, and Britain were ordered on September 27 to return to Turkey within three days. https://www.reuters.com/article/us-turkey-nato-exclusive-idUSKCN12C16Q.

formally as security contractors and informally as secretive armed forces that carry out clandestine operations that formal state institutions legally cannot implement (for example, SADAT); the second is a connection with criminal organizations in countries where large numbers of Turkish migrants and people of Turkish descent live; the third is related to youth clubs promoting the government's official line among new generations.

At the same time, the Jerusalem Institute for Strategy and Security and TRENDS Research and Advisory of Abu Dhabi in the UAE assert that Turkey has developed over the past decade a large pool of well-trained, easily deployed, and effortlessly disposable proxy forces as a tool of power projection, with a convenient degree of plausible deniability.[17] The researchers conclude that when combined with Turkish nonofficial but governmentally directed and well-established groups such as the Gray Wolves, it becomes clear that Erdogan now has a private military and paramilitary system at his disposal.

Incorporated in 2012, SADAT International Defense Consultancy is the creation of Brigadier General Adnan Tanriverdi, former military adviser to Erdogan and close to the Turkish military and intelligence circles. The company website describes "SADAT Defense as the first and the only company in Turkey, that internationally provides consultancy and military training services at the international defence and interior security sector."[18] SADAT Defense was founded, under the presidency of Brigadier General (Retired) Adnan Tanriverdi, by twenty-three officers and NCOs retired from various units of Turkish Armed Forces and began its activities after the official declaration of "articles of incorporation" by the February 28, 2012, dated and 8015 numbered issue of *Turkish Trade Registry Gazette*.

SADAT is neither Blackwater, Wagner, nor the Islamic Republican Guards managing Iran's proxies. Several overlapping tactical uses are present in the U.S., Russian, and Iranian use of contractors, mercenaries, and proxies with their Turkish peers. Still, SADAT is operating under its parameters that have centuries-old roots in the Ottoman Army. As long as President Erdogan is in power, the evolution of SADAT's modus operandi is going to influence the world of Turkish and Islamic PMCs.

A Western narrative on SADAT frames the company as a conduit between Ankara and Syrian proxy fighters, linking the Turkish military and security services while benefitting from a PMC's plausible deniability status. According to U.S. Joint Staff Major Matt Powers, "Despite a diverse and often provocative body of reporting, SADAT is best understood as a modern example in the evolution of the privatized military industry, serving as an indigenous Turkish alternative to both Western and Russian companies."[19]

THE EVOLUTION OF PMCS WITH TURKISH CHARACTERS

Since 2010, Turkey, as well as China and Russia, witnessed a thriving private security market with local PSCs offering traditional services from close security protection to infrastructure guarding services. For more than a decade in Turkey, PSCs have been able to use weapons; for example, Turkish PSCs tasked with protecting oil refineries, oil wells, and power plants use MP5 submachine guns and G3 rifles.[20]

SADAT is a step forward into state privatization of the monopoly on security with authoritarian characteristics. In Erik Prince's autobiography *Civilian Warrior*, Prince mentioned that a Christian and conservative background influenced his decision to create Blackwater. Later on, this part was conveniently forgotten because Prince shifted the company's sole contracting for the U.S. government toward the Middle East. In the SADAT company website's thirty-six pages, the founder's vision is influenced by religion, aiming to become the leading private military company in the Islamic world.* The company is neither shy nor hiding any secret plan; it is directly stated on page 1 of the document: "SADAT Inc. aims at establishing the cooperation among the Islamic Countries in the sense of military and defence industries, in order to assist the Islamic World to take the rank it deserves among the Super Global Powers as a self-sufficient military power."

The idea of SADAT came to the mind of Tanriverdi during the Yugoslav wars. While the Yugoslavian conflict was a timid step in the privatization of the U.S. military toward private military companies, it was a TSK colonel who was the linchpin between a U.S. military contractor and the local forces for the creation of the Bosnian Army. At that time, Tanriverdi was in the visiting delegation to Bosnia Herzegovina, and his

---

* SADAT official website English version, https://www.SADAT.com.tr/download/SADAT-eng -full-v02.pdf.

adverse reaction to the perception of the West in control of the Bosnian Army spurred him into action to create SADAT. His fear was related to Western private defense consultancy companies turning neighboring Muslim states into enemies:[21] "Although its geography is covered with forests and has a mountainous terrain, we learned that the Bosnian Army was transformed into a structure dominated by armoured units and tanks by the company in question. However, the Bosnian Armed Forces should have consisted of units capable of performing commando and air-mobile operations in accordance with the country's lands. But since the cost of forming these units would be less, it would not be in accordance with the interests of the Private Company and the country behind it."*

The American PMC Blackwater started in 1996 as a shooting range for the U.S. police and special forces; similarly, SADAT's business model began with a small core of ex-military personnel providing military training to foreign armed forces or individuals. The company's list of services also ranges from special forces training to ordnance services, a military term to say that SADAT could be a middleman in the supply of weapons.

While the SADAT website provides a long and detailed list of services that the company can provide to armies and individuals, the supporting services provided to Turkey's expansion in the MENA region are the real deal. U.S. Africa Command (AFRICOM) estimates that more than seven thousand Syrians are fighting on both sides of the Libyan conflict. AFRICOM reports that five thousand Syrian mercenaries are deployed in support of Libya's GNA, and another two thousand are fighting for the rival LNA. According to AFRICOM, "The Syrians fighting for the GNA are paid and supervised by several dozen military trainers from a Turkish company called SADAT, which also trains GNA-aligned militias."[22]

While General Tanriverdi has denied any role in subcontracting military and intelligence operations in the MENA region, the company is adamant that it is not a mercenary organization. However, drawing the line in the murky world of money for mayhem is anything but easy.

In 2020, the U.S. Department of Defense was not the only one to point the finger at SADAT in Libya for training Syrian fighters on behalf of the GNA. The UN Working Group on Mercenaries' Activities pointed

---

* SADAT official website English version.

out that the GNA received official support from Ankara, and the overall fluid situation in Libya has been utterly complicated by the presence of mercenaries.

Also, Libya is where SADAT met the Wagner Group, but on the opposite side of the front.

A subsequent set of accusations against SADAT came during the forty-four-day war in Nagorno-Karabakh, claiming that Turkey allegedly provided Syrian mercenaries supporting Azerbaijan's blitzkrieg against Armenia. Azerbaijan firmly denied that Turkey sent it fighters from Syria, and at the same time an Armenian envoy to Russia mentioned that four thousand fighters from Syria took part in hostilities after being deployed by Turkey.[23]

Again, SADAT denied any involvement in the South Caucasus conflict. At the same time, the Turkish company Baykar was pleased to claim the paternity of the armed drones that Azerbaijan deployed against the Armenian forces in the disputed zone. Considered a game changer, the TB-2 combat drone made in Turkey made a splash in the conflict, destroying an impressive number of Armenian tanks and artillery emplacements. Therefore Baykar was the first in line to reap the excellent media coverage that the UCAVs received. Quite dissimilarly, on the mercenary side, there is small and contradictory information on the deployment of Syrian mercenaries. Some data points to their use as cannon fodder for assault operations or even as the sacrificial lamb to spot fortified positions, attract fire, and provide a target for the incoming drones. The same narrative resurfaces during the Russian invasion of Ukraine. Similarly, the role of mercenaries from Syria was relegated to the shadows, while the Turkish-made drones were celebrated in Ukrainian song.

As the conflict in Ukraine is attracting all the attention on Russian and Syrian mercenaries moving from the MENA region to Donbass, reports of Syrian mercenaries not returning home from Libya and the Caucasus are emerging. Several organizations including Syrians for Truth and Justice (STJ), the Syria Justice and Accountability Centre (SJAC), and the Hevdestî Association for Victims in North and East Syria complained to the UN Working Group on Mercenaries' Activities concerning the involvement of Moscow and Ankara in the recruiting process of Syrian mercenaries. In a seventeen-page document submitted to the UN Working Group, the organizations present details on the recruitment of Syrian mercenaries tasked to fight in Libya and Azerbaijan.[24] According to the report, Syria's desperate economic conditions coupled with a local predatory recruiting system are conducive to human rights violations in Syria as well as in the foreign battlefields to which the Syrian mercenaries are sent:

> *Although Syrian mercenary groups have returned from Azerbaijan and begun to return from Libya under UN-brokered peace talks, there must be investigations into the violations that these groups committed in combat abroad as well as in Syria in the process of predatory recruitment practices. Moreover, the dire humanitarian conditions that incentivize mercenary recruitment in the first place have only worsened.[25]*

In a 2021 interview with AFP, Melish Tanriverdi, SADAT CEO and son of General Tanriverdi, was adamant in mentioning that SADAT Defense has no armed forces nor is the company a security force or have any relation with mercenary organizations. At the same time the SADAT CEO underlined how the company has never been in conflict zones and does not provide subcontracting services, which he mentions as "legionary services."[26] In his opinion the accusations of SADAT being a mercenary recruiter are part of a Western disinformation campaign designed to tarnish the image of Turkey and President Recep Tayyip Erdogan.[27]

Asserted Melish Tanriverdi:[28]

> *Should not the claimants prove their claims with evidence? If a company with a 10-year history has illegal activities, there must be financial, logistic or etc. evidence as the claimants suggest. Do you not think it is quite funny while we are having the space age, that our company cannot be proven to run global operations without leaving any trace, but to be gossip topic in the media? Do you really think we are professional enough to fool the global powers? Have we developed methods that no one else has discovered? Current situation has now turned into a conspiracy theory.*

SADAT—WHAT NEXT?

The existence of the Deep State predates the rise of Erdogan to the height of Turkey's power. In light of Erdogan's grip on power, it is possible to state that the Deep State Islamist version, sharing the president's Neo-Ottoman vision, will facilitate SADAT's rise and provide a fertile ground for the expansion of the Turkish private military sector internationally. Similar to the Russian private military industry, being supported by a central power guarantees a meteoric rise. The other side of the coin is that the fall of a "supreme leader" is going to create a domino effect embracing all the individuals and companies that have benefited from a proximity to absolute power. Similarly, the development of a professional Turkish private military sector, once the time for Turkey's foreign policy assertiveness has reached its zenith, could probably follow what happened to the Ottoman Army mercenaries when war ended: being employed by foreign countries. Something that could happen sooner to the Wagner Group forces that will survive Ukraine and MENA region deployments.

In light of the ongoing trajectory of Turkish foreign policy, Afghanistan and Somalia are the next logical steps. As soon as the United States left the Afghan capital's international airport in a hurry, Ankara was swiftly proposing Turkish private military contractors to provide security. The same modus operandi was used in the Mogadishu airport. Ankara's proposal to the Taliban did not explicitly mention SADAT, but the choices, at the time of writing, do not abound besides the Istanbul-based PMC. Tanriverdi himself noted that in Turkey only his company could provide expertise, consulting, and training that would ensure the airport's security.

Besides the experience with SADAT, Ankara knew early on that carefully placing mercenaries, from cannon fodder to special operations units, along Turkish geostrategic objectives could achieve one crucial objective: establish a beachhead with everyone knowing that Turkey is active in that region without incurring a domestic blowback. As the Wagner Group did for Mother Russia in Syria, establishing a foothold prior to the official involvement of the Russian Army and providing plausible deniability in Africa, similarly, Turkish PMCs are going to operate using a not too different playbook. The main problem is that both tactics are going to compete for the same geographical area. Knowing Putin's and Erdogan's firm belief that the geopolitical chessboard is a zero-sum game, it is yet to be seen when and how the two competing mercenary forces are going to fulfill the will of their master and survive doing it. Also is yet to be seen whether the use of Wagner contractors in the Ukrainian war is going to deplete the group's combat readiness and reduce its footprint from the Middle East to Africa, offering some leeway to Turkish PMCs to fill the gap.

The political and religious credo that embeds SADAT and the paramilitary organization that is part of Erdogan's power projection assets places them in between the Wagner Group and the Iranian Islamic Revolutionary Guard Corps (IRGC).

While Wagner and similar Russian PMCs are composed of contractors that share Putin's Eurasian vision, the monetary gain is a predominant driver, while in SADAT it is possible to witness the peculiarity of Tanriverdi's idea of an Islamic Army that is first and foremost motivated by Islamic values and secondarily by the coin.

In this respect, there are affinities between the Iranian IRGC and the popular mobilization units (PMU) in Iraq where the financial support is essential, but the forces are first and foremost composed of "political soldiers" that can be deployed abroad or internally in defense of the regime. According to Jonathan Spyer, an expert on Syria, Iraq, radical Islamic groups, and Kurds, "The proxy party-militia structures which the IRGC excels at creating and controlling, in turn, have the advantage of informality, and deniability, when compared with conventional forces."[29]

Therefore Afghanistan and not the Middle East could be the real litmus test for SADAT. While Turkey was at an early stage of its return to Afghanistan under the Taliban 2.0, SADAT took a step further, flirting with the idea of supporting the return of the Sharia-based Islamic Emirate of Afghanistan.

According to Ali Coşar, a retired colonel and board member of SADAT, Turkey will need to support building a new Afghanistan run by the Taliban in cooperation with Pakistan, Qatar, and Malaysia. Coşar, quoted on the Association of Justice Defenders Strategic Studies Center ASSAM's webpage, notes the historical parallel between modern Taliban religious warriors and Seljuk and Ottoman Turks following the Sharia law during their rule. Mr. Coşar considers the Taliban "the 21st century, religious warriors who once again prioritised asymmetrical warfare and embraced martyrdom and becoming veterans for their homeland prevailed over the conventional superpowers backed by special forces in the mountainous Central Asian terrain." It is not by chance that the ASSAM president is Adnan Tanriverdi. Also, Coşar expresses a commonality of intent on the SADAT website, envisioning an Islamic PMC that can provide the security training that the Taliban needs to develop a modern security apparatus.

In a declaration published in March 2022 Mr. Coşar summarized the scope of establishing the Joint Defense Industry Cooperation of Islamic Countries: "As the main geography where most of these countries are located, in the 'ASRICA' countries, besides the production of warfare weapons and vehicles, as a service sector application of the military art; by introducing the concept of 'Defense Service Industry,' this activity is becoming more and more widespread in every Islamic country; it will be mentioned that efforts should be made under the control of states, to be put into legislation by placing them on a legal basis, and to play a catalyst role in developing the Islamic Countries defense industry cooperation environment."[30]

His definition of Joint Defense Industry Cooperation is considered an "inevitable necessity" for Islamic countries to play a prominent role on the global chessboard, and it is achievable compounding the deep-rooted military traditions in Islamic countries and the flexibility offered by PMCs. In the declaration, the Western PMCs are considered to be an imperialistic tool to maintain control and expropriate the wealth of Islamic countries and a pivotal point in the rationale for the establishment of Islamic PMC is that if an "imperial country's PMC is assigned to give military consultancy to Islamic Countries, that PMC has never done anything for the good of the Islamic country it serves. By making wrong guidance with incorrect recommendations, it either led to unnecessary expenditure and waste, or caused attempts to be fruitless."[31]

Basically, this is the reason that pushed Adnan Tanriverdi to found SADAT. While the declaration is bent on criticizing the "Imperialist Christian West," the logical reasoning for creating a mature private military sector in Turkey is not dissimilar from the one present in the West:

supporting the state military function economically and efficiently locally or abroad. In the commentaries that populate the SADAT and ASSAM websites, it is constantly reiterated how the company and the future development of the Turkish PMCs need to be under the supervision and control of the Ministry of Defense. Also, in case of requests for support and cooperation from non-Turkish actors, the Ministry of Foreign Affairs is called to the fore.

NOT ONLY SADAT, AKADEMI SANCAK

Another company that populates the early development of the private military sector with Turkish characteristics is Akademi Sancak (ACS).* The company, having limited international media exposure compared to SADAT, is managed by another retired general from TKS, General Ahmet Can Çevik, who was appointed as the military advisor of the emir of Qatar. According to Intelligence Online, the ACS private military company is fast turning into Turkey's private relay to the Qatari military.[32]

ACS' website is not far from SADAT minus the Islamist narrative. Similarly to SADAT, ASC provides training to armed forces that have a good standing with Turkey. Qatar is a case in point as ACS has been providing training for many years, notably to the Qatari Emiri Navy (QEN) and special forces. Also the role of Turkey in support of Qatar in delivering top-level security services during the World Cup has been partially delegated to Turkey's security companies, ACS being one among them.

Besides Qatar, ACS also regularly trains security forces in countries that have historical relationships with Ankara ranging from Azerbaijan to Turkmenistan.

Similarly to Tanriverdi, Çevik spent time in Bosnia during the conflict. He was one of the highest-ranking Turkish military personnel in the International Security Assistance Force (ISAF) in Afghanistan. General Çevik's relationship with the Turkish military-industrial complex also is not to be discounted as he is a member of the board of the state-owned defense contractor Aselsan. Aselsan's subsidiary is tasked with producing the new electro-optical reconnaissance, surveillance, and targeting sys-

---

* ACS official website English version, http://asancak.com/eng/Default.aspx.

tem for the Bayraktar T-B2. Again, it is not by chance that Qatar is an important client for Aselsan.

Besides having a relationship in the Gulf with other monarchies such as the Kingdom of Saudi Arabia, ASC's close relationship with Qatar is related to the preferential relationship between Doha and Ankara and their shared view on the Muslim Brotherhood.[33]

Comparing the dawn of the Turkish private security sector with China and Russia, especially to forecast the future path that Ankara will force on its own breed of PMCs, is an overall lack of laws and regulations for the developing security sector. From a legal standpoint, while China has a very detailed law concerning the private security sector's domestic role and a new set of regulations is under scrutiny for expanding the Chinese PSCs abroad, Russian law still considers PMCs illegal. In Turkey, there is a vast legal gap. While Ankara could count on hundreds of years of experience managing free lances, there is an ample legal regulatory vacuum regarding PMCs in modern Turkey.

Considering the situation that Turkey does not have a signature in the Montreux Convention that regulates PMCs or in the ICoC for PSCs, there are plenty of opportunities for the application of modern standards and regulation as well as plenty of opportunities for abuses. As the privatization of the state monopoly on violence is just happening in Turkey, there is still a modicum of hope in the possibility that the leading PMCs are going to opt for an international code of conduct as stated on their website. Nevertheless, the ongoing trends from Libya to Ukraine beg to differ.

As China is finding its way in regulating the action of its PSCs abroad and the civil-military fusion at home, Turkey is probably going to follow its own path to develop PMCs with "Turkish characters." In a time of high uncertainty, Turkey will most likely continue to pursue a pragmatic foreign policy that is neither pro-Ukraine, nor pro-Russia, but entirely pro-Turkey.[34] Turkish security companies are nurtured in an environment different from their Chinese counterparts. They are likely to chart their own development. In contrast to Chinese companies, SADAT, rooted in in Islamic rather than Kemalist values, does not envision a future with at best limited access to weapons.

CHAPTER TEN

Drone Mercenaries

New Security Paradigms from China, Russia, and Turkey

THE RISE OF DRONES FROM THE MIDDLE EAST TO THE CAUCASUS
THE USE OF UAVs,[*] USUALLY REFERRED TO AS DRONES, WHETHER OVER
the Middle Eastern or the Caucasus battlefields, or delivering medicine
in remote African areas, is expanding. It is also at the forefront of the
search for an efficient and technologically driven new normal. During
the 2020 spread of COVID-19, UAVs were called on to perform new
roles, ranging from contactless delivery, to aerial monitoring, to supporting lockdowns. While the uses for civilian drones in the struggle against
the pandemic are developing, their military counterparts, which are
well ahead of the curve, have ushered in a new era of remote-controlled
conflicts. The French philosopher Gregoire Chamayou, author of *A
Theory of the Drone*,[1] wrote that the rise of the UAV catalyzed the emergence of a new paradigm for the ethical and political norms of warfare.

From Yemen to Libya, Syria, and Nagorno-Karabakh, armed drones
delivering precision munitions[2] or DIY flying bombs deployed by insurgents are a game changer. The Middle East and the South Caucasus have
become opening acts for drone warfare. In the 1990s, the United States
opened the proverbial Pandora's box by deploying drones for targeted

---

[*] The term *drone* will be used to define UAVs and UCAVs that are both parts of unmanned aerial
systems (UAS) that consist of (1) an aircraft with no pilot on board, (2) a remote pilot station, (3) a
command-and-control link, and (4) a payload specific to the intended operation.

killing. Since then, the evolution and diffusion of armed UAVs, with increased capabilities and decreased operational costs, have ushered in a new type of deterrence by turning conventional military doctrine on its head. In recent conflicts, warring parties resisted calls for a truce, emboldened by their confidence in newly acquired armed UAVs. In the forty-four-day war between Azerbaijan and Armenia, the belief in drone air superiority that bolstered Baku into choosing war over diplomacy is a case in point.

Mercenaries, private military contractors, and private security companies are taking note. Countering the drone menace is already a business opportunity that Chinese PSCs are offering. During large crowd events in Mainland China, it is quite common to spot PSC contractors operating long plastic tubes that look like a b-series sci-fi prop, or antennas while their colleagues are scanning the sky with binoculars. The antennas are jammers, machines that cut the communication between the drone and the remote operator, forcing the drone to land or return to its point of origin. The "long tubes" are microwave guns that fry the drone's electronics, causing an immediate crash. While the Chinese municipal authorities are confident in what they are paying for, most of the reported cases are related to takedown of amateur drones flying near to a public gathering to take a good picture. How the deployed drone's countermeasures will work in case of a terrorist attack with explosive-laced drones has yet to be seen.

Nevertheless, the Chinese authorities have started to look at the remote-controlled menace from the sky, and the local PSCs have been available to provide a solution, though for quite a price. The next step will witness the top Chinese PSCs operating outside Chinese borders to deploy Chinese commercial drones and tethered blimps to scout for threats or to provide aerial coverage for early warning systems around gated compounds.

Antipiracy drone solutions are still in their beta version, as the antidrone equipment carries a rent price tag that clients are not readily willing to pay. An increase of swarm drone attacks on sea lanes of communications (SLOC) around the chokepoints of Bab el Mandeb and the Strait of Hormuz or around South Africa and the Mozambique channel will change this attitude. Many chokepoints are close to weak nations, unable to provide security to the vessels in transit or even being part of the problem. An increase in navigation risks from a land- and sea-based drone menace will force the hand of the insurance companies to mandate the use of antidrone operators as a requirement for their insurance policies. "My guys are not yet able to send one email from a vessel, figure it out operating an anti-drone countermeasure," commented a manager overseeing a Chinese PSC maritime operation.[3] Therefore better financing could ensure access to a proper talent pool, but waiting for a severe accident before taking this step is a costly gambit. Examples abound.

The Houthis, an Iranian-backed group that operates in Yemen, developed a wide array of capabilities to deploy against commercial vessels in the Red Sea, ranging from acts of piracy to remote-controlled explosive boats, mines, and suicide drone attacks. Copycats are just waiting for a chance as nonstate actors and criminal organizations are learning from the Middle East combat drone playbook.

In less than three decades, armed drones evolved from highly sophisticated and expensive weapon systems that only a few nation-states' armies could deploy to a diffused and cost-efficient tool on the battlefield. Increase in GPS autonomous navigation software precision and a sharp drop in the price of components catalyzed a new era in remote-controlled warfare. Instead of a few multi-million-dollar military-grade drones, the new battle space is progressively saturated by cost-efficient and widely available armed drones. The abundance of Iranian-made combat drones on the side of Russia in the Ukraine war is a case in point. Several lessons may be drawn from the current rise of drone warfare:

- Reengineered commercial drones transformed into kamikaze bombs put the defender at a disadvantage by increasing disproportionally the cost of defense.
- Drone hybrid warfare offsets conventional military advantage.
- Drones lower both the political and economic costs of retaliation.
- Drones minimize the risks of loss of life and accountability.
- Drone data feeds are not only used for scouting and targeting but also for propaganda.
- The drone's characteristic buzz makes a psychological impact on a soldier's morale and is a cause of PTSD in the civilian population.

- Drones are used as an economic warfare tool, denying access to strategic waterways or damaging critical infrastructures.

- The deployment of drones increases the propensity for aggression, even during a pandemic.

- Drones are used by nonstate actors to coerce a political outcome.

The effects of this new drone era are just being perceived in the battlefield, but the ramifications on the future of warfare and the impact on society are far-reaching.

According to Chamayou, remote killing without the possibility of being killed is suspending the rapport of reciprocity in armed conflict: "the seduction of the drone has been the promised inevitable invulnerability."[4] Therefore remote-controlled violence is not only lowering the threshold for conflict and increasing propensity to aggression, but it is also presenting new ethical, moral, and legal problems spanning from precision to autonomous killing restrictions.

The use of drones that hover above the battlefield and rain death down on command is already here, and it is only going to increase in sophistication and diffusion due to further advancement in AI applications. AI lethal autonomous weapons systems will not need humans in the decision-making loop in terms of both target acquisition and the finger pulling the trigger. The day when humans will not be part of the conflict decision-making process is getting near, or at least the human variable in the equation will persist but just as a target.

U.S. EARLIER DRONE SUPREMACY: REMOTE ASSASSINATION

Three decades ago, the U.S. deployment of drones for targeted killings in Iraq and Afghanistan wrote the second chapter in the book of aerial drone warfare doctrine, following Israel's early adoption of drones as bait for aerial defenses. At that time, the drones' alleged precision strikes were represented in the popular perception of the War on Terror.[5]

Since 1991, drones have become increasingly recognized as a game changer on the battlefield as well as in the struggle against terrorism. The table, however, has turned. The upper hand once held by national armies has been reversed in favor of insurgents. An example is given by Saudi

Arabia's efforts to contest armed drone incursion inside the kingdom's borders. The Saudis appear to not have taken the venerable expression "don't bring a knife to a gun fight" very seriously. In 2017, the U.S. Patriot air defense system was used by Saudi forces in Yemen to shoot down a reengineered Houthi aerial drone. However, using a sledgehammer to swat a fly was hardly efficient: it cost more than a million US$ for one Patriot missile to shoot down a drone worth a few hundred dollars.

Similarly, both Hezbollah and ISIS have taken advantage of asymmetric drone warfare. Commercial drones have been reconfigured as flying bombs and used for surveillance. ISIS used professional photographic aerial drones for propaganda purposes by filming black-clad caliphate fighters in action.[6]

Many are familiar with the costly, highly efficient unmanned U.S. Predator and Reaper drones that cost $4 million to $16 million per unit, but the narrative is changing. The ability to weaponize inexpensive commercial drones is gaining momentum.

Most important, the efficiency of the commercial drones versus military defensive capabilities poses a disadvantage for the defender. The new cycle in remote-controlled warfare is shifting from military-grade drones in favor of relatively cheap, off-the-shelf hobby toys that can be weaponized for pennies on the dollar.[7]

China versus Turkey: The Real Drone War Is for Market Share

In a sign of the times, it is not the United States, producer of the world's most advanced armed drones, battling to maintain market share. Instead it is China, challenged by an upstart, Turkey. As the era of the deadly drone unfolds, Ankara is planning to win the race for the acquisition of combat drone market share. The binomial combination of Turkey's armed drone plus mercenaries could be soon on the table, while the Chinese offer of drones and PSCs' counterdrone solutions seems unable to compete with Ankara.

With Beijing feeling the heat, it has now turned to "acquisitions with Chinese characteristics," a euphemism for acquiring foreign technology by any and all means.

Ankara has adopted Beijing's playbook. Turkey is quickly eroding China's market position with its affordable and battle-tested combat drones, creating a one stop shop including ammunition. Moreover, Ankara offers localized production, as evidenced by the Ukraine deal.[8] This is attributed to two factors: limited legal restrictions on the sale of combat drones and a low price.

For example, the Stockholm International Peace Research Institute[9] reported that China, between 2010 and 2020, delivered 220 armed drones to sixteen countries. Not to be outdone, Turkish sales increasingly erode a sizeable part of the Chinese market, from Ethiopia[10] to Poland. According to the Turkish combat drone producer Baykar,[11] the company delivered Turkish armed drones to thirteen countries in 2021.

Therefore countries from the EU to Canada need to be aware that Turkey is pressing China by finding a new competitive edge in combat drone development, no matter what.

A review of the evidence reveals three critical aspects of the international market for armed UAVs.

First, the struggle for market share, which is well underway, is not defined solely by cost competition. In addition, the number of participants continues to expand. The United States and Israel, considered the market innovators that produce the gold standard MQ-9 Reaper and the Heron TP, no longer dominate the market. Turkey, a relative newcomer, produces the Anka, the ubiquitous Bayraktar TB-2 that is expanding its deadly buzz from Eurasia to the Middle East and Africa.

Second, the lack of any meaningful international regulatory regime has resulted in a bifurcated market, one part of which is composed of nation-states that abide by the Missile Technology Control Regime (MTCR).[12] In contrast, the other part consists of countries that comply with flexible regulations. As a result, the lack of terms and conditions expands the threat scenario dramatically.

Third, the various available UAVs range from inexpensive off-the-shelf drones that can be easily weaponized to the Turkish "air force for hire" affordable airpower. This diversity, more than creating a more competitive market, lowers the threshold of the ability to wage war. The TB2 deployment in the forty-four-day war in Nagorno-Karabakh is a case in point that illustrates that the challenge to develop and implement an effective deterrence regime that would inhibit state and nonstate actors is daunting.

Given that the United States produces the MQ-9B,[13] the Rolls-Royce of killer drones, one might assume that the United States dominates that sector of the drone market. But one would be wrong. The truth is that the United States does not have a dominant market share. In fact, the United States is a distant player in the war for armed drone market share, in which China and Turkey are the dominant players.

Nevertheless, Beijing, able to sell its drones with fewer strings attached and with financial support from its state banks, is suddenly feeling the pressure from Ankara.

To be fair, as with Rolls-Royce in the automotive sector, the MQ-9B drone is priced well beyond the means of many prospective buyers. For example, General Electric (GE), which advertises its highly praised Reaper drone as "unmanned and unmatched," has a significant sticker shock problem.

China's top-of-the-line armed drone, the CH-5 "Rainbow," sells for around half[14] of the MQ-9, while a Turkish TB2 is priced at around US\$2 million.[15] Compare those prices to the US\$32 million[16] price tag for the Reaper MQ-9B.*

But even those countries with big budgets, such as U.S. allies in the Persian Gulf, have found that price is not the only consideration. So are legal structures hindering the sales of U.S. drones, such as the aforementioned MTCR. None of these factors apply to Chinese or Turkish sales. Nevertheless, both countries, neither of which is a member of the MTCR, claim to abide by their own set of terms and conditions.

Ankara's military-industrial complex has been developing efficient and cheap combat drones and missiles, and their success in Syria, Libya, and especially in the forty-four-day conflict in Nagorno-Karabakh[17] has seized the headlines. In the early days of the Azerbaijan-Armenia conflict, Turkey's Bayraktar TB2 drone was a game changer that inflicted massive losses on Armenian troops and equipment. The TB2 has another advan-

---

* The Reaper price includes the accompanying ammunitions, sensors, ground control station, and Predator Primary satellite link, while the Chinese and Turkish counterpart estimates do not include accompanying ammunitions.

tage: Muslim countries in Southeast Asia are more likely to view it in a more favorable light. Countries such as Malaysia and Indonesia could conceivably feel threatened by data theft by China. A drone's video feed and geolocation tag could be rerouted to Beijing while the Chinese-made combat UAVs fly over disputed waters or sensitive military installations.

China is now scrambling to stay afloat in the game, and sales are not the only prize at stake. Pakistan signing a deal with Turkey to coproduce the Anka[18] drone is a case in point. The aircraft could soon be buzzing over Afghanistan, providing Ankara with valuable intelligence on Chinese moves in the area.

To achieve a technological advantage over Turkey, China is craving foreign combat drone high-tech. Israel, which is considered to be the father of combat aerial drones, is at the top of Beijing's list, but this is fraught with difficulty. Washington is extremely sensitive to any form of cooperation between the two countries: for example, Israel pulled the plug on a planned deal for the Phalcon[19] airborne early warning system after pressure from the United States. With the China-Israel relationship deepening beyond business and infrastructure investments, the United States will likely be even more eagle-eyed. At the same time, Tel Aviv will find it increasingly challenging to maintain its balancing act between Beijing and Washington. Nevertheless, many other countries worldwide are juicy targets for China's voracious appetite for technological secrets. Exhibit A: Italy.

Alpi Aviation, an Italian company that produced military drones deployed in Afghanistan by the Italian special forces, was a supplier to the country's Ministry of Defense. It also cooperates with the state-owned defense giant Leonardo. In 2018, a Hong Kong shell company[20] bought a majority share in Alpi and allegedly planned to transfer know-how and production capabilities to Wuxi in China. The deal, which came to light a few years later, has been investigated by the Guardia di Finanza, an Italian police force under the authority of the Minister of Economics and Finance. The acquisition violates laws that prohibit strategic companies in critical sectors, such as defense, from selling outside Italy without the government's authorization. Countries with sophisticated defense technology ought to be mindful of the lengths China will go to keep a leading position in the game or risk being blindsided by Beijing. It is the same situation on the Turkish side as several components critical to Ankara's military drone industries are supplied by third countries. The current Canadian federal government's decision to ban the export of high-tech Canadian drone optics and targeting systems to Turkey is a case in point.[21]

China's acquisition of foreign military drone technology follows the same pattern used by Beijing to acquire foreign high tech that is key for its rapid civilian and military development. However, the recent competition with Turkey forces Beijing to reduce the time in spotting and acquiring foreign technologies, increasing the political risk of being caught with their hand in the cookie jar.

According to James Mulvenon,[22] while economic development is the primary driver of China's nontraditional collection and espionage activity, improving the capabilities of its military is a close second. As the United States increases its effort to stop Chinese acquisitions of U.S. dual-use technology, the European Union is a weaker target. Without European centralized supervision, the highly innovative but cash-strapped European companies are easy prey for international shell companies, bidding on military equipment and technology that could find its way later to China.

While the combat drone market competition between Beijing and Ankara is in the making, the global competition to expand the drone arms race is already underway. PMSCs including drone warfare and counterdrone solutions is the next logical step. In this respect the Russian private military sector looks like a distant competitor to China and Turkey. Probably the Russian military ethos in always having humans in the loop is deferring the armed drone adoptions' inevitable consequence. At the moment of writing one of the few reported uses of drones by Russian PMCs and mercenaries is the Wagner Group's deployment of scout drones in Libya.

In order to compete with China and Turkey, the United States has tried to address the legal issues surrounding drone sales. The Trump administration moved to reinterpret the MTCR as part of an overall effort to sell more weapons overseas. The Biden administration is following suit, with a planned sale of MQ-9B drones totaling US$2.9 billion to the UAE as part of the US$23 billion deal that includes the F-35 fighter jet. Other potential customers for U.S. armed drones include Saudi Arabia, Oman, and Indonesia. Nevertheless, such planned sales are clouded by uncertainty. In the case of Indonesia,[23] for instance, concerns over whether it has the regulatory framework in place to protect U.S. technology—among other matters—have contributed to the debate in Washington over whether to allow the sale.

In contrast, Turkey and China have no such qualms. To sweeten the deal, Ankara and Beijing are ready to transfer an entire production[24] line for combat drones as in the case of China in Saudi Arabia or Turkey in Ukraine and Pakistan, enhancing the countries' long-term military relationship while simultaneously driving a wedge between Washington and its allies.

Even the proposed transfer of the MQ-9B to the UAE is encountering a difficult path. Following the IDEX[25] defense exhibition in Abu Dhabi, the Chinese state military equipment producer Norinco is ready to sell its Golden Eagle CR500 VTOL (vertical takeoff and landing UAV), which increases the UAE's acquisition of Chinese armed drones. The Norinco CR500 is an oversized version of a commercial drone. Still, the notion of the UAE being willing to partner with Norinco could help the UAE accelerate its cooperation with the United States. Playing the Chinese card is something that the Gulf state is increasingly apt to do, swiftly moving from one side to the other in the U.S.-Chinese competition in the Middle East. The recent suspension of talks over the US$23 billion deal could be part of the UAE's negotiating tactic. Ankara's willingness to enter the Gulf armed drone market could complicate U.S. and Chinese calculations.

Therefore the international market for combat UAVs is both increasingly diverse and increasingly lethal. The transfer of UCAVs from Tehran to Moscow intensifies an already complex landscape for sourcing and developing combat drone components, creating further constraints on countering the drone menace. In one crucial aspect, the militarization of UAVs is similar to the unrestricted use of chlorine gas in the early twentieth century. Eventually, the international community, which realized that unrestricted use of poisonous gas was a dangerous, destabilizing threat, concluded that chemical weapons had to be banned, which the Chemical Weapons Convention achieved. The solution is not to ban UAVs; rather, in the same way that the threat posed by chemical weapons was contained, the optimal way to deal with the UAV issue is to treat it as an arms control issue. The UAV genie is out of the bottle, and unlike poisonous gas, it cannot be put back again.

YEMEN: HIGH-TECH VERSUS LOW-TECH WARFARE

The role of armed UAVs is expanding. From Afghanistan to Nagorno-Karabakh, the unmistakable buzz of a drone is the foreboding soundtrack of a missile strike. In these regions, the unnerving sound is already a source of posttraumatic stress disorder (PTSD) among civilians, especially the young.[26]

The ongoing civil war in Yemen showcases how highly sophisticated armies could be countered by low-technology drones that impose a high toll on the defending soldiers' lives and matériel.

Yemen's civil war erupted in 2014 when the Ansar Allah movement, better known by the tribal affiliation as Houthi, a Shiite group with links to Iran, seized Sana'a, the country's capital. In March 2015, a coalition of Gulf states, led by Saudi Arabia, economically isolated the rebel's forces. The initial air strike campaign with U.S. logistical support[27] quickly drew the coalition into open conflict.

According to the Council on Foreign Relations Global Conflict Tracker,[28] the civil war

continues to take a heavy toll on Yemeni civilians, making Yemen the world's worst humanitarian crisis. The UN estimates that the civilian casualty toll has exceeded 15,000 killed or injured. Twenty-two million Yemenis remain in need of assistance, eight million are at risk of famine, and a cholera outbreak has affected over one million people. All sides of the conflict are reported to have violated human rights and international humanitarian law.

Throughout 2020, despite the repeated calls by Saudi Arabia for a ceasefire in Yemen, Houthi drones were used as flying bombs against the Riyadh-led coalition and also targeted strategic objectives inside the Kingdom of Saudi Arabia.

Since the beginning of the conflict, mercenaries and drones have been an integral part of the war effort.[29] Weaponized UAVs have been deployed by the rebel forces as the Iran-backed Houthis are using explosive-laced UAVs to offset the Saudi-UAE coalition's overwhelming military advantage. Reengineered Chinese commercial drones and militarized Iranian-looking models such as Qasef-1 have been deployed as scouting platforms as well as to harass the coalition's antimissile systems. While the cost and the capabilities of the Houthis' drones pale in comparison with their American counterpart, the effects are equally devastating on the troops' morale and are a boon for the insurgents' propaganda machine. The use of UAV attack videos posted online on social media is not an isolated case related to Yemen, but it has become a widespread propaganda tool that has reached its apex during the Nagorno-Karabakh war. Baku's official communications have flooded the Internet with videos of armed UAV strikes on Armenian defenses.

Incursions inside the Saudi borders, brazen attacks against Saudi civilian airports, and even an attack on oil refineries that culminated with the crash of the oil price are examples of the reach of the Houthis' drones. In addition, the Houthis' UAVs tried to adopt the U.S. preferred playbook in drone warfare: remote targeted killing.

In January 2019, in the southern part of Yemen at the al-Anad airbase, a drone attack aimed at a coalition military parade wounded several high-ranking officials including the Yemeni Army's deputy chief. The drone was zeroed in on the authority's podium in the attempt to strike at the core of the military command structure. The video of the attack, filmed by several bystanders, immediately reverberated across the Internet, which increased the propaganda effect of the aerial strike exponentially. According to Aaron Stein, director of research at the Foreign Policy Research Institute (FPRI), "the recent drone attack in Yemen hasn't received much attention outside the small circle of experts that pay attention to the conflict in Yemen or the proliferation of unmanned aerial vehicles, but it will likely be a historical footnote in the proliferation of unmanned technology to sub-state militants."[30]

In addition, the irony in the attack is related to the fact that the al-Anad airbase was used as a U.S. special forces attack platform for drone strikes against Al Qaeda supporters in Yemen and the Horn of Africa. Following the drone strike on the airbase, the Saudi-led coalition denounced the action as a blatant breach of the just-inked but feeble truce while the Houthis, in a tit-for-tat counter claim, and stated that the attack was payback for the ongoing Saudi airstrikes that killed numerous civilians.

During May of the same year, the Houthis' drone warfare reached a new level of sophistication when oil tankers and pipelines were targeted by remote-controlled bombs that forced the Saudi oil giant Aramco to suspend several pipeline operations. At the same time two Saudi, one Norwegian, and one Emirati tankers in international waters in proximity to the Strait of Hormuz were hit by a coordinated drone strike and by underwater limpet mines. Nonetheless, the Houthis claimed responsibility for the attack. Similarly, the group claimed responsibility for a drone attack that hit two Aramco oil drilling pumping stations west of Riyadh. A dress rehearsal prior to the attack was a strike on one of the major Aramco refineries well inside the kingdom's borders.

On September 2019, a combined drone and missile attack on the biggest Aramco oil processing facilities in Saudi Arabia, Abqaiq and Khurais, severely crippled the production of 5.7 million barrels of oil per day.[31]

The game to determine who was responsible for this attack is still ongoing. On the one hand, Saudi Arabia and the United States point at Iran as the mastermind behind the attack, for which Yemen's Houthi rebels have claimed responsibility.

While the Houthis have claimed responsibility for several drone attacks against high-value targets in Yemen and an oil refinery adjacent to Riyadh, the attack on the Aramco oil facilities is different. Western military analysts aired doubts that a "ragtag" militia could plan and carry out sophisticated aerial drone strikes involving twenty-five drones and cruise missiles. While the Iranian drones are not as technologically advanced as their Western counterparts, they are relatively inexpensive and can be assembled using off-the-shelf components. In this respect, the previous drone strikes carried out by the Houthis against Aramco oil refineries could be considered a dress rehearsal to probe Saudi aerial defenses before a much broader and brazen attack against Aramco's Abqaiq and Khurais oil facilities.[32] Nevertheless, doubts on the legitimacy of the

Houthis' claim persist. What these attacks have in common is that the drone is one of the easiest parts of the equation to obtain. Other elements required to carry out the September drone strike included advanced scouting and planning, deep knowledge of the objective to pinpoint weak links in the aerial defense, and the ability to identify high-value targets to cause the greatest damage given the warhead's weight limit.

Following the attack, satellite images provided by the U.S. government showed nineteen damaged facilities.

An examination of the wreckage revealed that cruise missiles were included in the drone attack. What stood out is the fact that this attack was not the work of amateurs. The command and control (CC) of the drones, which was robust as well as near instantaneous, was well beyond the capabilities of a marginal organizations such as the Houthis. This type of highly advanced CC indicates beyond a reasonable doubt that the Houthis had help from an organization, perhaps an intelligence bureau, or a military entity familiar with the CC required to deploy drones effectively.

Several conclusions concerning the remote-controlled bombing of a vital refinery located deep into Saudi territory have emerged. The first is that drones are capable of causing great damage far away from the operators/pilots. Second, the cost required to defend against drones is a multiple of the cost to launch such an assault, which places the disparity squarely on the purse of the defender, a shining example of asymmetric warfare. This is otherwise known as smashing an ant with a sledgehammer. Few countries can afford to use, on a routine basis, a million US$ Patriot missile to destroy a reconfigured few hundred US$ hobbyist drone purchased over the Internet.

Another lesson is related to the ability to determine who was responsible for the attack. If the operators/pilots are hundreds of miles away, then speed away after the strike, they could literally be anywhere. This complicates the calculus of retaliation. Who do you bomb, and with what level of intensity? Simply bombing the "usual suspects" because you know where they are is not a solution.

Then again, it is similar to the strategy used by President Thomas Jefferson to deal with the Barbary pirates (read: the Ottoman Navy) that were attacking American ships in the Mediterranean and elsewhere on the high seas. Jefferson concluded that while the American ships could not be defended, it was possible to determine the location of bases from which the attacks were launched, in and around modern Libya and elsewhere. Jefferson advised the sultan that if his navy did not stop attacking American ships, the U.S. Navy (what there was of it) would respond by bombarding the harbors on the Barbary coast. In other words, we might not know where you are, but we know where you live. This was an early example of what evolved into what became known in Latin America as "gunboat diplomacy."

Another lesson concerns the degree to which the cycle of military advancement has been compressed. This is due in large measure to the willingness of states to transfer weapons and the know-how to operate them to nonstate actors. The timeframe required to turn a group of sword-and-sandals fighters into a band of drone specialists with the ability to extend their threat radius hundreds of miles from their base has become remarkably compressed. The knock-on effect of this development will become manifest in a variety of sectors, especially in the money for mayhem world.

The negative externalities of a localized drone attack were revealed in an empirical index, that is, the price of crude oil, and they were almost immediately felt worldwide. Within minutes of the strike, the price of crude oil jumped 20 percent and fell back 14.6 percent the next day before settling on an 8 percent increase relative to the prestrike price.

The Houthis exploited their ability to expand their threat radius well beyond their limited sphere of influence. First, they admitted that they made the attack, then immediately stated that other targets were well within their ability to strike as far away as some of the Saudi coalition's allies, including the UAE.

The Saudi response to the attack was, to be charitable, ad hoc, taken directly from *Catch 22*. In the novel, Yossarian told the psychiatrist that he didn't want to fly because the Nazis were trying to kill him. The psychiatrist replied, "Yossarian, don't take it personally. They want to kill everyone." Asked Yossarian, "Then why are they shooting at *me*?"

The Saudi Energy Minister would have one believe that an attack on a key refinery on Saudi territory was not really an attack on Saudi Arabia. Instead the actual target of the attack was the global economy. One cannot attribute, with any reasonable credibility, to the Houthi planners sitting around a sandbag in an improvised bunker debating how to attack the global economy. The target was Saudi Arabia's Aramco oil field. That is why the Houthis shot at the kingdom but did not attempt to kill the entire world.

This is where the Trump administration photobombed the situation. Having announced that under Trump the United States was averse to foreign military engagements, including those that might be in America's national interest, the Trump administration was caught between a rock and a hard place. In light of the United States having achieved energy self-sufficiency, Trump has been caught between increasing weapons sales to the Saudis and reducing military engagement in the Middle East.

After repeatedly asserting that the United States would stay away from Middle Eastern quicksand, Trump authorized a drone strike that killed Iran's Major General Qassim Soleimani, which almost ignited a war with Iran.

Like clockwork, the Saudi government reacted to the Aramco attack by expanding their $51 billion defense budget by focusing on antidrone capabilities. This move was not ignored by the international military-industrial complex.

In Yemen, the UAV race between low-tech drones and military-grade UAVs has created a financial dilemma in the search to find a cost-efficient solution to deal with low-cost remote-controlled threats. According to Adam Smith's neoclassical economic theory, the market always finds a way to clear itself due to an "invisible hand." Smith concluded that if every market participant acts in its own self-interest, equilibrium will be achieved. When one looks at the drone market as a whole, one sees disequilibrium as well as inefficiencies.

For example, the drone market appears to be differentiated between low-cost explosive-laced UAVs that are also low-tech, and high-cost, high-tech armed UAVs. What they have in common, however, is the ability to conduct countervalue strikes. Neoclassical economic theory also describes the role of substitutes in market equilibrium; for example, if you don't have sugar, use honey instead. In the early days of drone warfare, the pilot/operator had to be close to the target. Today, GPS has become a proximity substitute. Both low-tech and high-tech drones may be directed to targets many miles away by GPS. As long as the drone market remains unregulated, meaning that there is no economically viable way to suppress the threat posed by low-cost, low-tech UAVs, the targets of this threat have no alternative to unilateral market intervention. In practical terms, the intended target's military solution is preemption, which is a destabilization strategy of note.

On January 17, 2022, drones deployed by the Iran-backed Houthi group blew up oil tankers in the UAE, killing three people and causing a small fire at Abu Dhabi International Airport. The damage on the Emirates capital's infrastructure has been minor, but the psychological impact of a strike on an international airport reverberated all over the world. This is a stern reminder of the mayhem that can be caused when cheap, easy-to-operate, and readily available flying bombs fall into the hands of those determined to use them for maximum effect. Nevertheless, the January 17 strike has even more ominous overtones: sending a message that the Houthis are able to reach the heart of UAE, in case of offensive operations carried out by Emirati-backed militias in Yemen. Just a week before the January strike, the UAE provided a crucial support to counter the Houthi fighters to occupy the city of Marib, a hydrocarbon-rich area. The drone strikes followed shortly after in order to coerce the UAE to increase their military footprint in the conflict.

The Houthis, who are learning fast, have become a source of inspiration for other nonstate actors bent on using the same tool to wreak havoc. The Houthi asymmetric approach to warfare evolved from primitive explosive-laden drones intended to harass the Arab Coalition land operations in Yemen to precise and far-reaching drone strikes. In this respect the group is not just adept at using armed UAVs but have evolved the ability to cause mayhem on state actors through the use of other inexpensive methods: remotely piloted, explosive-laden boats.

Moreover, following seven years of conflict, the Houthis have become proficient in assembling and reengineering armed drones. Nevertheless, the group's rapid proficiency in asymmetric drone warfare did not happen in a vacuum. The technology transfer and operational training for this form of asymmetric warfare could not have happened without state support.

Iran or its Lebanese proxy are considered suspect number one in providing expertise and matériel.

The evolution of the Houthis' tactics—from using drones to harass the Arab Coalition troops to precision strikes on vulnerable infrastructure—amounts to remote-controlled political coercion.[33]

The Emirates now face a conundrum: accelerate disengagement from the conflict or escalate its military involvement. Both decisions put the UAE between a rock and a hard place. Conceding to the Houthis is unlikely for a country that has been called "Little Sparta," but the option of getting mired in a costly escalation is going to exact an untenable toll on lives and resources. As Saudi Arabia and others have discovered, defending against cheap drones is anything but cheap.

The Middle East has again provided decision makers with a case study as they assess the need for new defensive measures, and the necessity to evolve their conventional deterrence toward nonstate actors and extremist menaces that are moving closer to national borders. The region's playbook on the use of mercenaries and private military contractors is now adding a new chapter: drone warfare.

CHAPTER ELEVEN

Drone Warfare

Lesson Learned?

DRONE'S PARADIGM SHIFT

A VENERABLE CONCEPT THAT HAS BECOME SOMEWHAT OF A TIRED CLI-
ché is "paradigm shift." The term refers to a material shift that changes
one's worldview, concepts, thinking, as well as standard practice with
regard to how something is done. The rise of the drone has caused a
paradigm shift in at least two areas: first, the conventional battlefield,
and second, the War on Terror. For example, in 2019 the advantage held
by the military of nation-states shifted to nonstate actors and insurgents
primarily due to the fact that the cost of drone defense is a magnitude
greater than a drone offense.

The ability of drones to inflict substantial damage on economic
infrastructure and populations, known as a "countervalue" strategy, differs from a strategy that targets military assets, known as "counterforce."
The inability to protect countervalue targets was a key factor during the
Cold War's first Strategic Arms Limitation Talks (SALT I) negotiations
between the United States and the Soviet Union. In the world of deterrence, defensive measures may be perceived as offensive. For example, the
Spartans perceived the Athenian wall to be an aggressive move, which
contributed to the outbreak of the Peloponnesian War. Likewise, the
Soviets perceived any effort by the United States to deploy an antiballistic
missile (ABM) system to be a shield that would allow the United States

to launch a nuclear attack, then avoid any retaliatory damage by shooting down Soviet missiles. What became crystal clear is that it is relatively easy to overwhelm any defensive measure. Both the U.S. and Soviet sides recognized that the development of multiple independent-targeted vehicles (MIRV), meaning one launch vehicle could be armed with ten or more warheads each with its own target, rendered any thought of an ABM system useless and obsolete. In the drone era, the ability to conduct a strike using a swarm of low-cost drones overwhelms any conceivable defensive measure, no matter how costly.

The Kingdom of Saudi Arabia followed by the other Gulf monarchies have already taken note, but the overall drone menace to civilian targets should not be discounted in the West.

Take, for example, the economic consequences generated in December 2018 by nothing more than the rumor that drones had been spotted at Britain's Gatwick Airport. The ensuing panic resulted in more than 140,000 passengers stranded for days and the cancellation of more than one thousand flights. Samira Shackle, in an article in the *Guardian*, noted:

> *The Gatwick incident was the first time a major airport was shut down by drones, and it distilled deep cultural anxieties—from the threat of terrorism and unconventional attacks by hostile states, to our fear of new technology. Two years later, it remains unsolved, despite a police operation that lasted 18 months, cost £800,000 and involved five different forces. Conspiracy theories abound online.*[1]

In this respect, the effectiveness of a countervalue drone strategy will be multiplied by the psychological effect that this type of attack induces. As already mentioned, in Afghanistan, the targeted killing program led by the United States has generated a new kind of PTSD that is related to the distinctive hum of the propeller of an armed drone.

PTSD is caused by the terror created by the sound of a UAV overhead. People on the ground, who have been through this before, know that a drone strike is on the way—it's only a question of when and where. Exactly the same type of terror caused by the use of the German V1 flying bomb (Vergeltunswaffe 1, the Vengeance Weapon). The V1, a "buzz" bomb that the English called the "Doodlebug," was designed to run out of fuel over London. When the ram jet stopped, everyone who heard it knew that an explosion was imminent, though it was impossible to know where. Ironically, in the tragic sense, PTSD has affected the ranks of the drone pilots and operators.[2] Even killing from far away on an airbase's container in the United States takes a psychological and emotional toll eventually.

A disturbing trend that has emerged over the past few years is how effective drones have been when used in economic warfare, meaning countervalue targets such as infrastructure, transportation (particularly oil tankers), and refineries. The use of drones to disrupt the flow of traffic through the SLOC is a direct threat to the global economy. In addition, armed submerged drones have not been studied adequately.

No maritime region is immune from the threat of both aerial and submerged drones. From the Strait of Hormuz to other naval choke points such as the Strait of Malacca, UAVs or unmanned submarine drones could easily wreak havoc in densely trafficked international waters. In light of this reality, major insurance companies have taken this into account, which affects the terms and conditions of policies, risk assessments, and premium rates. Even pirates have gotten into the act. Pirates in Somalia use low-cost drones to stalk their prey as well as to interfere with a ship's radio communications.

As demonstrated in several ongoing conflicts, including the Yemeni civil war and the wars in Syria and Libya, the effort to integrate low-cost drones with high-cost military versions has intensified. As previously mentioned, the substitution of geographic proximity by GPS has created a paradigm shift in drone design as well as in operations. Thus far, no drone swarm attack has occurred with serious outcomes, but it's only a matter of when, not if.

The clock is ticking. If UAVs are going to be controlled in any meaningful way by the international community, the tipping point is imminent. Once the Pandora's box of UAVs using artificial intelligence is opened, there will be no way to mitigate the consequences.

Unfortunately, very little in this scenario is hypothetical. Take the civil war in Libya, for example, where drones are used by both sides in the conflict. Chinese-made Wing Loong armed drones, supplied by the UAE, are the weapon of choice of the Libyan National Army. On the other side, Turkey supplies the Bayraktar TB2 to the Government of National Accord's forces. Turkey used the TB2s as well as the more potent Anka-S version during its incursion into Syria in February 2020. Drones accounted for much of Turkey's operations in Idlib against pro-Assad forces, including swarm attacks, jamming missions, or target spotting. Turkey's tactics have been adopted and improved by the Azeri military's operations against Armenia, with spectacular success.

Of all of the theaters where drone warfare is occurring, the Middle East stands out. Regardless of the source of the drone, the proliferation of drones has altered the concept of limited warfare. Prior to the drone era, combat operations would have been inhibited or even stopped by the COVID-19 pandemic's effect on readiness and logistics. This is not just a problem for small-time operators. At the height of COVID-19 diffusion, two of the U.S. Navy's nuclear powered aircraft carriers, the USS *Theodore Roosevelt* and the USS *Ronald Reagan*, were temporary sidelined in Guam and Japan, which kneecapped America's ability to project power in the South Pacific. In several countries soldiers are not able to conduct basic military training. None of this has affected the ability to fly drones, even in battlegrounds.

For the time being, drones are not independent when it comes to target acquisition and pulling the trigger. Before long, however, AI-enabled armed drones will have the capacity to fly, hover over a target, as well as decide whether to shoot or not. Despite the disruptions caused by the COVID-19 pandemic, drone operations have not been interrupted. A virus does not stop a drone from carrying out a lethal mission.

The era of totally independent, autonomous UAVs that operate without humans in the decision-making loop has yet to emerge, but it is not far off. In contrast, there is no technical or operational issue that prevents a handful of operators from releasing swarms, in the hundreds, of UAVs.

The remote-controlled assassination of Mohsen Fakhrizadeh, a leading Iranian nuclear physicist, riddled by bullets while traveling in his car on the outskirts of Tehran by a remote-controlled machine gun hidden in an empty pickup parked nearby, is a case in point.

ing an immediate escalation permitted Tehran to dodge a more severe counterstrike from Israel or the United States, both of which appeared to be spoiling for a fight as President Donald Trump's days in power were waning. Since the end of the Iran-Iraq War in 1988, Tehran has mastered a low-intensity conflict military doctrine to achieve its strategic and operational objectives. Iran's asymmetrical response encompasses a wide range of nonstate actors: Hezbollah in Lebanon, popular mobilization units in Iraq, the Syrian National Defence Force, and the Houthis in Yemen, to name just a few. This network of influence includes proxies with different degrees of capabilities and allegiance to Iran. Proxy warfare is an integral part of Iran's security doctrine, alongside more conventional capabilities such as advanced ballistic missiles and cyberwarfare. The use of long-range armed drone strikes just added an additional capability to Tehran and its security network.

TURKEY'S DRONES: SILVER BULLET OR POISONED CHALICE?

While the conflicts in Libya, Syria, and Yemen increased the security analysts' attention over the drones, the popular curiosity over this new combat tool was truly catalyzed during the conflict between Azerbaijan and Armenia over the disputed Nagorno-Karabakh region. Turkey's ubiquitous combat drones impeded several attempts to broker ceasefires by ratcheting up the brutality until the winner imposed its political will. The early advantage gained during the initial assault by Azeri troops shifted rapidly to static warfare. From artillery barrages to missile strikes, the war of movement shifted to trench skirmishes, as waves of volunteers, ex-soldiers, and others responded to nationalist appeals from both governments and rushed to the frontline. The latter part of the forty-four-day grinding war of attrition highlights an important fact that should not be overlooked.[3] One feature of the Nagorno-Karabakh conflict is the widespread Azerbaijani use of drones that hover above the battlefield and rain death down on command. The Azeri victory is temporary as Baku thawed a conflict that is going to restart as soon as there is a perceived shift in the power balance. In this respect, the use of armed drones also upends conventional military theory, which suggests that conflicts can be brought to a quick, victorious, and relatively bloodless end.

This misperception has been fueled by their success in asymmetrical warfare in a variety of theatres. As previously mentioned, on the one hand, the United States has used the most efficient and expensive combat drones to carry out remote assassination missions from Africa to Afghanistan. On the other hand, militant groups such as Hezbollah and the Houthis have taken advantage of inexpensive and widely available commercial drones reengineered as standoff weapons—flying bombs that can hit targets at a distance without endangering the operators. The Nagorno-Karabakh conflict is different. Azerbaijan has deployed Turkish military drones and Israeli loitering munitions at medium range—in other words, in the middle of a fight, as conventional air power—inducing fear in the opposing camp, but paradoxically rallying defenders to the cause.

In this regard, drones represent a dangerous new trend—a small state that acquires them in numbers and deploys them as a sort of expanded air force can significantly increase its power projection capability. This removes some limits to its aggression. As has happened with cyberweapons, drones have ended the monopoly of rich nations to visit violence on their foes. For countries such as Azerbaijan, which only has a few fighter jets, inexpensive drones have dangerously shifted the perception that their military capabilities are limited, leading to greater aggression. The promise of warfare without risk goes hand-in-hand with an alleged lower risk threshold, thus increasing the chances of conflict escalation. Baku's use of a "drone air force" has also dramatically changed the equation: it has tilted a marginal military power imbalance into a possibly decisive one, putting Yerevan on its heels.

The use of drones in an all-out conflict between two armies has produced some unexpected results. While combat drones are generally bad news in any conflict, they are easy prey for short-range air defense systems. The number of drones Armenia has claimed to have shot down was increased as soon as the Armenian soldiers started to develop a new situational awareness. As its armed forces overcame their initial drone-induced shock, the effectiveness of unmanned aerial vehicles decreased, although it was not completely lost. Questions have also arisen because of the large number of Azerbaijani armored vehicles that were lost. Both sides have lost a number of tanks, and the drone menace has increased the need for electronic warfare systems and short-range antiaerial defense for armored formations. During the forty-four days of war, poor training and obsolete tactics anchored to the use of tanks spearheading armored assaults are recorded in numerous videos on YouTube. The video clips present tanks and armored personnel carriers crossing open ground slowly while grouped together, being picked off easily by precision artillery and drone strikes.[4] Not long after the forty-four-day war, similar images surfaced on YouTube portraying Russian tanks and APVs destroyed by Turkish drones, just in a different scenario, Ukraine.

Taking a step back, several big picture developments can also be divined from this faraway conflict.

First, drone sales in the ravaged Caucasus should be seen in a broader political-military context. Increased military drone transfers and training from Turkey imply not only better economic deals for the Turkish military-industrial complex but have also expanded Ankara's diplomatic reach for building new security allegiances and a new security architecture with President Recep Tayyip Erdogan at its helm. Similarly, Israel has been asked to reduce its weapon sales to Azerbaijan. As with Turkey, such sales serve commercial and strategic purposes. In Tel Aviv's case, they go hand-in-hand with its effort to constrain Iranian ambition—Azerbaijan is a close ally, and a Muslim one at that. It is thus unlikely that Israel will stop the sales. These developments signal once again an increasingly complex strategic rivalry in the Middle East.

Next, attention should be focused on the evolution of drone warfare. The next step is probably the introduction of UAV swarms that saturate air-defense systems. Swarming systems are lightweight and cheap drones that operate networked together in high numbers, mimicking bird or insect swarm cooperation patterns. Drone swarms have not appeared in the Nagorno-Karabakh conflict, as they are not yet available on the market. Nevertheless, Chinese CH-901 and U.S. Coyote tube-launched drones are already moving from the testing phase to production.

Finally, despite the effectiveness of drones in conflicts from Syria to the Caucasus, their inability to become a decisive force confirms that wars still need to be ended with boots on the ground. However, this issue should not just be viewed through a tactical lens. In Nagorno-Karabakh, the use of drones has raised all sorts of questions, including their propaganda value, as well as the ethical and legal aspects of this form of warfare. One notion that must be consigned to the dust heap is the Cold War mentality that technological development has reduced the propensity for war. The other is the widespread adoption—among a generation of warriors or diplomats for whom "precision strikes" are an article of faith—of the idea that technology can deliver a rapid, bloodless, and decisive victory.[5]

Too many times, scientific developments, considered a silver bullet, have become a poisoned chalice instead.

UNDERWATER DRONE MENACE

Submersible drones are an increasingly important but less popular variable in the automated warfare equation.

Unmanned vehicles are not confined to the air. Submersible drones, which are partial substitute for submarines with a crew of sailors, are already active in the East China Sea and the Persian Gulf. The unmanned subs are a substitute for submarines in which the crew members are packed tight. In the COVID-19 era, social distancing on surface ships, though problematic, could be achieved. In a submarine, social distancing is physically impossible due to the confines of the vessel. For example, "hot bunking," which means that one bunk is shared by two sailors, is still in practice on some ships.

Due to the proliferation of underwater unmanned vessels, the meaning of the word *drone* must be expanded to include both aerial and underwater devices. Underwater drones that are capable of traversing the East China Sea, the Malacca Straits, or the Gulfs of Oman and Aden without being detected present a paradigm shift in maritime intelligence gathering. But like their aerial counterparts, the range of operations will evolve and expand, just as aerial drones started off as reconnaissance vehicles. Then one fine day a clever technician wondered whether it would be possible to hang a Hellfire missile under the drone's wings.

During the year 2020, several Chinese Sea Wing underwater drones have reached the Indonesian shores or have been caught in Indonesian fishermen's nets. The drones were an ocean glider-type UV utilized to conduct underwater explorations. Hydrographic surveys are fundamental in drawing accurate maritime charts for commercial shipping and other civilian activities such as underwater fiber optic cable deployment. At the same time, a precise underwater map allows submarines to plot in advance a preferential insertion route. In this respect, the area between the South China Sea and the Indian Ocean is already a possible flash-point where increased underwater activity could lead to unnecessary friction in an already tense area.[6]

The evolution of the role of submersible drones from passive operations (for example, surveillance and reconnaissance) to combat operations is motivated, in part, by the way COVID-19 has changed as well as restrained traditional navy operations. This trend not only affects U.S.-China relations concerning territorial claims and freedom of the sea, it also will be seen when regional states and their allies begin to exert their ambitions for a greater piece of the sea.

URBAN DRONES: SAFER SMART CITIES OR FLYING BIG BROTHER?

In a textbook example of unintended consequences, the COVID-19 pandemic has created additional opportunities for the use of drones for non-military purposes. Drones have already demonstrated that they are an efficient and economical solution for restrictions created by the virus. Governments have realized that drones are useful for another purpose, that is, crowd control. Governments around the world have emulated China's use of drones for surveillance, fever scanning, contact tracing, and crowd mapping. Military drones, which often are equipped with high-definition cameras and thermal sensors, are ideally suited for these purposes.

The question is whether drones can be used to save lives as well as used to kill.

Though driverless vehicles are not delivering groceries as many antic-ipated, UAVs are gaining acceptance and additional government support. It comes as no surprise that China is out front. The cities of Shenzhen and Hangzhou produce industry-leading civilian drones (DJI) and security cameras (Hikvision). The latest move is to produce and export crowd-tracking solutions.

In August 2019, the U.S. defense bill signed into law effectively banned Hikvision products in the United States. Shortly there after DJI was added to the U.S. Department of Commerce's Entity List,[7] designating the Chinese company as a national security concern and banning U.S.-based companies from exporting technology to DJI and consequently impairing DJI's commercial operations in the United States.

As usual, an Israeli facial recognition company, AnyVision, is leading the private sector pack, being among the first to have produced commercial drones capable of performing facial recognition while flying. This feature sounds quite normal as contemporary sci-fi movies take it for granted that small drones are able to perform visual recognition at any angle, speed, or climate. Reality differs as it is quite a daunting task to perform a proper facial recognition at steep angles without incurring a false positive result. While there are not yet any commercially available drones with this full capacity, there is an expectation from the security sector and especially the police sector to be able to employ this tool in a future not so far away. AnyVision also provides the technology for monitoring the border crossing checkpoint between Israel and the West Bank.

In 2020, following a barrage of media reports on an alleged mass surveillance program conducted by Israel in the area, M12, the investing arm of Microsoft that previously invested in the company, declared in an official statement[8] that "after careful consideration, Microsoft and AnyVision have agreed that it is in the best interest of both enterprises for Microsoft to divest its shareholding in AnyVision. In the meantime, AnyVision has already launched a new partnership with Rafael, an Israeli defence company that produces drones under the brand name SightX." According to the joint venture statement, the new drones with AI-driven computer vision will be deployed for urban warfare. The drones' augmented visual capacity could autonomously differentiate between civilians and armed combatants while scanning buildings in a densely populated area.

In the smart cities of today, the balance between an increasing adoption of surveillance technology and right to privacy is already a highly debated subject. Merging drone face recognition capabilities with a city web of surveillance cameras, business-owned cameras, and a specific AI to digest in real time the gargantuan amount of data is not a matter of if but when.

While civil society is still debating the needs for accountability and limits to be imposed on the government's use of unmanned aerial surveillance, several criminal organizations all over the globe have more than a decade of experience in the use of drones for illegal purposes. From flying drug mules to the delivery of mobile phones inside prisons, the variety of drone employments for illicit activities is finding new venues by the day.

In this respect, the aphorism that what happens in the Middle East does not stay in the Middle East is appropriate when it comes to unmanned aerial vehicles.[9] The fight against the Islamic State and the conflicts in Syria and Libya showcase how off-the-shelf commercial drones could be deployed to deliver explosive payloads, scout enemy positions, or even perform kamikaze attacks on high-value targets.

One lesson from this is that readily available commercial technologies provide a low barrier to entry for illicit actors.

The Middle East–North Africa region was where the use of commercial drones for illegitimate purposes dawned, and other actors soon noted their value and efficacy and began to copy these actions, though for different purposes.

Over the past decade, improvement in GPS autonomous flight, payload capacity, and battery life in commercial drones have increased their use as drug mules. From South America to Europe, the police seizure of drones carrying an illicit payload brought home the dark reality that it is not just militant networks that are using the technology but criminal organizations too. Even in the tightly controlled Singapore, drug smugglers tried to use a relatively inexpensive and easily available Chinese-made commercial drone to smuggle 278g of crystal methamphetamine from Malaysia, just to get caught by the police while using the same landing spot three times in a row in the same day.

Drones have been put to some rather creative uses. In Pennsylvania, for example, a drone was used to detonate a homemade bomb. A drone was used to deliver contraband into a prison, which illustrates a new type of threat for which governments and the police thus far have no solution. In light of the fact that these challenges have been created by what is basically the first generation of drones, the next generation will create even greater threats and danger. For example, commercial drones, which have been modified for military purposes, have already been deployed on the battlefield in Syria and Libya. One would be naïve to think that criminal enterprises have not been paying attention to the ways drones may be deployed for nefarious purposes. One fact, which is beyond reasonable dispute, is that governments and regulatory bodies always lag behind paradigm-shifting devices and events. By the time they begin to pay attention, the horse is always out of the barn.

There are multiple reasons that draw the interest of amateurs to drones. Commercial drones are inexpensive, easy to fly with little or no knowledge or training, may be operated with great precision by using wireless communications and GPS navigation, are easily equipped with high-resolution cameras, and navigation errors may be mitigated by autonomous obstacle avoidance sensors, meaning it is difficult to fly such a drone into a brick wall. All of these characteristics will draw the attention of the aforementioned nefarious actors like a sinister moth to a flame.

Battlefield experience is not confined to the battlefield. The police in many jurisdictions have learned the hard way that the drone menace manifests itself one step ahead of the authorities. In addition, there is no blanket solution, as there are many variants of the drone threat. That said, the recipe used to create antidrone countermeasures is well known. The ingredients consist of detection, identification, tracking, and mitigation. But like all recipes, the ingredients must be tweaked for each location, environment, and threat scenario. For example, defending a large area such as an airport requires both fixed and mobile antidrone systems. An antidrug drone operation, on the other hand, requires the capacity to follow the perpetrators in order to collect probative evidence.

During the space race that occurred during the Cold War, NASA spent millions trying to produce a ballpoint pen that would function in zero gravity. The Soviets solved the problem by using pencils. The point is that devices produced for one reason do not necessarily work well when removed from a specific set of circumstances. For example, air defense systems designed to detect large aircraft, or in the case of the Patriot system a missile, or in the case of NORAD incoming nuclear warheads, are utterly useless if the incoming object is a golf ball.

Intercepting civilian-grade drones is another kettle of fish, due to the fact that they are small, slow, and can creep along at treetop altitudes. The first problem is to see them. This requires several layers of radars, radio frequencies, acoustic sensors, as well as electro-optical and infrared cameras, not things one just has laying around in the equipment shed. In the absence of any coherent drone regulation regime, the authorities have turned to the solution for any failed regulatory regime: prohibition. As demonstrated by any state that has attempted to ban alcohol, the ban merely creates a black market. Urgent attention has been applied to trying to stop drones zooming around airports, sports stadiums, or vital infrastructure such as dams or power grids.

The problem is compounded by the fact that the decision window is small. Just because you have all sorts of gear and gizmos doesn't mean that you know what to do when a "threat" appears on the screen. One has one minute to decide if the drone is the high school kid's birthday present or a dedicated terrorist UAV intended to bring down a passenger jet that is rotating on takeoff. Unlike a battlefield, choosing to jam a drone's radio frequency to break the connection to its pilot/controller is not the optimal solution in an urban setting. What if the drone is on autopilot? What if jamming disrupts the police radio frequency? What if you interfere with the air traffic controller's instructions?

Lenin stated that the capitalists would sell the Bolsheviks the rope that would be used to hang them. Using hard-kill options—basically, shooting down a drone—is difficult and also presents a possible threat to the community, especially if the drone is flying over a densely populated area.

As previously mentioned, arms control theory may provide an offramp for the drone dilemma. The movie *Dr. Strangelove* drove home an essential element of a risk reduction regime. If one does not disclose the existence of a doomsday device, it has no deterrent effect. The registration of commercial drones is no more intrusive than the registration of personal automobiles. The ideal solution is to require drones to have friendly transponders that will advise the status of the drone.

Flying registered drones not only enables quicker forensic work but also lays the foundation for a future active friend or foe mechanism that will enable tracking in real time. To find the right solution, active "red teaming," or realistic testing of defenses against simulated foes, is vital. These exercises allow security agencies to layer equipment so that gaps are covered and to expose holes in defenses. Constant vulnerability assessments and improved postforensic analysis are not going to eliminate the threat, but they can mitigate or even prevent the most dangerous ones as they are already happening in the cybersphere. At the global level the private sector has already understood that this state of affairs presents lucrative business opportunities.

As previously mentioned, Israel, the so-called Start-Up Nation, already has private companies and universities at work translating the lessons learned on the battlefield to the civilian sector.

CHAPTER TWELVE

Drone Casus Belli

WAR CATALYST

ON JUNE 20, A U.S. NAVY RQ-4N BROAD AREA MARITIME SURVEIL-
lance drone, a variant of the US$180 million Global Hawk, was downed
by the Iranian military's aerospace defense. A direct military confrontation
between the United States and Iran was avoided at the last minute.

The increasing presence of combat UAVs and the future role of
lethal autonomous aircraft are still not clearly defined by the laws of
war. There is a pressing need to regulate a proportional response in the
case of drone strikes and define how drones may constitute a casus belli.
Similar to cyberattacks, the regulatory efforts are hampered by several
problems that range from the rapidly evolving technologies behind drone
offensive capabilities to a rapid and broader accessibility and diffusion of
remote-controlled weapons. Nevertheless, the main problem is related to
the certainty in attributing the responsibilities. From Aramco oil fields
to Caracas or even Gatwick there is still not a clear attribution of who is
the mastermind behind the attacks.

The evolving pattern of UAV deployments from the Middle East to
North Africa, which has showcased how wars still need to be ended with
boots on the ground, has also exposed how conflicts can be ignited by a
remote-controlled vehicle.

Even though Iran possesses the sophisticated Russian S-300 air
defense system, the Islamic Revolutionary Guard Corps claimed that
the U.S. drone had been shot down by a locally developed surface-to-air
missile (SAM). While the debate among military experts is centered on

Iranian air defense capabilities to deny access to U.S. airpower projection, a compelling set of questions needs to be answered.

- How does a technological innovation in the military sphere constitute a casus belli?
- When does a drone shootdown constitute an act of war?
- What constitutes a proportional military response to an attack on a drone?

The U.S. Navy RQ-4N Broad Area Maritime Surveillance drone, shot down by the Iranians, brings to mind when the Russians shot down the Cold War–era U-2 spy plane, the Dragon Lady. Both the drone RQ-4N and the U-2 are bulky planes, thirty-five- and thirty-two-meter wing spans, respectively. Both lack effective countermeasures to deceive or outmaneuver a SAM. Nevertheless, this time, compared with the May 1, 1960, U-2 incident, the United States did not have the compelling need to rescue a pilot by getting entangled in endless negotiations and a propaganda skirmish. At the same time, the downing of the U.S. drone was almost the precursor of a severe military retaliation on human targets or even a full-scale conflict.

The airspace in conflict zones is going to be progressively saturated with armed UAVs. The submersed space from the Strait of Hormuz to the Bab el Mandeb Strait is sharing the same fate.

The past decade, which was characterized by U.S. Predator drones' man hunting from Afghanistan to Somalia, carried the promise of power projection without vulnerability. The U.S. Navy drone downed by Iran revealed the contrary. The chain of events that might have been spawned by the shootdown could have led to the loss of several "real lives."

The promise of warfare without risk is accompanied by a lower risk threshold, which contrary to predictions increases the risk for conflict escalation. Therefore the speculation on the effect of the next wave of technological changes on state versus state conflict and hybrid warfare does not have to be solely related to tactical aspects of a new weapon system.

The Cold War mentality anchored to the notion that technological development reduced the propensity for war is outdated. Drone or cyber-deterrence has yet to be efficiently postulated and put into practice, avoiding the trap of the allure of technology. Scientific developments have too many times been regarded as a silver bullet. In the 1999 publication *Unrestricted Warfare*, Qiao Liang and Wang Xiangsu, colonels in China's PLA, stressed the speed and the severity of new technological innovations.[1]

New technologies coexist in the military and civilian sphere, allowing weaker actors to compete against more powerful ones via asymmetrical confrontation. At the same time, both armed drones and cyberweapons carry a low barrier to entry into the weapons market compared to former monopolies of violence retained by few countries.

Finding a legally and morally acceptable middle ground is not a short-term task. It is quite probable that the military-industrial complex has learned the lesson of the June 20 Navy drone downing, which is that the next generation of surveillance drones will have antimissile countermeasures and additional maneuvering capabilities—for a price, of course.

Unfortunately, in a not-so-distant future, these problems will be solved with solutions that are economically affordable and technically viable. As the dawn of drone warfare nears, the true potential and effect of AI lethal autonomous systems will be revealed.

For the time being, humans are still in the decision-making loop in terms of both target acquisition and the final order to attack. While the moral debate over whether it is necessary to keep a human decision maker in the kill decision loop intensifies, the day is coming when humans will not be part of the conflict equation until the drone is well past the fail-safe point. Or, at least, the human variable in the equation will persist but just as a target. Several organizations such as Campaign to Stop Killer Robots[2] are advocating for banning entirely autonomous lethal weapon systems; even UN Secretary-General António Guterres stated on his Twitter account that "autonomous machines with the power and discretion to select targets and take lives without human involvement are politically unacceptable, morally repugnant and should be prohibited by international law." A total ban is an unlikely event, mentioned Zachary Kallenborn in the *Foreign Policy* article "A Partial Ban on Autonomous Weapons Would Make Everyone Safer," considering that a partial ban is also in the interest of the great powers.[3] Similar to the norm that constrains mercenaries but lets a small door open, just in case.

While the line between the man and machine interface is progressively blurred, the next generation of drones controlled by AI will further complicate the moral and ethical challenges.

WEAPONIZED DRONE BUSINESS AND AERIAL DEFENSE: A CONTRADICTION IN TERMS?

While the Baykar Turkish manufacturer of the UCAV TB2 is stealing the spotlight from famous combat drone producers such as Raytheon and General Atomics, it is still the Israeli military-industrial complex that is leading the development of drone combat platforms and counterdrone technologies.[4] If the year 2020 could be considered the year of the rise of the drone, 2021 is definitely the year of antimissile and antidrone systems. From the Gatwick airport incident to the attack on the Aramco oil field or the Iranian missile barrages on U.S. military bases in Iraq, the made-in-Israel counterdrone systems are increasingly seizing a considerable portion of the market. A proper aerial defense system costs in the range of several billion US$. It is also a certainty that a nation-state could acquire it without constraints or even creating a diplomatic incident, as happened with Turkey.

A NATO member, Turkey acquired the S-400, a state-of-the-art Russian antimissile system, incurring the wrath of the United States. In this respect the Russian S-400 Triumph air defense missile system (NATO designation SA-21) is perceived by several of the world's armies as a "must buy" item for their strategic and tactical defense, particularly because this defensive missile system has a proven effectiveness on the ground in different operational scenarios from the Middle East to Eurasia. Similar to its American counterpart the Patriot, the S-400 high-performance high-altitude missile aerospace defense system (HIMADS) was designed to track the latest generation of stealth aircraft. What differentiates the Russian HIMADS from its direct competitor is the proven capabilities in dealing with armed UAVs. The effectiveness of the S-400 is related to the integration of the surface-to-air missiles, mobile radars with airborne early warning systems, and additional components such as the one that can detect very low observable aerial targets. The weapon system doesn't come cheap as it carries a price tag of more than a billion US$ per regiment; nevertheless the Russian system looks less picky than the U.S. version when it is time to sell. The United States sanctioned Turkey in December 2020, with Secretary Pompeo declaring that the United States "will not tolerate significant transactions with Russia's defense and intelligence sectors." While the Obama administration stopped the sale of the Patriot defense missile system to Ankara, the Trump administration in the words of Mr. Pompeo sounded more accommodating: "Turkey is a valued ally and an important regional security partner for the United States, and we seek to continue our decades-long history of productive defense-sector cooperation by removing the obstacle of Turkey's S-400 possession as soon as possible."[5]

India, China, and lately Turkey, which received four S-400 missile batteries in 2020, are a statement on the profound changes and rebalancing of the global security architecture. Several countries, such as Iran, that operate the previous S-300 model are on the S-400 delivery waiting list. Countries such as Qatar and Saudi Arabia, two important allies of the United States in the Middle East, expressed interest due to the evolution of Iran's missiles and drones.

In the same way that missile defense systems are sold and distributed, the transfer of armed drones involves different layers of economic and geostrategic interests. Drone technology transfer, which is not only related to economic gains, also engages notable strategic and political dimensions. This is especially so when the military hardware transfer involves sophisticated weapons platforms that need specialized training and maintenance.[6] While the allegedly Iranian drones operated by the Houthis in Yemen are easy to assemble and to control, the Turkish drones that buzzed over the Syrian and Caucasus skies need specialized maintenance and piloting skills. Therefore the more sophisticated the drone, the more the military transfer doesn't end with a single financial transaction. Instead it creates a long-term relationship that strengthens the geopolitical relationship between the contracting parties. The outsourcing of high-tech weapons platform maintenance and training to PMCs has already been embraced by the West. It's highly likely that Russia and China will soon adopt this approach as well.

In this respect Israel is betting on both sides of the global race for combat drones, on the one hand increasing the drone's innovative combat capabilities, and on the other hand creating new air defense systems. The Chinese idiom that represents the word *contradiction* (maodun) is a combination of shield (mao) and spear (dun). The word derives from a story in which a weapon trader was advertising in his stall a spear that can pierce any shield and at the same time a shield that cannot be defeated by any weapon. Considering the increasing orders that the Israeli military-industrial complex is witnessing, there is no contradiction of terms in this business model.

To make the example clearer, the Israeli IAI is constantly developing new jammers compounded with kinetic antidrone systems. These platforms basically jam the communication between the remote operator and the drone, while the kinetic component, being a laser, a projectile, or a microwave beam, then intercepts the incoming threat and destroys it. At the same time, Israeli researchers have announced that they have developed a drone that is capable of flying without GPS assistance, nullifying any jamming efforts.

While the Russian S-400 is still dominating the market for aerial defense against an aging U.S.-made Patriot missile defense system, the Israeli Iron Dome multilayered aerial defense system has come to the fore.

The combat drone and the parallel antidrone production is sustaining a booming global industry. It is not by chance that Israel, the "Start-Up Nation," is spearheading aerial menace research and development. During the 1973 war, Israel was the first to deploy existing UAVs in an active combat situation, using its own drone fleet to draw the enemy's surface-to-air missiles into the open, which gave precious time to its own pilots to carry on with bombing raids. During the 1983 conflict, the Israeli drones manufactured by IAI were tasked with reconnaissance objectives, hence the name *Scout*. In 2001, the first drone strikes carried out by the U.S. MQ-1 Predator had their roots in three decades of Israel's indigenous UAV research and development.

Drone Mercenaries

The transfer of armed drones and scouting drones with military-grade surveillance systems is on the rise. It will not take much longer to witness mercenary companies providing pay-per-use drones with armed payloads. While local government regulations are evolving rapidly, trying to avoid drone hobbyists slamming their UAVs into a landing airplane, there is a dire need for robust international regulatory norms. A global armed drone standard norm could tackle a dangerous and uncontrolled proliferation of weaponized drones.

PMCs or even mercenaries powered by remote-controlled armies are going to be available to state and nonstate actors with money. Three-dimensional printing and additive manufacturing will allow the deployment of cheap and easy to assemble drone forces. These on-demand drone armies could be even on lease for the sole duration of the conflict, increasing economic efficiency and effectiveness and decreasing the willingness to engage in diplomatic negotiations. Drone combat applications, being a versatile tool that can be adapted to a fast-changing combat environment, are going to increase the speed in the evolution cycles of remote-controlled warfare. Drone mercenaries operating in weak states, as happened during the 1980s and 1990s on the African continent, could easily morph into local warlords with augmented capabilities and at the same time being safely distanced from the ongoing violence and civil disorders. Coupling AI with readily available drones will allow small but technologically savvy private military companies to operate as a force multiplier not only as a combat asset but also as a social control private police at the service of unscrupulous authoritarian regimes, employing drones with biometric scanning capabilities and Big Data analytical capabilities in a proprietary machine surveillance intelligence network. During the African postcolonial wars, helicopter pilots and mechanics due to their scarcity were among the most well-paid mercenaries. In a not-too-distant future, drone pilots, drone intelligence analysts, drone software engineers, and mechanics are going to be at the top of the mercenary roster's payroll.

The deployment of combat drones from the Middle East to the Caucasus has witnessed the passage from the first drone age of U.S.-led targeted killings to a second drone age of hybrid drone warfare. The third age of drone warfare featuring autonomous weapon systems and AI-controlled drone swarms is at the door. The lack of effective oversight over drone proliferation and transfer not only as a kinetic offensive tool but also as an intelligence and policing tool could generate severe, negative ripple effects. The first drone-age cycle started with using unarmed drones as a scouting tool, which morphed into becoming a precise killer armed with antitank missiles. Leaked reports on the effectiveness of the precision targeting in Afghanistan and Iraq led to severe questioning of the moral and legal implications of increasing collateral damage and targeted assassination in countries not at war. Chamayou rightfully asserts that "the precision of the strike has no bearing on the pertinence of the targeting in the first place. That would be tantamount to saying that the guillotine, because of the precision of its blade—which, it is true, separates the head from the trunk with remarkable precision—makes it thereby better able to distinguish between the guilty and the innocent."[7]

It took more than two decades to evolve into the second drone age. Several considerations on the first drone age that are still being researched include first strike theory and casus belli as well as the extraterritorial use of drones for force and surveillance. Considering the constant pace of progress in technology cycles, it is probable that the evolution from the second drone age to the third one will be faster and more destructive.

The second drone age also has several unanswered questions, such as the psychological impact of drones on the affected population or the ethical implications of automated weapon systems. Definitely, during the third drone age, nation-states are going to be back on the scene with a vengeance. The Defense Advanced Research Projects Agency better known by its acronym DARPA, a research and development agency of the U.S. Department of Defense specialized in gazing at the crystal ball of emerging military technologies, is working in close cooperation with the U.S. military-industrial complex juggernauts General Atomics, Lockheed Martin, and Northrop Grumman on project LongShot.[8] The goal of the LongShot program is to develop air-launched UAVs with interchangeable air-to-air weapons that can perform autonomous aerial dogfights. The LongShot drones are supposed to benefit from another futuristic project funded by DARPA, AlphaDogfight, which is AI dedicated to aerial combat.

Neither Moscow nor Beijing want to lose the drone game with Washington, and the Russian and Chinese versions of an intelligent drone are allegedly in the advanced development stage. The Russian Okhotnik (Hunter) stealth fighter drone is a jet stealth bomber equipped with advanced reconnaissance systems.[9] At the same time several seventy-year-old Tu-95 bombers have been refitted as air-based control stations for drones. Deploying the Tu-95 with drone swarms or the new Hunter drone will extend the range limits to that of the bomber. The invasion of Ukraine highlighted the Russian indigenous UAV program's limits in terms of quality and quantity. Moreover, Russia's reliance on Iranian drones, notably the Shahed-136, underlined how Moscow's relations with Tehran have strengthened as both countries are under severe sanctions. China's WJ-700, a high-altitude, long-endurance, and high-speed armed reconnaissance drone, which was developed by China Aerospace Science and Industry Corp., is designed for a complex battle space that targets the enemy's aerial defenses and fortified positions thanks to a large payload. As has already happened with the previous models, the Chinese combat drone is easily acquired by foreign countries, especially the ones that were not allowed to buy the U.S. models, as happened with the Kingdom of Saudi Arabia.

The proliferation of drones is spearheading a new arms race and the dawn of a new global security architecture. Nevertheless, several questions on drone proliferation from what is going to happen when every state and nonstate actor has combat drone capability to the impact assessment of emerging AI technology risks are still dangerously unanswered. The future of drone warfare is not stemming from the U.S.-led conflict in Iraq and Afghanistan but from Yemen and Nagorno-Karabakh. The impact of the 2019 and 2020 drone warfare in the global security architecture is set to increase considerably uncertainty and threats and demands due attention. Nevertheless, following Clausewitz's dictum, while technology changes, the enduring nature of war—primordial violence, uncertainty, and purpose—is eternal.[10]

CHAPTER THIRTEEN

Cybermercenaries

From Boots on the Ground to the Metaverse

SOLDIERS OF FORTUNE MEET CYBERSPACE

IN THE 1980S, A MANUAL FOR WANNABE FREE LANCERS—SOLD VIA AN international mail order included in a magazine for soldiers of fortune— presented a set of rules that aspiring mercenaries must follow including, *inter alia*: you are not superman, always try to look unimportant as the enemy may be low on ammunition, and avoid any suicide mission just before payday. Nevertheless, one of the core recommendations that looks less ironic but fits very well in today's cyberdimension is that local talent that can use a Kalashnikov is easily available and cheap to recruit. In contrast, a mechanic who can repair a helicopter in a battle zone is not common, and his services are sometimes literally paid for in gold. PSCs and PMCs that are adding cybertools to their arsenal or entirely pivoting their business model to cyberspace are expanding, but the main constraint is finding skilled operators. The pool of talent with the necessary IT and security skills is progressively shrinking as both state and top corporations compete for the same dwindling recruiting pool.

In this respect, while the debate on the future of warfare is gravitating toward the use of AI, autonomous weapon lethal systems, and bloodless cyberwars, mercenaries are silently returning to a place of prominence, not only with boots on the ground but also in the cyberarena. In the 1992 sci-fi novel *Snow Crash*, the author Neal Stephenson coined the term *metaverse*, which predicts a virtual reality–based world where people interact through digital avatars.[1] In *Snow Crash* reality is set in a hypercapitalist society that exists within a dystopian framework, and it is not by chance that Hiro, the protagonist, is both a hacker and good with a sword.

From a three-decades-old novel, fast-forward to today: following a keystroke, in another part of the world, a malicious code is activated that destroys a network of computers, a power grid shuts down, and chaos surges. Cyberswords for hire that can perform such attacks are already here. The quest to define if an individual or an organization was paid to launch a malware attack or to collect intelligence and is considered a cybermercenary is not easy. In this respect the cyberarena's veil of anonymity offers one of the core characteristics of mercenarism: plausible deniability.

As happens in the real world, both state and nonstate actors are harnessing defensive and offensive cybercapabilities that utilize services offered by the private sector. Similarly, in the never-ending search for a straightforward definition of PSC and PMC based on their passive and active stance in the provision of kinetic services, the cyberarena is also mired in the same quagmire. The distinctions between offensive and defensive services in cyberspace are even more difficult to pinpoint as the overall sector lacks transparency by design. Since the dawn of the Internet, states are bent on harnessing the cybersphere potential for intelligence and increasingly as a catalyst to ignite coercive power. In this respect nonstate cyberoperators can operate across borders with a small digital footprint and at a very low cost, both desirable outcomes for a state willing to project power through cyberspace.

Both in armed conflict and in peacetime, some actions in the cybersphere may be considered mercenary-related activities. Such actions could include a wide range of hostile cyberactivities conducted by individuals or groups across national boundaries. In this respect hostile cyberactivities are understood as entailing the use of cybertools to disrupt or destroy computer systems or networks or acquire the control of remotely or automatically managed machinery ranging from SCADA* systems to UAVs that have immediate impacts outside the computer network.

---

* SCADA is a control system that is designed to collect, analyze, and visualize data from industrial equipment.

As noted earlier, if it is a difficult task to define who is a mercenary, then the definition of cybermercenary requires an even more nuanced approach as cyberspace is populated by an increasingly diverse number of actors, from script kiddies to state-supported hacking groups. For example, drawing a clear line between legal operators that provide red team network probing and incorporated hacking groups that offer pre-emptive hacking attacks or even spyware is still amply debated. A small step in the definition of cybermercenary starts with narrowing down how PSCs and PMCs are adding cybercapabilities to their list of services. Yet pivoting from a gun for hire to a hacker doesn't automatically make one a cybermercenary. Nevertheless, private military companies and private security entities adding to their list of services cyberattack capabilities and spyware are already reachable, for a price.

You may not be interested in cyberwar, but it's interested in you, mentioned Frank Hoffman, a senior research fellow at the Institute for National Strategic Studies, adapting Trotsky's trope on war while discussing Thomas Rid's publication "Cyber War Will Not Take Place."[2] Rid confutes the common notion of incoming doomsday scenarios such as a Cyber Pearl Harbor or a Computer Waterloo, as there are no body bags in cyberland. On an opposite stance Leon Panetta, former U.S. Defense Secretary, warned of a Cyber Pearl Harbor. Echoed by Robert Mueller, at the time the FBI director, that while terrorism remains the Bureau's top priority for the moment, in a not-too-distant future cyberthreats will pose the greatest threat to the United States. Again, China and Russia come to the fore as leading culprits in the U.S. perception of the cybermenace. While Russian boots on the ground pose a direct threat to the West's interests from the MENA region to Ukraine, China's state-sponsored hacking activities rise to the top in the global cyberarena threat. While Washington is pointing the finger at Beijing as a perpetrator of state-led hacking operations that target foreign civilian and military networks, China is bringing the same accusation to the fore. According to a report the *Global Times*[3] obtained from the Chinese National Computer Virus Emergency Response Center, China captured a spy tool deployed by the U.S. National Security Agency (NSA), which is capable of lurking in a victim's computer to access sensitive information and was found to have controlled global Internet equipment and stolen large amounts of users' information. While the unspoken cyberconfrontation between China and the United States is raging, the role of cybermercenaries operating on the fringe of a declared cyberwar is set to increase.

Mark Galeotti, an expert on global affairs, acknowledges that part of the cybermenace's[4] unspoken but unavoidable challenge is to define the nexus between cybercriminals, cyberterrorists, and cyberwarriors. The cyberarena is populated by a wide range of actors from government and corporate information warfare specialists, a whole subculture of hackers, Internet-savvy criminal organizations, hacktivists, and the so-called script kiddies, who deploy off-the-shelf hacking tools devised by others. In this respect, the discussion on the impact of cyberwar and cyberweapons is still raging on, especially considering the defense budget that governments are allocating to defend and to attack cyberobjectives, yet the evolution of intelligence for hire and cybermercenaries is still a blip on the security sector's radar.

The world of cybersecurity preemptive attacks, intelligence for hire, provision of spyware, and more generally cyberweapons is the new Wild West. Therefore, in order to regulate and differentiate lawful from unlawful operators there is a pressing need to keep the focus on how the private security sector is transiting from boots on the ground to cyberspace, and how to define the cybermercenary.

In this respect, the requirements of modern warfare and data-related security are already forcing mercenaries, private military outfits, and even private security companies to upgrade their game. In *@War*, Shane Harris mentions that the wars of the future are already being fought today, and the private and public sectors in the United States are already teaming up for the rise of the military-internet complex.[5] President Dwight Eisenhower's warning in 1961, that the United States was threatened by the military-industrial complex, was widely quoted during the rise of Western PMCs in Iraq and Afghanistan. Harris' wakeup call is a modern version of Eisenhower's warning on the threat posed by the private military-industrial complex, in this case the privatization of cyberoperations and Big Data analysis. The privatization of cyberarsenals from the state or available on the dark net for a price allow the private sector and criminal and militant organizations to engage in a range of operations in the cyberarena from surveillance to sabotage that were once the prerogative of a limited number of nation-states. In this respect cybermercenaries are already here, though they are not yet recognized as such.

The UN Working Group on Mercenary Activities considers companies that use war-grade cyberweapons to do the bidding of foreign powers, nonstate actors, or even criminal and terrorist organizations as cybermercenaries.[6]

In the report, the Working Group on the Use of Mercenaries as a Means of Violating Human Rights and Impeding the Exercise of the Right of People to Self-Determination examines the provision of military and security products and services in cyberspace by mercenaries, mercenary-related actors, and private military and security companies and their human rights impacts.

There is a wide range of military and security services provided in cyberspace, including data collection, intelligence and espionage. Private actors can be engaged by States and non–State actors in various proxy relationships to conduct offensive or defensive operations and to protect their own networks and infrastructure, as well as to carry out cyberoperations to weaken the military capacities and capabilities of enemy armed forces or to undermine the integrity of other States' territory. Individuals carrying out cyberattacks can cause damage remotely, across various jurisdictions. As such, they can be regarded as undertaking a mercenary-related activity, or even a mercenary activity, if all of the qualifying criteria are met.[7]

Again, the necessity of defining what is a cybermercenary comes to the fore and it is even more complicated than the one related to boots off the ground. The definition of what is a cyberweapon or even a cyberattack is still amply debated. For example, considering malware as "war ammunition" could cost millions of dollars in insurance claims, as happened with the food giant Mondelez's cyberinsurance claim.

After being infected by NotPetya ransomware, Mondelez claimed US$100 million in losses, but the Zurich Insurance Group refused to settle the claim as the United States and other governments labeled the NotPetya attack an action by the Russian military. Therefore the claim was excluded under the circumstance of war exemption. As the U.K. government and the CIA blamed the attack on Russian state-sponsored hackers, claiming it was the latest act in an ongoing cyberwar between Russia and Ukraine, Zurich Insurance Group appealed that NotPetya was an act of war.[8]

NotPetya is a type of malware that looks like Petya, a common ransomware, but at the end it is a computer virus designed to wipe out the target's computer network without any chance to fix the problem even if the ransom was paid in full.[9]

The case of Zurich Insurance highlights the damages that weapons-grade apps could generate when used outside war zones, and in cyberspace the gray areas are ample and vague. At the earliest stage of diffusion, NotPetya hit Ukraine totaling more than 80 percent of the computer infection cases, but it soon spread around the globe.

Another example is offered when intelligence for hire is compounded by offensive hacking. In the murky world of espionage, intelligence for hire is not new, but recent trends in the commodification of military-grade spyware have raised awareness of private cybersecurity companies that offer spy-for-hire services.[10]

The previously mentioned lack of regulation compounded by a low barrier to entry and a huge demand have all helped to make cyberespionage a fast-growing industry. As it seems unlikely that cybersecurity companies are going to add boots on the ground capabilities to their services, the idea of PSCs and PMCs probing the cybersecurity market is already a reality. The booming market for spyware is a case in point. Spyware is a kind of malware that allows hackers to control a system remotely, enabling them to monitor their targets' computers and mobile devices. While Israel is a world leader in the field, it does not have a monopoly on the spyware market.

In 2020 and 2021 the Israeli private firm NSO came under a media barrage for the sale of its Pegasus spyware from the Persian Gulf to Canada, the United States, and Switzerland. In the same way, the Italian firm Hacking Team was engulfed in scandal after the revelation that its

Galileo software had possibly been sold to Egypt. This came to light in 2016 after Giulio Regeni, a young Italian researcher from Cambridge University, was found dead in Cairo following days of torture by the Mukhabarat, the Egyptian intelligence. Widespread reports that the Egyptian intelligence service had used Galileo to track the researcher later led to the Italian government placing export restrictions on the software. Hacking Team's client list includes government agencies around the world and commercial entities, including banks.[11]

Cheap and widely available spoofing tools are altering the landscape of the already murky world of surveillance. Even the European Union, which bills itself as a leader in privacy and digital rights protection, is having trouble regulating private espionage among its members.[12]

In addition, PMCs specialized in very niche services such as hostage recovery are morphing their skill sets from real-life ransom payments to recover a hostage to negotiating a ransom's payment when some sort of ransomware virus is holding hostage a hospital computer network. Ransomware is a malicious form of cyberattack that is used to extort its victims into paying large sums of money to retrieve their own data that has been encrypted by the ransomware app that has infiltrated the victim's computer network. Ransomware has proven to be quite lucrative for cybercriminals, especially when used against health care providers, who often pay the ransom to regain access to their data and avoid not only missed profit but especially a loss of life.[13]

As described earlier, Chinese PSCs are benefitting from Beijing's expansion of the Digital Silk Road to sell and manage high-tech security solutions. In this respect, China presents another challenge altogether. Several Chinese companies are among the global leaders in AI facial recognition applications for a variety of uses, and their cheaper solutions make them competitive players in the global market. The country's national cybersecurity law carves out Chinese cyberspace as sovereign territory, and Beijing's strict control over Big Data flow and storage, as well as the authorities' unfettered access to companies' servers, all stand to compound the impact of private technology companies with Chinese characters.

Is it too late to put the genie back into the bottle? The 2022 call by the United Nations for countries to exercise greater oversight on the sale of military-grade cybertechnologies is timely.[14] The first step toward this is to challenge the traditional regulatory framework that deals with dual-use technologies. All technologies tend to be susceptible to more than one use, and there is a need for updated rules delineating commercial applications from governments' national security requirements.

A more daunting task is differentiating private cybersecurity companies from cybermercenaries and identifying when private sector efforts to augment government espionage capabilities cross the proverbial red line—the Wild West nature of the Internet only makes this more difficult.

HACKING AS A SERVICE

Hacking as a service is a very fluid area, and the line that separates cyberdefense from cybermercenaries is easily blurred. The cybersecurity industry is poorly regulated and prone to abuse, but it is rapidly growing and very profitable. Societal trends sparked as a result of COVID-19—working from home, using online meeting platforms, and the burgeoning use of cloud computing—have increased the opportunities for nonstate actors to satisfy governments' ravenous appetites for spyware and automated intelligence gathering: "In short, there is a threshold at which a small group of people, or even an individual, can acquire the ability to cause harm, including physical harm, across vast distances at a global scale. This threshold is lower for hacking than for most conventional military capabilities,"[15] acknowledged Tim Maurer, author of *Cyber Mercenaries*.

States are already using proxies to commit criminal acts in cyberspace. The logical next step will be an increase in offensive cyberoperations—aimed at disabling, disrupting, or destroying digital infrastructure or functions—carried out by private cybersecurity companies. Leaving this dangerous business to mercenaries motivated only by profit risks escalating matters into dangerous uncharted territory.

In this respect, the United States is still the precursor in terms of privatization of the cybersecurity function. As happened with the private sector contactors in war zones, the cyberspace domain that affects all aspects of U.S. national security has witnessed an important and not much discussed trend to privatize the military and intelligence cyberservice. According to Charles Mahoney, an expert in defense outsourcing,

After almost two decades of contracting, the cybersecurity market functions efficiently because it is competitive and information about the capabilities of corporate suppliers is widely available. Conversely, the small number of suppliers in the offensive cyber market coupled with the limited commercial utility of offensive cyber tools suggests that the sector may develop into an oligopoly in which the United States government is highly dependent on contractors.[16]

During the past two decades, the role of cybersecurity contractors in the United States has been well documented,* and the public-private relationship looks efficient and economical due to the presence of a multitude of contractors and a transparent market. Analyzing the public-private interaction in the Big Data security arena and more importantly in the private market for cyberoffensive operations, the available data is limited at most. The cyberoffensive tool developed and managed by private entities on behalf of the state has a limited function outside of the cyberwarfare sphere and carries heavy legal liability baggage. The legal dispute in the United States involving NSO and the big tech companies Apple, Google, Meta, and Amazon is a case in point. The Israeli private company NSO tried to have the U.S. Supreme Court consider its role as a foreign government agent and therefore be entitled to immunity under U.S. law limiting lawsuits against foreign countries.[17] The NSO filing mentions:

Many nations, including the United States, rely on private contractors to conduct or support core governmental activities. . . . If such contractors can never seek immunity . . . then the United States and other countries may soon find their military and intelligence operations disrupted by lawsuits against their agents.[18]

Looking at Russia, Turkey, and especially China the reality differs as the state-led development of cyberoffensive tools and civil-military

---

* In 2017, the U.S. government authorized $19.8 billion in unclassified spending for all cyber-related activities performed by defense contractors, an increase of 120 percent over 2012 levels. *Federal Cybersecurity: FY18 Standard Market Taxonomy of Unclassified Spending* (Alexandria, VA: Govini, 2017), 1, in Charles W. Mahoney, "Corporate Hackers: Outsourcing US Cyber Capabilities," *Strategic Studies Quarterly* 15, no. 1 (2021): 61–89.

integration well reflect how the state is bent on squeezing every capability out of its private sector toward national security long-term objectives.

Another challenge in analyzing the trends on cybermercenaries, with special reference to China, is the distinction between cyberoperations aimed at influencing a defined political outcome and cyberoperations focused on economic espionage.

TRADITIONAL PRIVATE MILITARY AND SECURITY COMPANIES MOVING INTO CYBERSPACE

Discussing with Gene Yu, a former U.S. Special Forces Green Beret who has served in Iraq and the Philippines and is a computer studies graduate from West Point, concerning how PMC and PSC are pivoting to cyber-security services, it seems clear that the trend has already begun.

Initially Yu, as has happened with several PMCs from the United States, founded a niche special risk insurance consulting firm with former comrades in arms, looking to monetize their military experience that matured during high-risk deployments. His Hong Kong–based company, Blackpanda, provided security consulting services in ASEAN for mining, IT, and casino companies. Blackpanda soon discovered its niche special-ization in kidnapping negotiations. After several years of activity in Hong Kong, Blackpanda moved its headquarters to Singapore to pivot its busi-ness model toward cybersecurity, focusing on ransomware negotiations. Yu noted,

> *Ultimately, cybersecurity is not an IT problem, it is a security prob-lem. It's not a computer that is hacking you from the other side—it's a human being. That human being has friends, possibly organisation, and may be even sponsored by the government. So, that aspect of that human element is always very important to understand when looking at cybersecurity.*

Pivoting the business model of a private security company into cybersecurity started considering the cyberarena as the digital extension of the physical security world. In physical security, the fundamentals, like terrain analysis, looking at obstacles, administering approach, cover and concealment, and key terrain are not going to differ when applied to cybersecurity. Still, from a business perspective the booming cybersecurity industry is more scalable and offers a long-term perspective for profits.

While the market for force in Iraq and Afghanistan provided a fast-growing source of income for the PMCs that operated in those regions, cyberspace's need for security is going to provide long-term growth.

In this respect there are very intriguing similarities between private military and security companies and private cybersecurity companies. First and foremost, business is one of these commonalities. Today the cyberarena still looks like the Wild West, not far from the early days of the private military industry in the Middle East in the early 2000s. While the PMC sector in the West has pivoted to certifications and accreditations, the role of legitimate cybersecurity companies will gradually move in this direction.

In the IT cybersecurity sector, there is only a handful of certifications, but the role of PSCs or PMCs that offer cybersecurity capabilities and how to differentiate them from cybermercenaries lies in uncharted territories.

Differentiating from red teaming, preemptive offensive hacking or even ethical hacker penetration testers is a daunting task and from a legal point of view is not so straightforward to draw a line when an operation is defensive or is offensive and breaching the law.

Acquiring cybercapabilities or outsourcing cybersecurity to the private sector doesn't make it necessarily a declaration of intent to support cybermercenaries. Nevertheless, both the public and private sector noticed that outsourcing to individual or external organizations offensive hacking is an efficient way to build several layers of disso-ciation and achieve plausible deniability, one of the mercenaries' core components. The Middle East, and not only Israel, is spearheading this trend. In 2014 the company Dark Matter based in the UAE attracted former intelligence and cyberoperatives from the United States in what the media defined as cybermercenaries in the service of the UAE. An investigative report by Reuters discovered that the company "Proj-ect Raven" was set to build a clandestine team that included more than a dozen former U.S. intelligence operatives engaged in surveillance of other governments, as well as militants and human rights activists critical of the monarchy.[19]

Project Raven also proves that there's a major shortage of cyber-security professionals in the world. Cybersecurity talent needs a long learning path that includes important technological expertise coupled with hundreds of "hours on the keyboard." A couple of weeks of courses and a paper degree as a cyberincident responder don't fit the bill. The cybermercenary's arena has a very high entry bar as the technical skill set requires constant evolution.

FROM KIDNAPPING AND RANSOM TO RANSOMWARE
In this respect framing the analysis on the human part and not exclusively on zeroes and ones calls to the fore the long-standing experience that PSCs and PMCs have in dealing with real-life ransomware negotiations from Manila's suburbs to the outskirts of Baghdad's green zone. Therefore one of the main reasons that the boots on the ground security sector can pivot to the metaverse is that both the real and virtual world share important similarities and modus operandi; kidnap and ransom and ransomware negotiations' similarities are a case in point.

A ransomware attack on a company's network is basically a kidnap and ransom situation where the company's critical data and not an employee is held hostage. That doesn't mean that lives are not at risk, as the example of a hospital paralyzed by a ransomware attack well reflects how the disappearance of patients' data and lifesaving machines suddenly halting could lead to a perilous domino effect.

Not only from the defender's perspective but also from the attacker's perspective, the differences between real life and virtual reality are not so daunting. For the attacker in the real world and in the cybersphere the final objective is the same: extorting funds or coercing political outcomes. Examples abound on the similarities, starting with the negotiation procedures that the security company needs to implement, including proof of life.

Kidnapping and ransom proof of life procedures are not so different from the cyber kind: once contacted by a demand for a ransom payment, the hackers need to prove that they can decrypt the ransomware data set and defuse the situation after the ransom is paid. Also, according to Yu, another aspect that is often overlooked during the negotiations for both the kidnapped victim and ransom or ransomware is the actual exchange.

In both cases the role of a third party or facilitator is called to the fore. But paying the right person is not the only problem; in case the receiving party is listed as a terrorist organization the cyber private security company could be accused of terrorist financing.

Specifically, to Blackpanda, the company is a partner with the U.S. Secret Service in the Asia Pacific and needs to abide by local and international law. The U.S. government regulations on ransom payments are quite stringent, and there is not much room to maneuver around them. In the case of a Chinese PSC transiting to the cybersecurity sphere, adhering to China's Cyber National Security law is going to keep the company on the safe side of the law while on the Mainland. But as soon as the operation relocates overseas, legal constraints are going to create operational problems. For example, the EU privacy laws supported by the GDPR are a complete antithesis to China's legal definition of cybersovereignty.

At the same time, a traditional PSC boots on the ground company specializing in ransomware doesn't immediately qualify to make a successful jump into the cyberarena. The technical requirements and the constant updates that are needed necessitate a technical team that is constantly aware of threat intelligence and the evolution of ransomware and malware variants. For example, being able to analyze the ransomware level of sophistication that is being used can change the tone of the negotiation as well. Being able to look at the cyberweapons used by an attacker could help profile if the attacker is a cybermercenary or just a wannabe trying to make a name for itself and some bucks in the process.

On the dark web it is not a difficult task to purchase ransomware and other malware to be deployed without knowing much about hacking. Cybercriminals that follow this modus operandi are called script kiddies, and the threat level of the attack is quite low. This all plays into the calculus when it comes to the advice to the client to pay or not, or at least how much.

Moving from a business perspective in protecting companies' data and reputation to a war zone, the role of cybermercenaries and PMCs with cybercapabilities will increase thanks to the adoption of UAVs. Cybermercenaries being able to hack combat drones and loitering ammunitions, reverse engineering their video feed to see what the enemy sees, or even shoot their own troops are an unfortunate byproduct of remote-controlled warfare.

Nevertheless, in the coming decade the PSC sector with embedded cybersecurity professionals is going to be the norm, while PMCs that will match kinetic services with cyberattacks and deployment of remote-controlled combat platforms are not so far away.

With regard to cybersecurity, governments and businesses are still living in a time with limited laws and regulations. The world of hybrid PMCs with cybercapabilities and cybermercenaries is anarchy where wealth and power can afford to have any degree of security they desire.

New technologies shine, but in the end they are not actually new things. They are just a different setting and new playing field with the rules played in the digital world. Recall Yu's observation that it's not just an IT problem, it's a security problem.

In the end, as mercenary is the second oldest profession, cybersecurity is an extension of an older problem.

CYBERSPHERE EXTENSION OF PRIVATE MILITARY AND SECURITY CONTRACTING

Cyberoperations have become a reality in contemporary armed conflict. The International Committee of the Red Cross (ICRC) is concerned by the potential human cost arising from the increasing use of cyberoperations during armed conflicts. The ICRC[20] underlines how cyberwarfare is quite similar to conventional warfare; therefore it must comply with international humanitarian law.

In countries such as the United States and Israel, the private market for offensive cyberoperation and intelligence gathering is growing rapidly. The same trends that supported the growth of the Western private military and security industry are present in the cybersphere: limited regulation compounded by the promise of significant profit. Since the beginning of the new millennium an ongoing cyber arms race has been moving from the West, China, and Russia to the Middle East. In this respect, while Turkey is trying to step up its game, other countries especially in the Middle East from Israel, Iran, to the rich Gulf monarchies are attempting to grab hacking weapons and cyberoperators faster than their rivals.

The Project Raven investigation also opened a Pandora's box that is quite common with the boots on the ground counterpart, when state-trained former special forces and operators move their combat skills abroad for the best offer. In this respect the case of the DarkMatter race to acquire abroad talent and tools not available at home calls to the fore an old dilemma of former intelligence and cyberoperators being hired for offensive hacking by foreign countries or foreign companies. Bob Anderson, who served as executive assistant director of the FBI until 2015, mentioned in a Reuters report that "within the U.S. intelligence community, leaving to work as an operative for another country is seen by some as a betrayal. There's a moral obligation if you're a former intelligence officer from becoming effectively a mercenary for a foreign government."[21]

The ethical dilemma faced by a former special forces operator, whose country has invested millions of dollars in training, moving their skill set to other countries for a price has been amply discussed. The dilemma also applies to former intelligence contractors that are moving their trade abroad. In the United States, from a legal standpoint it's illegal to divulge classified information after the operator leaves his official position, but there is no specific law that blocks contractors from distributing general spy craft know-how, including spyware.

Therefore many conventional private military and security companies in the West who are jumping into the cybersphere are counting on their preferential relationship with previous clients in the government and corporate sectors. In China and Russia there is only one client: the state.

Also, the answer to the question of why someone would want to be a cybermercenary is not far from an the boots on the ground counterpart. In the world of money for mayhem, financial gain is the primary driver. Other justifications can range from bitterness accumulated during years of working for the government stemming from the perception of being exploited or underappreciated or from ideological stance in making it right. Adrenaline can play its part as well in the world of kinetic action where adrenaline junkies and violent psychopaths are part of the equation. Nevertheless, the most important motivational factor for cybercontractors is still the coin. The private sector and foreign government with money but a small talent pool are able to offer salaries that Western governments are not able to match.

Following the money trail, even if it is cryptocurrency, is one of the most efficient solutions in linking a cybermercenary to their client, but the legal framework that states are able to muster to cope with the cyber-mercenaries' threat is underdeveloped and limited in scope and action.

The regulatory frameworks at the national and international level are all limited looks at advice and nonlegally binding prescriptions such as the *Tallinn Manual's*[22] rules for cyberconduct, a kind of Montreux and International Code of Conduct for PMCs and PSCs in cyberspace. The manuals are a tool for policy and legal experts as to how international law applies to cyberoperations, especially the cyberincidents that states encounter on a day-to-day basis but that fall below the threshold of the use of force or armed conflict.[23] Besides being not legally binding, the evolving publication that is set to soon reach the third edition is intended to provide an objective restatement of international law as applied in the cybercontext. While the specific notion of cybermercenaries has not surfaced in the current editions of the manual, the role of attribution of action conducted by proxies is amply debated. As discussed previously, the attribution of action conducted by mercenaries is not always straightforward. In contrast, in cyberspace it is much easier to identify and state the rule than it is to apply it in factual situations.[24]

In the cyber realm, that might be translated as a state providing the cyber tools, identifying the targets, and selecting the date for the cyber operation to take place and it would still not implicate state responsibility. As states continue to be the victims of cyber activities that are unattributable to a state, and the rules of sovereignty and due diligence don't allow victim states to require effective action by the host state, the pressure on the attribution standard will increase as a method of allowing victim states to have broader access to countermeasures.[25]

In this respect the top-down approach in defining cybersovereignty used in China and Russia allows for swift action against perceived culprits and at the same time offers an ample but temporary protection to operators contracted by the state.

For example, hacktivists monitoring the movement of Russian troops in Ukraine via hacked CCTV or the Russian counterattacks online by hackers for hire exemplify the transnational character of cyberconflict, its implications in an ongoing conflict, and the complicacy in attributing responsibilities. In this respect Tim Maurer underlines the dynamic relationship between hackers for hire and the state in peacetime, wartime, and the increasingly blurry space in between. In this respect the preoccupation is not solely focused on the impact of cyberoperations during a conflict but also on nonmilitary outcomes such as information operations aimed to influence a political outcome.[26] Looking at the development of cybersecurity applied to border control management from a Chinese and Russian point of view, in case of a privatization of this security function the existing regulations are detailed to promote and protect the state interest. For example, in China the core perspective on information threats is not related to individuals' privacy concerns but to the spread of a "politically incorrect message" and the exploiting of the state's vulnerabilities. Considering the limited functions of the Chinese PSCs in Mainland China and overseas, including the ban on carrying weapons, it is possible to foresee that Beijing is going to keep close control on the state use of technology to project coercive power. In the short term, the use of cybermercenaries with "Chinese characteristics" is going to be more related to proxy operations aimed to obfuscate any link with Beijing than a true privatization of the state monopoly on the use of cyberforce.

In this respect, the emergence of Big Data applied to border management profiling and new surveillance technologies is already raising concerns in the West.

The West and especially the U.S. liberal approaches to cyberspace offer an ample gray area prone to abuse not only by cybermercenaries but also PMCs and PSCs that are bent on exploiting a profitable and fast-growing market. On the other side of the coin, authoritarian states do not offer even a glimpse of what is happening behind the cyberfirewall as all the Big Data management is pertinent to the realm of national security.

CHAPTER FOURTEEN

Two Opposites

Noncombatants Contractors and Jihadist Mercenaries

INDIVIDUAL COGS IN THE WAR MACHINE

IN THE SIXTEENTH AND SEVENTEENTH CENTURIES, THOUSANDS OF Scots went to Europe as soldiers of fortune under any available banner. At that time mercenaries were recruited in bulk; a local fixer was used to scout villages in search of men willing to fight and ready to sail to foreign lands.[1] Similarly, today's mercenaries, PMCs and PSCs, are recruited in groups. Nevertheless, the discourse around the motivation that moves someone to decide to follow the money for mayhem path has been studied and debated for centuries looking at the individual decision to get on this specific career path. The effect on the person and the society when a contractor comes back from the frontline is also a social problem that has profound impact on the communities that are providing the small cogs in the much larger machine of violence for hire.

From an anthropological point of view, three leading authors, Joshua Reno, Noah Coburn, and Adam Moore, have been looking at contractors through the prism of individuals participating in the support for the war machine from Iraq to Afghanistan.

In *Military Waste: The Unexpected Consequences of Permanent War Readiness*,[2] Reno focuses on how the pressure of constant war readiness produces military waste that in turn animates places and people far from the battlegrounds. He argues that "war waste" should be central to calculations of social, political, and economic costs of war. Also, being ready for war accumulates an impressive amount of wastage. Even worse, after a conflict is over there are plenty of toxic legacies, from depleted uranium ammunitions to decommissioned satellites.

Looking at the twentieth century as the return of professional soldiers and using the analytical lens of waste, it is possible to frame the definition of contractors coming back from a war zone as a kind of "retired surplus human military instrument." In this respect the states and armies that contract them often don't take into consideration what will happen next. From Afghanistan to Chechnya, retired contractors could join criminal organizations, DIY private military companies, or just fall into PTSD-induced oblivion, including drug and alcohol abuse.

Discussing with Reno, he mentions that an unexpected outcome of a heavily militarized society is related to mass shooters:

There have been some shootings over the course of the long 20th century and early 21st, where shooters were trained with military training and used that to attack civilians in a mass shooting episode. That's the most obvious example but there are less obvious forms too and veterans' organisations will point to the mental impact or the mental toll taken on these men and women and the vast majority of them are not a danger to anyone; they're a danger to themselves because they're at high risk of suicide, drug and alcohol abuse.[3]

Reno also underlines how war veterans are going to be an asset in the global marketplace of money for mayhem:

If you have too many people produced with those skills and they can end up "leaking out" from regular military actions like a "pollutant" in a waste-like sense and infecting other social systems. I think that's a fair way of describing it because most people would say it is a destructive force when people who are very good at killing, are put in positions in the black market or in criminal networks.[4]

The market for force is also at the center of Noah Coburn's book *Under Contract: The Invisible Workers of America's Global War*,[5] in which he elaborates on how colonial-era structures for recruiting Gurkha soldiers from Nepal came to be remobilized for providing low-cost temporary labor for the American war in Afghanistan. Gurkha or French Foreign Legionnaires often come to the fore when discussing mercenaries, but it is not the case as both are a kind of soldier for hire and not a mercenary. This means that they are part of a military chain of command and related legal responsibilities. Similarly, the Swiss Guard protecting the life of the Pope in the Vatican falls into this category, and today not many have pointed the finger at the well-groomed Swiss halberdiers to call them mercenaries.

From an ethnographic point of view, Coburn underlines how the military-industrial complex is increasingly relying on what the military refers to as third country nationals (TCNs) who are mostly citizens of the Global South, from poorer countries who migrate toward these conflict zones and are paid by contractors or, more frequently, subcontractors. He argues that

this, of course, creates some odd contradictions when you go to a US military base in Afghanistan. Until recently, oftentimes it was not a US soldier who will be standing in that watchtower; it was a Nepali contractor who was doing the work of guarding that American base. . . . What we see here is a real outsourcing of labour but also an outsourcing of death and injury where the political consequences of a wounded or killed American soldier are so high that they have been replaced by non-western bodies. Inherent in this is also a fundamental lack of transparency in this new system—it makes the war less visible to everybody, even to the soldiers themselves who are on the ground.[6]

As already witnessed in several norms that states enact to control the privatization of the market for force, the lack of transparency is also inserted by design in order to exploit contractors especially when they are a liability to the company by ending up wounded or dead. In this respect, the role of fixers in sixteenth-century Scotia is still alive and doing well under different names, from brokers to curators. Coburn's bottom-up analysis of the recruiting network in Nepal could be easily applied to other countries from Syria to Venezuela.

Coburn mentioned:

You have at the earliest stage, village brokers who will go to the village in Nepal and connect you with a broker who is in Kathmandu and that broker in Kathmandu will promise you a job in one of these war zones. Oftentimes, you then get handed off to a broker in India and you might spend some time in India waiting for a visa or a contract to come through. There's really this global network of brokers . . . you have other contracts supplying not just labour but goods too, goods to these bases. You have, oftentimes, Afghan firms that are connected to international firms who are providing fuel and food and a lot of this work is being done by a similar network of brokers. Ultimately, it is this group that profits the most from the war, not the individual contractors themselves.[7]

Contrary to Reno, Coburn addresses the contractors not as "military waste" but almost as "military fuel." Coburn's field study of the Nepalese "contractors diaspora" underlines how after Afghanistan everyone is on the lookout for the next war. Iraq is still a preferred destination as the United States maintains a contracting presence and Gulf countries that rely on private contractors use them to expand their militaries, especially since the beginning of hostilities in Yemen.

Looking at the present trends in the world of money for mayhem, Russia and Turkey have their own pool of cannon fodder and military talents to refer to, even at the time that the Ukraine war is consuming at alarming speed Moscow's military and paramilitary resources. China differs as the Chinese PSCs are still mired in one serious ambiguity, the need to remain Chinese and the imperative to use foreign resources to upgrade their capabilities.

While the pool of foreign trainers is shrinking by the day due to the ongoing friction with the United States, Gurkhas demobilized from Western PMCs or even from the British and Indian armies as well as the Singaporean police can find employment in China. Since the nineteenth century's British Empire, the "Gurkha brand" is still quite alive and profitable, and it is related to the fact that Gurkha fighters are considered brave, ruthless, but extremely loyal. Today in China, the Gurkha brand resonates extremely well. Nevertheless, the invisible hand of the market for force is not working optimally in allocating resources efficiently. A Shanghai-based PSC tried to teach Chinese to the Nepalese contractors as their own operators were able to communicate only in Chinese.[8] The experiment did not end well. Also, China is facing the problem of "fake Gurkhas," Nepalese citizens with no prior affiliation to the British Army that pumped up their CV with a nonexistent military background as a Gurkha. While in China it is now easy to deal with the huge number of copycats in the fashion luxury brands, the issue of "fake Gurkhas" and other foreign personnel claiming to overblow their military capabilities is still a problem for the Chinese private security sector.[9] Screening wannabe Rambo from contractors with solid military backgrounds is not an easy task, especially in times of high demand and when the brokers are willing to throw anything to their clients just to make a quick buck. It is not uncommon that Chinese security managers introducing their Israeli consultant whisper with a grin that they are from the Mossad.

The "fake Gurkhas" are not only China's problem; Western PMCs operating in Iraq and Afghanistan experienced the same issue, usually with one or two professional former British Army Gurkhas contracting an entire team composed of Nepalese with less field experience.

Adam Moore in *Empire's Labor: The Global Army that Supports U.S. Wars*[10] shifts the focus from Nepalese contractors to Filipino and Bosnian migrant labor to sketch out the vast transnational logistical infrastructure employed in running day-to-day U.S. military affairs around the world. For example, in Afghanistan only about 8 percent of military contractors were directly involved in soldiering and the rest were hired for various other tasks ranging from cooking to construction, logistics, and communications.[11]

Using ethnographic research, Moore illustrates how U.S. Army foreign deployments depend on TCN and only a fraction is involved in kinetic action:

As for motivation, I would say one reason for writing this book was the general annoyance with how much attention has been given to mercenaries that they make up only a fraction of the military contractor workforce. Indeed, I don't really engage with these writings at all in this book; instead, one of my main aims is to give voice to the agency, the aspirations and experiences of the majority of labourers who perform logistics work which may not be appealing to most observers but is far more important in sustaining the US' overseas forces.[12]

While Russia, China, and Turkey are not set to follow the U.S. Army's example in outsourcing logistics and noncombat functions in terms of scale and reach, it is important to trace the future development of the U.S. market for force. This may be done by evaluating if Moscow, Beijing, and Ankara are going to absorb the surplus of contractors and determine the new areas where the United States is going to reallocate them, which is an indicator of future conflicts.

According to Moore, several Bosnians and Filipinos are now working on bases in Africa for a U.S. logistics contractor for the Africa Command. At the same time, the limited request from Africa left an important number of unemployed contractors desperately applying for the dwindling number of jobs.

NO MORE HOLLYWOOD: FROM *WOLF WARRIOR* AND *TOURISTE*

Moving from an anthropological analysis to a propaganda perspective, in Hollywood most of the past decade's movies portray PMC contractors as the bad guys with some notable exceptions such as *13 Hours: The Secret Soldiers of Benghazi*,[13] which narrates the real story of a group of U.S. contractors defending the American diplomatic compound in Benghazi, Libya, against Ansar al-Sharia armed militants on September 11, 2012. The attack cost the lives of four Americans, including U.S. Ambassador Chris Stevens.

In China and especially in Russia, the patriotic narrative is focused on the glorification of their PSCs and PMCs.

Looking at the Russian state media angle on the Wagner Group, Candace Rondeaux hints that there is a kind of glorification and mythization of the Russian contractors coming back from the Middle East.

The early narrative of Russian heroes supporting struggling African countries against terrorist threats and postcolonial corporate greed plays well with the nostalgia of Russian heroes during World War II and the myth of the Spetsnaz special forces' superhuman capabilities during the Cold War. According to Rondeaux, reality differs:

Unfortunately, I think signs of deep post-traumatic stress disorder in this cohort of military actors, a kind of obsession with very graphic violence. That is not to say that it doesn't exist elsewhere, but there are a number of signs where you see a kind of glorification of very graphic violence, trophy violence or performed violence that I think is definitely disturbing.[14]

The macabre obsession with the sledgehammer by Wagner's mercenaries is a case in point. The filming of the killing of a Syrian Army deserter with a sledgehammer has given rise to a culture within the group that glorifies violence against civilians, and even the founder Prigozhin has embraced this ghastly culture and incorporated the sledgehammer into Wagner's propaganda.

Russia tried in two instances to spin the narrative toward a popular view of the Wagner Group's fight in Africa against colonialist powers. In 2021, two Russian productions hit movie theaters in Africa and in Russia, the film *Touriste*, which totaled fourteen million views on YouTube, and *Granit*. Both movies represent the actions of the Russian fighters, without directly mentioning Wagner, in a positive light. At the same time Blue Helmet peacekeepers are portrayed as inept and the French military as neocolonialist bad guys. *Granit* also tries to reverse the narrative of the Wagner Group failing to keep its promises to fight insurgents in Mozambique.[15] The movie narrates the story of a top-notch Russian PMC fighting terrorists that have pledged their alliance to ISIS. The Russian PMC is not in Africa for money but to guarantee peace and stability in Cabo Delgado. Basically, the film showcases money for mayhem without money and mayhem, but with a good dose of Kalashnikovs. The movie ends when the Russians defeat a private military company from South Africa that was supporting the militants. Something that really happened in Cabo Delgado, just it was a South African company saving the day while the Wagner Group was not able to quell the militants' menace. Similarly, the movie *Touriste* is narrating the exploits of a Russian police officer, whose call sign is Touriste, training CAR's military amid the ongoing civil war. The difference is that the supposedly unarmed Russian instructors sent to CAR have been augmented by several thousand heavily armed mercenaries.[16]

Both movies were filmed in CAR. And according to the *Financial Times* the film rights are owned by Aurum, a company founded by Prigozhin.[17] It's not by chance that Prigozhin is the owner of a Russian "troll farm," Internet Research Agency, that was sanctioned by the U.S. Treasury following the accusation that the troll farm meddled with the 2016 U.S. presidential election.[18] According to the U.S. Department of the Treasury,

The Association for Free Research and International Cooperation (AFRIC), . . . facilitates Prigozhin's malign operations in Africa and Europe while primarily operating from Russia. AFRIC has served as a front company for Prigozhin's influence operations in Africa, including by sponsoring phony election monitoring missions in Zimbabwe, Madagascar, the Democratic Republic of the Congo, South Africa, and Mozambique.

In this respect, the role of the two movies is not a naïve attempt to put the Wagner Group under a positive spotlight, but it is a part of a broader disinformation strategy. Even during the early days of the invasion of Ukraine the Russian propaganda machine in Central Africa was working at full speed to extend Moscow's influence in the region. On March 2, 2022, the UN General Assembly in New York was asked to vote on a resolution calling for Russian troops to withdraw from Ukraine. It is not by chance that twenty-six out of fifty-four African countries abstained or voted against the resolution.[19]

While the Russian impact of the movie on contractors is a limited attempt to influence the African perception in favor of the Russian nonofficial paramilitary presence, it is with the Chinese blockbusters where the rubber meets the road. In China the impact of the *Wolf Warriors* movie has been substantial, albeit limited to a Chinese-speaking audience. The success of the *Wolf Warrior* narrative has been endorsed even by the Chinese

Ministry of Foreign Affairs that praised its diplomats for being a "wolf warrior" in defending China's interests and culture against foreign disinformation and representing their country's nationalistic pride.

China, as usual, can count on its huge population and the first *Wolf Warrior* (2015) depicting a Chinese PLA commando destroying single-handedly a group of foreign mercenaries, which was a blockbuster that earned US$82 million.[20]

In *Wolf Warrior II* (2017), a Chinese contractor is not only a capable martial arts fighter but also a selfless hero devoted to the motherland bent on saving a group of Chinese workers in an unspecified African country ravaged by violence. The action movie has earned US$780 million, doubling down on the success of the first *Wolf Warrior*.[21] In the final fighting scene, a callous American mercenary is defeated by the Chinese hero in hand-to-hand combat, and the workers are taken to safety by just showing the Chinese flag.

Contrary to Russian productions that are aimed at the African public, the message from Chinese movies is for the national audience's consumption: in any crisis Chinese nationals overseas are going to be taken to safety by Beijing, no matter what.

One of the problems of successful summer action movies is that the public is inclined to identify with the hero, taking for granted capabilities that are not yet there. The previously mentioned case of the Chinese embassy in Ukraine advising to show the national flag while traveling in the war-ravaged country is a case in point.

MORE HOLLYWOOD THAN REAL LIFE

While the focus of Moscow, Beijing, and Ankara is on the privatization of the monopoly of violence that encompasses Eurasia, the Middle East, and especially Africa, it doesn't mean that other regions are immune to the expansion of money for mayhem.

A quick list of cases from Venezuela to Haiti and even Japan underlines how mercenaries are on the rise. Even an uncommon case proves that the promise of efficient fighters to be recruited and deployed on the spot is perceived as valuable among militant groups.

On July 7, 2021, a group of twenty-six Colombian mercenaries took part in the assassination of Haitian president Jovenel Moise in the capital

Port-au-Prince. According to the Associate Press (AP), the kill team was mostly composed by former Colombian military personnel. Interviewed by the AP, the commander of Colombia's armed forces General Luis Fernando Navarro recognized that the recruitment of retired Colombian soldiers to serve as mercenaries is not only related to the event in Port-au-Prince and has been going on for years, but he stated there was no rule preventing it.[22]

Colombian, Peruvian, and Venezuelan mercenaries were an important component of the U.S. privatization of the monopoly of violence in Iraq and Afghanistan, being well-trained soldiers and costing a fraction of their American counterparts. As soon as the demand for the support of the U.S. "forever wars" began to dwindle, well-trained soldiers with a taste for private contracting started to look to new avenues of employment.

In the murky world of mercenaries, money talks. According to a *Los Angeles Times* report, profit is the first and probably only driver of the assassination of Haiti's president by a team of Colombian mercenaries, allegedly paid around US$3,000 each.[23] The Haitian crisis is not only a reminder of the "war waste" described by Reno but also a premonition when the remaining veterans from the Wagner Group will need to find a job outside mother Russia. Previous PMCs and paramilitary organizations that served only one master, once the master is gone, are probably going to splinter into nimbler groups. Their previous network with former clients could still provide money for mayhem, but their smaller size could make it more difficult to track their actions. Historical examples abound; during the Italian Renaissance, the peninsula was plagued by war bands turned bandits when their prince stopped paying.

If the murder of the Haitian president at the hands of mercenaries cast some light on the role that Latin American mercenaries and soldiers for hire play from the ongoing war in Yemen to the protection of oil fields in the Middle East, the story of Carlos Ghosn's exfiltration from Japan by the hand of U.S. contractors showcased how the murky world of money for mayhem in the Americas is not only restricted to the South. In November 2018, Mr. Ghosn, chairman of Renault and Nissan, was on house arrest in Japan facing a trial for financial misconduct, according to Nissan's accusation. After one year of house arrest, Mr. Ghosn was transported in a large box for a musical instrument by men posing as musicians and embarked on a private jet that flew to Lebanon, his home country.[24] A former U.S. special forces veteran, Michael Taylor, and his son were extradited from the United States to Japan over claims they were responsible for Carlos Ghosn's escape from Tokyo. They are facing three years' detention. According to the BBC, Taylor oversaw American International Security Corporation, a private military contractor that focused on helping people escape difficult situations overseas.[25] The Japanese prosecutors stated that the couple received US$1.3 million for their operation; quite a difference from the US$3,000 paid to each Colombian mercenary to kill the Haitian president.

Another reference to the fact that in the United States recruitment and deployment of contractors for questionable operations is all but difficult is given by the bizarre case of Jordan Goudreau, a former U.S. special forces Green Beret contracted to overthrow the Venezuelan government. In May 2020, what seemed like a bad rehearsal of the Bay of Pigs ended up with eight mercenaries killed by the Venezuelan security forces. Among the arrested were two former members of the U.S. Army special forces, which created light embarrassment for the Trump administration. Mike Pompeo, at that time secretary of state, mentioned with sarcasm that if it was him behind the operation, things would have gone differently. According to an AP investigation, Goudreau's Florida-based company Silvercorp was providing training in Colombia for Maduro's opponents.[26] The Colombian police were reported to have seized US$150,000 worth of military equipment including assault rifles. While the U.S. mercenaries' raid failed, other boots on the ground were setting up their base in Caracas to protect the Venezuelan president: the Wagner Group, thanks to Maduro's close relationship with his Russian counterpart.[27]

If the contractors recruited to exfiltrate the Nissan CEO inside a box for musical instruments or former U.S. special forces invading Venezuela looks more like a trope for an action movie than a real story, the case of Malhama Tactical and its recruiting and funding activity on social media as a Syrian jihadist PMC dials the shock down a notch.

The Blackwater of Jihad

Malhama Tactical, an unusual militant group formerly based in Syria, is considered the "Blackwater of jihad." The name stems from the fact that the group was run as a for-profit business that advertises itself on social media as the first jihadist private military training company.[28]

Initially the group was composed of jihadist veterans from the Muslim republics of the former Soviet Union and Russia, notably Chechnya; later on the number of Arabic-speaking fighters increased. Malhama started as a training outfit to augment the fighting capabilities of jihadist groups affiliated with Hayat Tahrir al-Sham (HTS), an Al Qaeda–linked jihadist alliance in Syria. Following a barrage of criticism that the group was perverting the notion of jihad by asking for money and not participating in the fighting, it soon started combat operations in proximity of the Syrian city of Idlib.

Abu Rofiq, a former soldier from the Russian special air forces from Kyrgyzstan, founded the group in 2016. To avoid being hunted by Russian forces in Syria, he faked his death during a Russian airstrike, then resurfaced a year later under the name of Abu Salman al-Belarusi.[29] Nevertheless, the ruse granted him only two more years. He was killed during a Russian air force bombing campaign in the Syrian city of Idlib in 2019. While Chechen president Kadyrov supported Putin's invasion of Ukraine by sending thousands of his battle-hardened fighters, the Chechen fighters belonging to Malhama in Syria are on the other side of the wall. Their struggle in Syria is partly an extension of their domestic separatist battle against Russia, which is keeping Assad's regime alive.

Since 2019, Malhama's new leader from Chechnya Al-Shishani claimed that by fighting against Syrian government forces, Chechen jihadists were debilitating Moscow's military expansion by diverting the Russian Army presence in Chechnya. Also, an undisclosed number of Chechen fighters signed up under the Ukrainian Army foreign battalion demonstrate this trend.[30] After the change of leadership, Malhama Tactical's primary role remains as a force multiplier that provides tactical training to HTS. In a pro–Al Qaeda Telegram channel, Abbottabad Documents, Malhama Tactical is mentioned as "the elite of the elite forces."[31]

Since its inception, the group has been a skillful user of social media platforms, including Twitter, to create its unique brand and an appeal among young wannabe jihadists that are more apt with video games than real fighting. As happens with Wagner's actions in Syria, most of the available information on Malhama Tactical could be collected from its Russian-language blogs, and since its new leadership the group increased its presence on online platforms such as YouTube, Twitter, and Facebook not only for recruiting but also for pledging funding. The pages were taken down, but the group tends to resurface on a new media platform as soon as an opportunity arises.

New militant groups looking to emulate the "Blackwater of jihad" have been spotted since the end of 2019; Chechen Tactical is one of them and it is part of Liwa al-Muhajireen wal-Ansar, another jihadist group predominantly composed of Chechens from the Caucasus.[32]

Following an increasing presence of foreign fighters not just from post-Soviet countries, Malhama has expanded its online outreach activities by posting in Russian, Arabic, Turkish, English, and German. The group's evolution is disturbing evidence that newer organizations following in its initial footsteps are emerging. With the changing security architecture in the Middle East, conflict-ridden regions such as Libya and Yemen could serve as new markets for jihadist mercenaries to seek their fortunes. Likewise, the resurgence of terrorist groups in Africa could make the region conducive to the growth of similar groups.[33]

CHAPTER FIFTEEN

Mercenaries, PMSC, and the Future of Warfare

SI VIS PACEM, PARA BELLUM (IF YOU WANT PEACE, PREPARE FOR WAR)

MORE THAN TWO MILLENNIA AGO, TITUS LIVIUS IN AB URBE CONDITA quoted Cato the Elder saying, *bellum se impsum alet* (war feeds itself). With a rising trend of conflicts to be fought over decades and not years, the quote is very relevant and well summarizes the world of money for mayhem.

Since the beginning of the new millennium, the international geopolitical situation has grown much more complex and increasingly volatile. Great powers and regional actors alike are competing to carve out their own spheres of influence, while jostling for influence has become more polarized.

Russia's invasion of Ukraine, the U.S. withdrawal from Afghanistan, and the recalibration of its military presence sent shock waves through the world. Although the United States had signaled its intention to return to its previous role of off-shore balancer since the Obama administration with fewer boots on the ground, regional allies and global competitors alike are still finding it problematic to accept the idea that the United States would leave.

The ongoing uncertainty and anxiety are casting serious doubts on how the global security architecture is transitioning. Now, regional recalibration is the name of the game, with mercenaries, private military, and security companies as significant players.

In Europe, the war in Ukraine has rocked the uneasy order that has been in place since the end of the Cold War. China's successful mediation for détente between Saudi Arabia and Iran in the MENA region is paving the way for new possibilities, including the potential for peace in Yemen. Meanwhile, Turkey and the Kingdom of Saudi Arabia are mending fences, fueled by concerns that sanctions and weapon transfers are driving Iran even closer into the arms of Russia. Turkish Islamist private security and defense companies are training Erdogan's allies from the Caucasus to Africa, while the Kingdom of Saudi Arabia is counting on foreign hired soldiers. Simultaneously, Iranian proxies are increasing their explosive-laced UAV capabilities from Yemen to Syria and increasing combat drones' transfers to Russia.

The competition for the monopoly of the state over the use of violence is here. Like everything else in modern market economies, state after state is outsourcing the use of force. What we can learn from history is that buying a force for hire is not necessary a guarantee for the desired outcomes: when one looks in detail at the impact of private military forces on military effectiveness, especially when they're deployed alongside allied military forces, the problem spans from major CC issues to structural communications problems. Strategic and tactical goals differ. There can be friendly fire incidents, there can just be sort of a lack of awareness about who's doing what on their side unless they're integrated systematically alongside the military. Also, the will to fight comes to the fore, especially when recruitment is linked to human trafficking. More often than not, contractors that show up are often assigned a job that they were neither planning to accomplish nor able to do, especially when their background is not up to special forces levels.

This is not just a Western phenomenon. To put it colloquially, private armies are mushrooming all over the place. Another fundamental question that has been around for centuries but is still overlooked in today's environment is, what is to be done with ex-soldiers who are looking for another combat gig or private military contractors returning home?

In the contemporary world, today's combat veterans around the world, disillusioned with the way they have been dismissed by the army they take an oath to serve, are not content to return to the apathy and monotony of civilian life. Even the ex-military who never saw the business end of a gun on a battlefield are attracted to life as an itinerant mercenary. What could surpass the opportunity to be deployed to Africa by a private company that pays well while giving you a gun and a get-out-of-jail-free card if you shoot the wrong wedding party?

As discussed throughout this book, the concept that the state retains a monopoly on the use of violence has been around since the time of Aristotle. What is odd about today's international environment, however, is that while a state may delegate authority, in common law it may not delegate responsibility. In theory, the state may delegate the authority to a mercenary group to use force, but at the end of the day it is the state, not the mercenary group, that is responsible for what the mercenaries do.

This relationship has been turned on its head. Mercenary groups, even those with close ties to national governments, are portrayed as independent actors, unrelated to the national command authorities. It is, after all, cheaper to hire mercenaries on a contract basis than it is to go to all the time, trouble, and expense to form, train, and sustain your own national army. In addition, it is not unknown for bored standing armies in unstable countries to send the government packing or, worse, to the firing squad.

Then there's the pesky issue of international law. The League of Nations determined that aggressive war was a violation of international law. Since then, every war has been declared as a defensive operation. Hitler claimed that Poland had attacked Germany. Japan rationalized its assault on the United States as a response to America's attack on Japan's economy, particularly cutting off oil and scrap metal. The Japanese and German bigwigs went to the gallows, or poisoned themselves, in reaction to being held accountable as war criminals. Today, Putin's delusional attempt to justify Russia's unprovoked, unjustified, and unsustainable attack on Ukraine is expressed as defensive war. NATO's coming!

While China's PSCs are considered latecomers in the private security arena, Turkey's PMCs are the latest to show up in the crowded private military industry. Their role in the market for force is raising serious concerns on what "private" really means and how their geopolitical expansion is going to alter the already complex security environment. At the end of the day, which is nowhere near, in the Russian definition of private military it is already clear what "private" means: paramilitary and mercenary forces under the control of the state without a traceable link. As the few Russian PMCs operating abroad have been phagocytized by the Wagner Group, the future of Russian operators is linked to the survivability of the regime that pays for their service.

While attention is polarized on Russia, there is a surprising unawareness that there is a new player in the market for free lances—Turkish contractors. While Turkish PMCs are a relative newcomer, Turkey counts on hundreds of years of experience in dealing with money for mayhem.

What is new is the fact that Turkey under president Erdogan's assertive international policy is going to offer not only an army for rent but also an air force for hire with the ubiquitous Turkish UCAVs. Bayraktar took the world of combat UAVs by storm. Turkish PMCs could replicate the same success by taking the West, China, and Russia by surprise.

A PRIVATIZED FUTURE OF WARFARE?

The future of warfare and an increasing presence of mercenaries, PMCs, and PSCs even during peacetime could be defined by several concurring factors that are part of the challenges of the modern world:

- Global diffuse collapse of trust and progressive erosion of norms and treaties based on the U.S. post–Cold War status
- Globalization and democracy crisis of confidence
- U.S. retrenchment to off-shore security balancer role and over the horizon missions with fewer boots on the ground
- China's rise in a multipolar world
- Eurasia security architecture reassessment following the invasion of Ukraine
- Middle East security architecture in transition toward a tripolar structure with Saudi Arabia, Iran, and Israel at its core
- Increasing role of UAVs deployed by state and nonstate actors
- Race for cyberoffensive capabilities and complex cyberthreat landscape
- Pivotal role of the private sector in the space race

In the transition to a new global security architecture, rising complexity augments the capabilities of small countries and nonstate actors by setting the stage for a return to the age of mercenaries. In a time when the war in Ukraine and the pandemic coupled with growing long-term problems such as the climate crisis are fanning the flames in the competition for scarce resources, states will keep the trend on the privatization of the monopoly on violence. Even nonstate actors and terrorist organizations are experiencing the convenience of an army for hire, Malhama Tactical being a case in point.

Considering the narrative on money for mayhem, mercenaries are not going to dispel the distinctly negative connotation acquired in the past anytime soon. In this respect the notion of private military contractors is more neutral compared to the definition of mercenary, but PMCs also retain the negative media perception acquired during the conflict in Iraq and Afghanistan. Of particular interest is the misuse of the term *contractor* when referring to the Wagner Group as a PMC. This is not going to improve the status of the PMCs that are playing by the book and are part of international stabilization operations.

As happened during the postcolonial wars in Africa, the number of PSCs was greater than the number of PMCs, but there was scarce attention paid to the phenomenon. Similarly, in modern warfare, the peacetime role of PSCs is on the sidelines and often misquoted when the PSCs' line of distinction is blurred with the definition of mercenary and PMC. In the past, in order to differentiate between the three definitions, following the money has always been one of the most efficient methods to ascertain the link between mercenaries and their patrons. In an age of diffused ledgers and cryptocurrencies, the privatization of the state monopoly of violence has another tool to keep its action in the dark: not Bitcoins but stable coins, cryptocurrencies that maintain their value pegged to the US$ or precious metals.

Besides the global attention that the Wagner Group received during Russia's invasion of Ukraine, the collection of timely data for future analysis on the evolution of mercenaries, PMCs, and PSCs is not going to improve in the short term. Especially when dealing with weak states or in a war zone, the information space is contested and lack of transparency combined with disinformation is going to pose a difficult challenge to overcome.

That an allegedly staggering number of forty thousand Syrian mercenaries are fighting for Russia in Ukraine,[1] for money or for free as mentioned by President Putin himself, is proof of how in an era of ubiquitous CCTV and sensors, it is still a daunting task to get a clearer picture of how many mercenaries have their boots on the ground. The irony, portrayed in Bellingcat's Wagner-gate report, is that mercenaries also fall for fake news. Since the increasing footprint of Wagner contractors from the Middle East to Africa and even in Ukraine, the Wagner Group morphed into an umbrella concept with several spinoffs such as Liga, Shield, and other groups that share one common trait: being unofficially tied to the Kremlin and the Russian security apparatus.

Discussing with Molly Dunigan, a RAND expert on Russia's military and security, she mentioned that[2]

Russia is also concurrently deploying thousands of mercenaries at this point under the guise of Wagner and other groups, it really does call into question if they are doing this sort of sleight of hand in some ways to cover up the shortcomings in their own military? That facts and data about these forces are so difficult to come by and that is one of their strengths. Certainly, it's what I call backdoor deployments of PSC and PMC. As you know, they can be deployed without the eyes of the public on them and this can be advantageous both in terms of international views as well as domestic views. Democratic presidents will often deploy them to get around domestic political opposition to war but I do think that the fact that you have significant personnel shortcomings, is one of the reasons they've been trying to deploy Wagner mercenaries in their place.

During modern conflicts, however, it is essential to remember that the market for the privatization of force is a multi-billion-dollar business that pales in comparison to weapons sales.

Peering into the crystal ball of the future of warfare, there are already clear indicators that the battle space is going to be congested by an increasing number of sophisticated weapon systems. Most of the armed conflicts worldwide will be fought by state and nonstate actors that do not have the capacity to produce sophisticated indigenous weapons. The diffusion of the Russian S-400 air defense missile system from Asia to the Middle East, deployed on both sides of the Himalayas, where India's and China's armies are still disputing contested territories and even reaching NATO countries, is a case in point.

The world is at an inflection point. Significant uncertainty and the framing of a new post–Cold War global security architecture calls for bigger defense budgets. While wealthy countries from the Persian Gulf are increasing their shopping list for high-tech defensive systems, Australia is looking to develop a nuclear-powered submarine fleet in light of the new quadrilateral security dialog. Even Germany and Japan are set to return to big military spending.

During the COVID-19 pandemic, the world's leading defense companies did not see a fall in their profits. On the contrary, even as the COVID-19 pandemic shook the global economy, arms sales increased. According to SIPRI, the top one hundred military contractors sold US$531 billion in arms and military services in 2020, a 1.3 percent increase compared to 2019.[3]

In this respect, the role of private military contractors in the West will increase in the provision of maintenance and training services for high-tech weapons platforms. It is not difficult to forecast the same pattern for Chinese and Turkish private contractors. While the entire Russian military-industrial complex is going to be mired in a network of overlapping economic sanctions following the invasion of Ukraine and the dismal performance of weapons systems that did not deliver as advertised, both China's and Turkey's weapons manufacturers are going to fill the gap.

The United States' perceived abandonment of the Middle East is already favoring an increase of orders for Chinese weapons systems from Saudi Arabia and the UAE. Ankara is not losing time starting with the Emirate of Qatar. In the recent past, a wave of criticism in countries like Jordan or Pakistan for the lack of after-market support by China for its Wing Loong UCAV is calling for the Chinese PSCs to add weapons platform maintenance to their services list. Therefore the rise of a new breed of Chinese PSCs that offer local support services in foreign countries that acquired Chinese weapon systems and advanced security equipment from AI facial recognition to cyberdefensive solutions is not to be discounted. Also, the case of Turkey's development of its own

PMC sector spearheaded by SADAT could likely follow the path in com-
plementing the ubiquitous Bayraktar UCAVs with Erdogan being able to
offer combat drones and deniable boots on the ground as a single package.
For example, the provision of TB-2 to Kyiv enraged the Kremlin; however,
Ankara was adamant that UCAV sales before the war were a private deal
and not Turkey providing weapons to Ukraine. Therefore the presence of
future Turkish PMCs in conflict zones will keep supporting Ankara in
walking the tightrope of public deniability.

While the future of Chinese PSCs and Turkish PMCs seems bent on
an expansion drive, the crisis ignited by President Putin with the invasion
of Ukraine is going to increase the scope of Russian mercenaries and PMCs
under a different name. Some sort of post-Wagner entity will provide the
Kremlin with strategic reach while competing in the shadow with the West.
When the FBI arrested El Chapo Guzman in Mexico or the DEA killed
Pablo Escobar, the most wanted drug lord in Colombia, it did not end
the plague of narcotraffic. Cartels simply splintered into smaller organizations. The Wagner Group could easily follow the same path. Just a small
fraction of the Wagner Group is based within Russian special forces, and
the continuous friction, especially in Syria, has severely limited the group's
professionalization. Nevertheless, the group's network of local patrons from
the Middle East to Venezuela could provide the necessary lifeline. At the
time of writing, two scenarios stem from Putin's invasion of Ukraine. The
collapse of Putin's grip on power following an untenable cost of war with
the Wagner Group splintering into numerous fighting units all over the
world. In a nutshell, more mercenaries. The other scenario is related to the
survival of Putin's system of governance, not necessarily Putin himself, but
with the Russian Army needing more than a decade to rebuild its core
structure due to the lack of military equipment and personnel to recruit.
Mercenaries will fit the bill with Russia returning to hybrid operations with
limited but efficient power projection. In a nutshell, more mercenaries.

Nevertheless, it is central to take into consideration not only the price
for mayhem but also the capabilities. Following Dunigan's analysis of the
Russian mercenaries' will to fight,[4] based on their performance in Syria,
it is always imperative to remember that most of the time the capabilities
are overrated. In this respect the motivation by the coin is not sufficient to
preserve high morale, and the lack of timely payments could lead to acts of
violence against the local population.

Also, another trend seems to be on the rise, following the conflict in Libya and the South Caucasus: human trafficking to increase the ranks of mercenary forces. For example, the case of contracted personnel being promised a relatively safe job as oil field guard abroad while being shanghaied into combat operations at their arrival. Without passports or any means of communication, the only choice is to try to survive in an alien high-risk environment. From Syria to Nagorno-Karabakh human trafficking to augment the ranks for mercenary forces is also a convenient way to cover up the deaths of Russian mercenaries without incurring a public outcry.

The Russian population, even during the constant information barrage from Russian state media, was not inclined to accept body bags of young conscripts coming back from Ukraine or other conflict zones. Contractors' activities are not much in the media spotlight, especially in Russia which, indicates that there is just less concern among the general public for dead contractors. Also, the families of deceased contractors are entitled to death payments that are paid in installments and that can be truncated is a case of grievances aired to the press or online.

Death payments to the relatives also shed a macabre light on the shadowy world of money for mayhem as several Syrian households complained that the promised benefits to be paid never materialized nor were sufficient to cover funeral expenses or even fly back the body of the deceased contractor. As the Ukrainian conflict showcased a prominent role played by battle-hardened Chechens, the fact is that future Russian PMCs will increase their recruiting process among foreign nationals belonging to the post-Soviet space. Besides the previously mentioned Syrian proxies, the nationalities that the Wagner Group was drawing from for its prior conflicts included Ukrainians, Moldovans, and Serbians. Also, with the invasion of Ukraine demanding more troops, an increasing number of Central Asian migrant workers residing in Russia are being cajoled into military service, effectively becoming mere cannon fodder in the Russian Army's grinding war machine. At the same time Chinese PSCs, besides the cooperation with local public and private security entities in their operational environment, are going to count specifically on Chinese nationals with few foreign nationals in managerial or training positions. Similarly, Turkey's PMCs are going to count on a core force of former Turkish military and police personnel and proxies from the conflict zones where they will operate.

From a legal point of view, Beijing intends to improve law and regulations related to the expansion of its own PSCs overseas and the private security sector standard operating procedures in communicating with embassies and consulates as well as with the PLA. While Putin's disappearance from the scene is going to profoundly influence the evolutionary trajectory of the Wagner Group, in China the evolution of the private security sector is not exclusively linked to Xi. The Communist Party of China (CPC) is going to define how the PSCs are going to behave even in a post-Xi scenario. Nevertheless, at the time of writing, President Xi Jinping controls the barrel of the gun and the pen, meaning the military and security services as well as the propaganda system. At the Boao Forum for Asia in April 2022, Xi launched his vision of a global security architecture named the Global Security Initiative (全球安全倡议), a road map for an international system as an alternative to the U.S.-led security architecture.[5] Xi's initiative outlined China's preferred strategy for 2023 and beyond: a global security order that is common, comprehensive, cooperative, sustainable, and separate from the United States' security umbrella. As usual in the CPC decision-making process, President Xi did not provide specific details about how to transform his vision into reality. Nevertheless, the expansion of Chinese PSCs overseas is going to play a role in the Global Security Initiative. At the same time, Beijing understands how a premature professionalization of the Chinese PSCs could create tension at home. Unaccountable and highly skilled Chinese PSCs operating overseas and paid locally by Chinese SOEs—that could have a different perception from the leadership—could be a constraint and not an asset for Beijing. Controlling the rise of Chinese PSCs with a detailed normative diminishes the chances of negative spillovers abroad and enhances the potential benefits especially where China cannot be seen to diverge from its declared "principle of peaceful rise."

Shifting the view from China to Turkey, Ankara is still at a very early stage of the definition of a legal framework to regulate the operation of its own PMCs abroad. A "Blackwater Bloody Sunday" could accelerate the need for timely laws during a time of expansion of the role of private Turkish contractors abroad. Russia will probably keep the legal lid of mercenaryism closed tight on the boiling pot, choosing to not legalize the use of private military and security firms abroad. Continued use of PMCs and mercenaries while at the same time considering them illegal is not only offering plausible deniability but also close control of the PMCs' activities in case they need to be disavowed or even arrested if orders are not followed to the letter.

As mentioned in chapter 1, over the past three centuries the prominence of state-run militaries that had been instituted following the Peace of Westphalia did not marginalize the role of mercenaries, just cast it in the shadows. Since the 1980s money for mayhem has returned into the open and states in the West have reinstitutionalized the role of private military and security organizations. In the new millennium, non-Western states are rewriting the PMCs and PSCs playbook, starting with the term *private* with a very different meaning.

Quoting McFate, we are witnessing a return to a new normal as it was the norm for a very long time. Since the explosion of privatization in the West with the United States and coalition partners craving to outsource various security functions, the next evolutionary steps are within Moscow, Beijing, and Ankara. In this respect the hidden hand of the market is going to play in a very different way when the creation of PMCs is subject exclusively to the state.

One truth from history will still hold: winning or losing a conflict is a bad outcome for mercenaries. Losing is bad because they end up dead, and winning is also a negative outcome because it will be the end of their business. Hence, they exist to preserve or continue insecurity, and that is one of the serious issues that apply to mercenaries all over the world. However, it is important to remember that the desired outcomes from the employment of mercenaries and PMCs cannot be taken for granted. From Syria to Ukraine there are multiple examples of how mercenaries carry many constraints while being deployed alongside allied military forces. Starting with CC issues, to losing the war on hearts and minds as happened with Western PMCs in Iraq and Afghanistan. Figure it out when it came to the efficiency mercenaries that have been forced or scammed to fight in a conflict they were unaware of.

While the United Nations and other international organizations are wholeheartedly committed to better regulate the role of PMCs and PSCs, and especially of mercenaries during conflicts, it is not going to happen anytime soon. To complicate the matter, the automatization of the combat function by UAVs and AI is already inserting new variables into an already intricate environment. Among the new variables, a trend that is not yet present in Beijing or Moscow is that Ankara is already looking at how to deal with the security, control, and management of migrants and refugees.

WALLS AND DESPERATION

Looking at future trends in the privatization of the state monopoly of force, it is already possible to witness how counterterrorism efforts and the increasing waves of refugees and migrants have amplified pressure on many countries to manage their border security and screening procedures. In the West, private security companies increasingly have been retained to provide support services to states to manage their border security.

In the West the private sector plays an increasing role in the development and operation of border management systems powered by artificial intelligence and biometric technology. In this respect border management and security functions are being outsourced to private companies but the rules and norms to monitor and control this niche security field have not caught up with the pace of development.

According to the OSCE Office for Democratic Institutions and Human Rights (ODIHR), the regulatory and legal space around the use of new technologies remains deficient, marked by discretionary decision making, privatized development, and uncertain legal ramifications.[6] Therefore states are primarily responsible for ensuring respect for human rights and must put in place clear human rights–based frameworks for the use of technology.

However, several compelling questions, from data privacy to the protection of human rights, are still unanswered. While in the West, the discussion of the benefits and constraints on a state's privatization of its border security and screening function has just begun, PSCs and PMCs are taking note in other regions. As a result, a new underregulated and highly profitable sector is rising.

In this respect, border security and management are the starting point in identifying possible threats, including individuals suspected of traveling to participate in terrorist acts. At the same time, counterterrorism operations must not clash with national and international laws that protect the human rights of every individual while taking counterterrorism measures. While the perception of the need for additional help from the private security industry is related to the management of gates and walls, the maritime dimension requires, even more, the participation of professional private security companies. The influx of refugees and migrants across the sea is growing in parallel with crime on the high seas. From smugglers to pirates, criminal organizations are becoming increasingly sophisticated, posing a threat to national security, and compromising the safety of the migration routes.

While the UN Security Council[7] reaffirmed that all counterterrorism actions must comply with international law, including IHR and refugee law, the new technologies coupled with the state privatization of border security is already impacting migration flow and the right to seek asylum when fleeing from persecution.

As happens in all the realms of the private security industry, from the boots on the ground to cyberspace, there is an ample gray area provided by lack of updated regulations and by a lack of understanding of the full implications that the new technologies entail, from opaque human control over AI and algorithm processing to discretionary power that the contractors have over the refugee.

Border control is another situation where the private sector is in dire need of accountability and oversight, at an early stage of this new business development.

While states have the right to control who enters their territory and an obligation to counterterrorism and other crimes, this must be done in full compliance with international human rights standards.

TREACHEROUS WATERS: PIRATES!

Another future scenario that stems from the current security vacuum at sea is the rise of piratical activity and the role played by the private military and security sector. It is not by chance that some of the top international Russian PMCs, prior to Wagner, such as Moran, started their activities protecting Russian vessels from Somalian waters to the Gulf of Guinea.

It's a common perception that pirates are a relic of the past and pirates are depicted in the media in very romantic tones. Even Steve Jobs was caught noting that "it's more fun to be a pirate than to join the navy." He was explicitly looking for pirates, in a way as someone that thinks different, while recruiting talent in the early days of Apple. In the new millennium, piracy on the high seas remains a real problem; it's escalating, and it is not romantic at all. In recent years, seafarers have been killed and abducted and vessels have been hijacked for ransom.

Since 2019 the Combined Task Force 151, an international task force set up to combat piracy near Somalia and the Gulf of Aden, reduced piratical activity to almost zero. However, during the last years on the other side of Africa in the Gulf of Guinea piracy is a clear and present danger, and it's on the rise.

Boarding to steal valuables from ships and crews is the most common type of incident, but an important element includes hijackings and/or kidnappings.

Different kinds of pirates infest the treacherous waters around maritime choke points, and vessels do not have many choices but to navigate these dangerous waters. However, the cost imposed by insurance companies to protect the SLOC from pirates is pushing the private security sector to increase their capability at sea.

The global sheriff's position appears to be vacant in a changing global security architecture in which the United States is retreating from being the policeman to being an off-shore balancer. As pirates are taking advantage of the increasing uncertainty along the SLOC, there is a call for much-needed professionalization of the sector, and at the same time antipiracy is perceived as a new source of income. Even individual mercenaries, while in between jobs, are boarding commercial vessels crossing the Gulf of Guinea as a temporary job placeholder.

Increased uncertainty is something that we must deal with in the coming years and proper planning and crisis management is essential for business to survive on land and especially at sea.

IT AIN'T OVER 'TIL IT'S OVER

The structure of the international security system is not just changing, it has already changed fundamentally. These changes in the external environment have resulted in equally profound internal recalculations: states have recognized that internal adjustment is a *conditio sine qua non* of successful adaptation to fluctuations in the external environment. Many states are revising their domestic polices, including the privatization of the monopoly on violence.

One of the most important conclusions from this discussion on money for mayhem is to be equally clear on what mercenaries do not do. Armed forces under the command of a national authority are often used to achieve political goals. The political use of military forces is a well-documented subject. Arguably the most salient example of this occurred in October 1973 during the Middle East war. The Soviet Union advised that it was contemplating the deployment of Soviet paratroopers to the region. The United States responded by raising the status of the U.S. nuclear forces to DEFCON 3. The Soviets backed down. Similarly, during the Cuban Missile Crisis, the status of U.S. nuclear forces was raised to DEFCON 2, one step short of a decision to use nuclear weapons. The Soviets got the message, again.

The American gangster Al Capone is attributed as saying, "You can get more with a smile and a gun than you can with just a smile." The point here is that sword rattling can be used to intimidate an adversary. As Clausewitz observed, war is an act of force to compel our enemy to do our will. This touches, of course, on the psychological aspects of threat making. At the end of the day, the questions are whether the adversary understands the threat, and whether the adversary considers the threat to be credible. The single unambiguous sign of an ill-conceived threat is the use of force. Diplomacy without the credible threat of violence is impotent.

What does this have to do with mercenaries? By definition, mercenaries are not subject to the chain of command of a nation-state. Today mercenaries are not in the business of intimidating national governments on behalf of other national governments. Mercenaries are paid to fight and kill according to the instructions of the current client. Modern mercenaries do not sit around composing letters to heads of government like the Zaporozhian Cossacks did in 1675 when they responded to Sultan Mehmed IV's order for them to surrender to the Sublime Port.

In the context of mercenaries being useless for signaling or deterrence, Hemingway was once asked to explain the message in his writing. He replied, "I don't write messages. I write stories. If you want to send a message, go to Western Union." Mercenaries don't send messages.

The lessons that are emerging from this fluid state of affairs are twofold. First, the proliferation of long-range UAVs should keep every national security official around the world up late at night. Second, the appearance of "little green men" follows the rule for army ants. For every one you see, there are ten that you do not. Unlike army ants, however, little green men can be bribed or, more accurately, be given a better deal.

Mercenaries are on your side until they are not. Hiring mercenaries is the equivalent of the venerable tale that if you choose to ride the tiger, you must stay on as long as you are able, otherwise you return inside the tiger. In terms of regulation and accountability PSCs offer a better deal. Regulating PSCs is possible, and there are already many international and national initiatives that promote accountability, transparency, and positive outcomes for the local stakeholders including the ICoC. PMCs are a different beast compared to PSCs and the attempt to regulate them is beleaguered by the definition of active and passive use of force as well as augmenting a state's fighting capability. The Montreux Document is a case in point. Nevertheless, norms and regulations are in the open, but many states are unwilling or incapable of enforcing them.

Finally, thus far any attempt to regulate the mercenary market is the equivalent of trying to pick up a blob of mercury with a fork. You can poke and jab all you want, but when it comes time to pick it up, you get nothing. There is a reason why mercenaries have been around for over three thousand years. The ability to vanish, when need be (army ants), to avoid any form of accountability (blobs of mercury), then reappear as if by magic—armed to the teeth—is a recipe for longevity.

An important thing to bear in mind as the international security system continues to evolve, nothing is inevitable until it occurs.

It ain't over 'til it's over.

From Mercenary to Cybermercenary

1977—Protocol Additional to the Geneva Conventions of August 12, 1949, and Relating to the Protection of Victims of International Armed Conflicts (Protocol I), June 8, 1977, https://ihldatabases.icrc.org/applic/ihl/ihl.nsf/Treaty.xsp?action=openDocument&documentId=D9E6B-6264D7723C3C12563CD002D6CE4.

1977—Convention for the Elimination of Mercenarism in Africa, Date of Adoption July 3, 1977, Date of Entry into Force April 22, 1985, https://au.int/en/treaties/convention-elimination-mercenarism-africa.

1989—International Convention against the Recruitment, Use, Financing and Training of Mercenaries (December 4, 1989), United Nations General Assembly Resolution 44/34, https://www.ohchr.org/en/instruments-mechanisms/instruments/international-convention-against-recruitment-use-financing-and.

Article 1

1. *A mercenary is any person who:*

    a. *Is specially recruited locally or abroad in order to fight in an armed conflict;*

    b. *Is motivated to take part in the hostilities essentially by the desire for private gain and, in fact, is promised, by or on behalf of a party to the conflict, material compensation substantially in excess of that promised or paid to combatants of similar rank and functions in the armed forces of that party;*

c. *Is neither a national of a party to the conflict nor a resident of territory controlled by a party to the conflict;*

d. *Is not a member of the armed forces of a party to the conflict; and*

e. *Has not been sent by a State which is not a party to the conflict on official duty as a member of its armed forces.*

2. *A mercenary is also any person who, in any other situation:*

a. *Is specially recruited locally or abroad for the purpose of participating in a concerted act of violence aimed at:*

i. *Overthrowing a Government or otherwise undermining the constitutional order of a State; or*

ii. *Undermining the territorial integrity of a State;*

b. *Is motivated to take part therein essentially by the desire for significant private gain and is prompted by the promise or payment of material compensation;*

c. *Is neither a national nor a resident of the State against which such an act is directed;*

d. *Has not been sent by a State on official duty; and*

e. *Is not a member of the armed forces of the State on whose territory the act is undertaken.*

2005—Working Group on the Use of Mercenaries as a Means of Violating Human Rights and Impeding the Exercise of the Right of Peoples to Self-Determination Established in July 2005 Pursuant to Commission on Human Rights Resolution 2005/2. It succeeded the mandate of the Special Rapporteur on the use of mercenaries, which had been in existence since 1987. https://www.ohchr.org/

en/special-procedures/wg-mercenaries. Reports listing: https://www.ohchr.org/en/documents-listing?field_content_category_target
_id%5B186%5D=186&field_entity_target_id%5B1318%5D=1318.

2008—The Montreux Document. On pertinent international legal obligations and good practices for states related to operations of private military and security companies during armed conflict, it is the result of an international process launched by the Government of Switzerland and the ICRC. It is an intergovernmental document intended to promote respect for international humanitarian law and human rights law whenever private military and security companies are present in armed conflicts. It is not legally binding as such but, rather, contains a compilation of relevant international legal obligations and good practices. The Montreux Document was finalized by consensus on September 17, 2008, by seventeen states. https://www.icrc.org/en/doc/assets/files/other/icrc_002_0996.pdf.

Private military security companies are private business entities that provide military and/or security services, irrespective of how they describe themselves. Military and security services include, in particular, armed guarding and protection of persons and objects, such as convoys, buildings and other places; maintenance and operation of weapons systems; prisoner detention; and advice to or training of local forces and security personnel.

2013—The International Code of Conduct Association (ICoCA). ICoCA is a multistakeholder initiative formed in 2013 to ensure that providers of private security services respect human rights and humanitarian law. It serves as the governance and oversight mechanism of the International Code of Conduct for Private Security Service Providers (the "Code"). https://icoca.ch/the-code/.

Private Security Companies and other Private Security Service Providers (collectively "PSCs") play an important role in protecting state and non-state clients engaged in relief, recovery, and reconstruction efforts, commercial business operations, diplomacy and military activity. In providing these services, the activities of PSCs can have potentially positive and negative consequences for their clients, the local population in the area of operation, the general security environment, the enjoyment of human rights and the rule of law.

2017—*Tallinn Manual 2.0 on the International Law Applicable to Cyber Operations*, second edition (Cambridge: Cambridge University Press, 2017).

2021—A/76/151: "The Human Rights Impacts of Mercenaries, Mercenary-Related Actors and Private Military and Security Companies Engaging in Cyberactivities," Report of the Working Group on the Use of Mercenaries, July 15, 2021, https://www.ohchr.org/en/documents/thematic-reports/a76151-human-rights-impacts-mercenaries -mercenary-related-actors-and.

More recently, mercenaries, mercenary-related actors and private military and security companies have become active in cyberspace. In its report on the evolving forms, trends and manifestations of mercenaries and mercenary-related activities (see A/75/259), the Working Group referred to so-called "cybermercenaries" as constituting one category of actors that can generate mercenary-related activities.

The Duma and Russian Pmscs

Maria Zabolotskaya, Legal Division, Russian Ministry of Foreign Affairs (June 2, 2016):

> *Under Russian law, it is not possible to set up a PMC or use one abroad. Russia is not taking part in the Montreux process, as we rarely use PMSCs and the process primarily brings together States that do. However, we are interested in international rules to regulate PMSCs. Such companies have attracted public attention by breaking the law, and there are still many questions regarding the status of PMSCs, that of their staff, and individual and State responsibility for their conduct. Confirming that IHL applies to PMSCs is not enough, and the Montreux Document doesn't solve the problem. This requires proper regulation, preferably in the form of an international treaty.*

https://www.icrc.org/en/document/russian-federation-regulating-private-military-security-companies.

2008—Gazprom and Transneft Russian Energy Companies are granted permission to set up their own armed forces to protect their production facilities.

2009—Duma proposal for an amendment to the law on PSCs operating abroad.

2012—Duma proposal for framework of law to regulate PMCs (Chastnye Voennie Companiy ChVK) by Alexei Mitrofanov.
https://www.rbth.com/articles/2012/04/17/private_military_companies_in_russia_to_be_or_not_to_be_15499.

Prime Minister Vladimir Putin supports the idea of creating a system of private military companies in Russia that could provide services for the protection of facilities and training of foreign military abroad without the participation of the Russian state. https://ria.ru/20120411/623227984.html.

2014—Duma proposal for PMCs operating abroad in antipiracy and demining operations by Gennady Nosovko.
https://www.themoscowtimes.com/2014/11/12/blackwaterru-the-future-of-russian-private-military-companies-a41291.

The Evolution of the Chinese Private Security Laws and Regulations and the Data Security Law

2005—"Opinions on Strengthening the Safety Protection of Institutions and Personnel of Overseas Chinese-Funded Enterprises," Establishing Project Safety Full Risk Assessment and Security Cost Accounting System (关于加强境外中资企业机构与人员安全保护工作的意见" 建立项目安全风险评估和安全成本核算制度), Ministry of Commerce, Ministry of Foreign Affairs, State-Owned Assets Supervision and Administration Commission.

2008—"Regulations on the Administration of Foreign Contracted Projects" (对外承包工程管理条例), State Department.

2010—"Overseas Security Risk Early Warning and Information Notification System for Foreign Investment and Cooperation" (对外投资合作境外安全风险预警和信息通报制度), Ministry of Commerce.

2010—"Regulations on the Safety Management of Institutions and Personnel of Overseas Chinese-Funded Enterprises" (境外中资企业机构和人员安全管理规), Ministry of Commerce, Ministry of Foreign Affairs, Ministry of Public Security, State-Owned Assets Supervision and Administration Commission, General Administration of Safety Supervision, National Industry Chamber of Commerce.

2011—"Guidelines for the Prevention of Overseas Security Risks of Chinese Enterprises" (中国企业海外安全风险防范指南), Department of Consular Affairs of the Ministry of Foreign Affairs.

2012—"Guidelines for the Safety Management of Institutions and Personnel of Overseas Chinese-Funded Enterprises" (境外中资企业机构和人员安全管理指), Foreign Investment and Economic Cooperation of the Ministry of Commerce, China's Foreign Contracted Projects Chamber of Commerce.

2013—"Regulations on Emergency Response and Handling of Overseas Security Incidents in Outbound Investment and Cooperation" (对外投资合作境外安全事件应急响应和处置规定), Ministry of Commerce, Ministry of Foreign Affairs, Housing City Township Construction Department, Health and Family Planning Commission, State-Owned Assets Supervision and Administration Commission, State Administration of Safety Supervision.

2014—"Notice on Further Strengthening the Supervision and Administration of Work Safety in Overseas Chinese-Funded Enterprises" (关于进一步加强境外中资企业安全生产监督管理工作的通知), Ministry of Commerce, State Administration of Safety Supervision, Ministry of Foreign Affairs, Development and Reform Commission, State Assets Supervision and Administration Commission.

2015—"Administrative Measures for Issuance of Certificates of Escort by Private Armed Security on Ships" (私人武装保安在船护航证明签发管理办法), China Maritime Safety Administration.

2017—"Several Opinions on Improving the Safety of Overseas Enterprises and Outbound Investments" (关于改进境外企业和对外投资安全工作的若干意见), Ministry of Commerce.

2017—The Cybersecurity Law (CSL, 中华人民共和国网络安全法), in force since. This law does not stipulate enforcement mechanisms for the regulations (see "Data Security Law").

The Personal Information Security Specifications (个人信息安全规范) are the main benchmark for personal data protection in China, a nonbinding standard issued by the National Information Security Standardization Technical Committee effective from May 2018. Its revision is effective from October 2020. This standard requires explicit consent and encryption to collect sensitive information like biometric data, travel history, or health information.

2018—(Revision of the 2012) "Guidelines for the Safety Management of Institutions and Personnel of Overseas Chinese-Funded Enterprises" (境外中资企业机构和人员安全管理指), Foreign Investment and Economic Cooperation of the Ministry of Commerce, China's Foreign Contracted Projects Chamber of Commerce.

2019—"Guidelines for Safety Training of Overseas Enterprises Expatriate Personnel (2019 Edition)" (境外企业外派人员安全培训指南(2019年版), Ministry of Public Security, Ministry of Foreign Affairs, Ministry of Commerce, State-Owned Assets Supervision and Administration Commission, All-China Federation of Industry and Commerce.

2019—"Guidelines for Overseas Operation and Services of Security Enterprises" (保安企业境外经营服务指引), China Security Association.

2021—"The Data Security Law (DSL, 数据安全法)," effective from September 1, establishes a hierarchical data categorization system. Key categories include "national core data" (that is, related to national security, important public interests, etc.), for which mishandling could carry penalties or criminal charges, and "important data" (introduced by the CSL), stating that a consortium of national-level agencies will develop catalogs of "important data," while local governments and regulatory agencies are required to develop more detailed catalogs to identify the scope of "important data" based on their region and sectors. At the same time, the DSL focuses on the general principles regarding data security, without specific reference to personal information.

2021—"The Personal Information Protection Law (PIPL, 个人信息保护法)" marks China's first comprehensive legal attempt to define personal information and regulate the storing, transferring, and processing of personal data. Like the European Union's General Data Protection Regulation, the PIPL states that personal information gathered by a company must be limited to the minimum amount necessitated by the purpose of the data (art. 6). The law also defines the concept and scope of personal information and introduces the principle of minimization (art. 28–30).

2021—"Outbound Data Transfer Security Assessment Measures (Draft for Comment)" (数据出境安全评估办法（征求意见稿).

NOTES

CHAPTER ONE

1. United Nations General Assembly, "Use of Mercenaries as a Means of Violating Human Rights and Impeding the Exercise of the Right of Peoples to Self-Determination," seventy-fifth session, Item 71 of the provisional agenda, Right of peoples to self-determination, July 28, 2020, https://digitallibrary.un.org/record/3883092.

2. See appendix I.

3. Oldrich Bures and Jeremy Meyer, "The Anti-Mercenary Norm and United Nations' Use of Private Military and Security Companies," *Global Governance* 25, no. 1 (2019): 77–99, accessed through Gale Academic OneFile.

4. African Union, "Convention for the Elimination of Mercenarism in Africa," July 3, 1977, https://au.int/en/treaties/convention-elimination-mercenarism-africa.

5. United Nations General Assembly, "Use of Mercenaries as a Means of Violating Human Rights and Impeding the Exercise of the Right of Peoples to Self-Determination."

6. Human Rights Council, "Promotion and Protection of All Human Rights, Civil, Political, Economic, Social and Cultural Rights, Including the Right to Development," Report of the Working Group on the Use of Mercenaries as a Means of Violating Human Rights and Impeding the Exercise of the Right of Peoples to Self-Determination, fifteenth session, agenda item 3, July 5, 2010, https://documents-dds-ny.un.org/doc/UNDOC/GEN/G10/151/55/PDF/G1015155.pdf?OpenElement.

7. Xenophon, *Anabasis*, trans. Carleton L. Brownson, Vol. III in Loeb Classical Library, (Cambridge, MA: Harvard University Press, 1998).

8. William Urban, *Medieval Mercenaries: The Business of War* (London: Greenhill Books, 2006).

9. Evan Andrews, "Legendary Mercenary Armies from History," History Stories, August 22, 2018, https://www.history.com/news/6-legendary-mercenary-armies-from-history.

10. Urban, *Medieval Mercenaries.*

11. Bilahari Kausikan, "ASEAN & US-China Competition in Southeast Asia," third IPS-Nathan Lecture, March 30, 2016, https://www.todayonline.com/world/bilahari-speech-us-china.

12. BBC, "Belarus TV Shows Arrest of 'Russian Mercenaries,'" July 31, 2020, https://www.bbc.com/news/av/world-europe-53606887.

13. Seth Jones, *Three Dangerous Men: Russia, China, Iran, and the Rise of Irregular Warfare* (New York: W. W. Norton, 2021).

14. P. W. Singer, *Corporate Warriors: The Rise of the Private Military Industry* (Ithaca, NY: Cornell University Press, 2003).

15. Sean McFate, *The New Rules of War: Victory in the Age of Durable Disorder* (New York: William Morrow, 2019).

16. Sean McFate, *The Modern Mercenary: Private Armies and What They Mean for World Order* (Oxford: Oxford University Press, 2014).

17. Jeremy Scahill, *Blackwater, The Rise of the World's Most Powerful Mercenary Army* (New York: Nation Books, 2007).

18. Aaron Stein, "From Ankara with Implications: Turkish Drones and Alliance Entrapment," *War on the Rocks*, December 15, 2021, https://warontherocks.com/2021/12/from-ankara-with-implications-turkish-drones-and-alliance-entrapment.

19. Christoph Bilban and Hanna Grininger, "Labelling Hybrid Warfare: The 'Gerasimov Doctrine' in Think Tank Discourse," in *Building Military Science for the Benefit of Society*, ed. Wolfgang Peischel and Christoph Bilban, Think Tank Discourse, November 2, 2020, https://www.academia.edu/44424163/Labelling_Hybrid_Warfare_The_Gerasimov_Doctrine_in_Think_Tank_Discourse.

20. Åse Gilje Østensen and Tor Bukkvoll, "Private Military Companies—Russian Great Power Politics on the Cheap?" *Small Wars & Insurgencies* 33, no. 1–2 (2021), DOI: 10.1080/09592318.2021.1984709.

21. Richard A. Bitzinger and James Char, eds., *Reshaping the Chinese Military: The PLA's Roles and Missions in the Xi Jinping Era* (London: Routledge, 2019).

22. David Shambaugh, "The Illusion of Chinese Power," *The National Interest*, no. 132 (2014): 39–48.

23. Alessandro Arduino, *China's Private Army: Protecting the New Silk Road* (Singapore: Palgrave, 2018).

24. Arduino, *China's Private Army*.

25. Alessandro Arduino and Nodirbek Soliev, "Malhama Tactical—The Evolving Role of Jihadist Mercenaries in the Syrian Conflict," Middle East Institute, National University of Singapore, Insight 262, June 22, 2021, https://mei.nus.edu.sg/publication/insight-262-malhama-tactical-the-evolving-role-of-jihadist-mercenaries-in-the-syrian-conflict/.

26. Reuters Staff, "Russia Jails Think-Tanker for Seven Years for Selling Secrets to German Firm," July 2, 2020, https://www.reuters.com/article/us-russia-germany-trial-idUSKBN2431S1.

27. Bloomberg, "Russian Journalists Killed in CAR Were Investigating Mercenaries with Links to One of Putin's Allies," *South China Morning Post*, August 1, 2018, https://www.scmp.com/news/world/russia-central-asia/article/2157830/russian-journalists-killed-car-were-investigating.

28. United Nations, "Working Group on the Use of Mercenaries as a Means of Violating Human Rights and Impeding the Exercise of the Right of Peoples to Self-Determination," November 2, 2020, https://www.ohchr.org/en/statements/2021/02/working-group-use-mercenaries-means-violating-human-rights-and-impeding-exercise.

29. The Montreux Document is the result of an international process launched by the government of Switzerland and the ICRC. It is a nonbinding intergovernmental document intended to promote respect for international humanitarian law and human rights law whenever private military and security companies are present in armed

conflicts: https://www.icrc.org/en/publication/0996-montreux-document-private-military-and-security-companies.

30. ICoCA is a multistakeholder initiative formed in 2013 to ensure that providers of private security services respect human rights and humanitarian law. It serves as the governance and oversight mechanism of the International Code of Conduct for Private Security Service Providers: https://icoca.ch/about/.

31. Sorcha MacLeod, interview by Alessandro Arduino, *Boots Off the Ground: Security in Transition in the Middle East and Beyond*, podcast episode 7, "United Nations Working Group on Mercenaries," Middle East Institute, National University of Singapore, October 23, 2020, https://mei.nus.edu.sg/event/boots-off-the-ground-security-in-transition-in-the-middle-east-and-beyond-episode-7-united-nations-working-group-on-mercenaries/.

32. See appendix I.

33. Jelena Aparac, "Mercenaries 'Impede' Peace, Must Leave Libya to Allow Elections," *UN News*, July 30, 2021, https://news.un.org/en/story/2021/07/1096752.

34. Luke Harding and Jason Burke, "Russian Mercenaries Behind Human Rights Abuses in CAR, Say UN experts," *The Guardian*, March 30, 2021, https://www.theguardian.com/world/2021/mar/30/russian-mercenaries-accused-of-human-rights-abuses-in-car-un-group-experts-wagner-group-violence-election.

35. Eric Schmitt et al., "Russia Is Recruiting Mercenaries and Syrians to Ukraine, Western Officials Say," *New York Times*, April 6, 2022, https://www.nytimes.com/2022/04/06/us/politics/russia-military-ukraine-war.html.

36. Christopher Spearin, "Private, Armed and Humanitarian? States, NGOs, International Private Security Companies and Shifting Humanitarianism," *Security Dialogue* 39, no. 4 (2008): 363–82.

37. Matt Apuzzo, "Blackwater Guards Found Guilty in 2007 Iraq Killings," *New York Times*, October 23, 2014, https://www.nytimes.com/2014/10/23/us/blackwater-verdict.html?_r=0.

38. Arduino, *China's Private Army*.

39. McFate, *The New Rules of War*.

40. Sean McFate, interview by Alessandro Arduino, *Boots Off the Ground: Security in Transition in the Middle East and Beyond*, podcast episode 1, "New Rules of War—Durable Disorder," Middle East Institute, National University of Singapore, April 24, 2020, https://mei.nus.edu.sg/event/boots-off-the-ground-security-in-transition-in-the-middle-east-and-beyond-episode-1-new-rules-of-war-durable-disorder/.

41. Singer, *Corporate Warriors*.

42. ISOA website, https://stability-operations.org/?.

43. ICoCA website, https://icoca.ch/.

44. Deborah Avant, interview by Alessandro Arduino, *Boots Off the Ground: Security in Transition in the Middle East and Beyond*, podcast episode 19, "The Future of Private Military," Middle East Institute, National University of Singapore, October 21, 2021, https://mei.nus.edu.sg/event/boots-off-the-ground-security-in-transition-in-the-middle-east-and-beyond-episode-19-the-future-of-private-military/.

45. Sarah Percy, *Mercenaries. The History of a Norm in International Relations* (Oxford: Oxford University Press, 2017).

46. Simon Chesterman, interview by Alessandro Arduino, *Boots Off the Ground: Security in Transition in the Middle East and Beyond*, podcast episode 8, "Regulation and Accountability of Private Military in the Eyes of International Law," Middle East Institute, National University of Singapore, November 25, 2020, https://mei.nus.edu.sg/event /boots-off-the-ground-security-in-transition-in-the-middle-east-and-beyond-episode-8-regulation-and-accountability-of-private-military-in-the-eyes-of-international-law/.

47. Simon Chesterman, interview by Alessandro Arduino.

48. Kevin Lanigan, "US Military Court-Martialling Civilian Contractor Ali While DOJ Slumbers," *Jurist*, May 19, 2008, https://www.jurist.org/commentary/2008/05 /us-military-to-court-martial-ali-while/#.

49. U.S. Government Accountability Office, "Statement before the Commission on Wartime Contracting in Iraq and Afghanistan. Contingency Contracting: Observations on Actions Needed to Address Systemic Challenges," April 25, 2011, https://www.gao .gov/assets/gao-11-580.pdf.

CHAPTER TWO

1. Seth Jones, *Three Dangerous Men: Russia, China, Iran, and the Rise of Irregular Warfare* (New York: W. W. Norton Company, 2021).

2. Frank Hoffman and Andrew Orner, "The Return of Great-Power Proxy Wars," War on the Rocks, September 2, 2021, https://warontherocks.com/2021/09/the-return-of-great-power-proxy-wars/.

3. Eugene Rumer, "The Primakov (Not Gerasimov) Doctrine in Action," Carnegie, June 5, 2019, https://carnegieendowment.org/2019/06/05/primakov-not-gerasimov-doctrine-in-action-pub-79254.

4. Qiao Liang and Wang Xiangsui, *Unrestricted Warfare* (Beijing: PLA Literature and Arts Publishing House, February 1999).

5. Kimberly Marten, "Russia's Use of Semi-State Security Forces: The Case of the Wagner Group," *Post-Soviet Affairs* 35, no. 3 (February 2019): 181–204, DOI: 10.1080/1060586X.2019.1591142.

6. From FY2011 to FY2019, obligations for all DOD-funded contracts performed within the Iraq and Afghanistan areas of operation totaled approximately $187 billion in FY2021 dollars. From "Department of Defense Contractor and Troop Levels in Afghanistan and Iraq: 2007–2020," Congressional Research Service, updated February 22, 2022, https://sgp.fas.org/crs/natsec/R44116.pdf.

7. "Department of Defense Contractor and Troop Levels in Afghanistan and Iraq: 2007–2020."

8. Gordon Lubold and Yaroslav Trofimov, "Afghan Government Could Collapse Six Months After U.S. Withdrawal, New Intelligence Assessment Says," *Wall Street Journal*, June 23, 2021, https://www.wsj.com/articles/afghan-government-could-collapse-six -months-after-u-s-withdrawal-new-intelligence-assessment-says-11624466743.

9. Paul D. Shinkman, "Number of Private Contractors in Afghanistan Drops Precipitously as Biden Pushes Withdrawal Plan," *US News*, July 21, 2021, https://www .usnews.com/news/world-report/articles/2021-07-21/number-of-private-military-contractors-in-afghanistan-drops-precipitously-as-biden-pushes-withdrawal-plan.

10. Åse Gilje Østensen and Tor Bukkvoll, "Private Military Companies—Russian Great Power Politics on the Cheap?" *Small Wars & Insurgencies* 33, nos. 1–2 (2021): 130–51, DOI:10.1080/09592318.2021.1984709.

11. Molly Dunigan and Ben Connable, "Russian Mercenaries in Great-Power Competition: Strategic Supermen or Weak Link?" The RAND Blog, March 9, 2021, https://www.rand.org/blog/2021/03/russian-mercenaries-in-great-power-competition-strategic.html.

12. Ben Connable et al., *Russia's Limit of Advance*, RAND Report, May 27, 2022, https://www.rand.org/pubs/research_reports/RR2563.html.

13. Kirill Shamiev, *Understanding Senior Leadership Dynamics within the Russian Military*, Center for Strategic and International Studies (CSIS), July 20, 2021, https://www.csis.org/analysis/understanding-senior-leadership-dynamics-within-russian-military.

14. Since the fall of the Soviet Union, the Russian military has undergone "Grachev's reform," "Rodionov/Baturin's reform," "Sergeev/Kokoshin's reform," "Ivanov-Kvashnin's reform," "Serdyukov-Makarov's reform," and, finally, "Shoygu-Gerasimov's period." Shamiev, *Understanding Senior Leadership Dynamics within the Russian Military*.

15. Mordechai de Haas, E. Gaberščik, T. Jenkins, and A. Kumar, "Russia's Military Action in Syria Driven by Military Reforms," *The Journal of Slavic Military Studies* 33, no. 2 (2020): 292–99, DOI: 10.1080/13518046.2020.1756705.

16. Svetlana Stephenson, "It Takes Two to Tango: The State and Organized Crime in Russia," *Current Sociology* 65, no. 3 (May 2017): 411–26, https://doi.org/10.1177/0011392116681384.

17. Anne Le Huérou and Elisabeth Sieca-Kozlowski, "A 'Chechen Syndrome'? Russian Veterans of the Chechen War and the Transposition of War Violence to Society," in *War Veterans in Postwar Situations: Chechnya, Serbia, Turkey, Peru, and Côte d'Ivoire*, ed. Nathalie Duclos (New York: Palgrave Macmillan, 2012).

18. Natalia Yudina and Alexander Verkhovsky, "Russian Nationalist Veterans of the Donbas War," *Nationalities Papers; Abingdon* 47, no. 5 (September 2019): 734–49, DOI:10.1017/nps.2018.63.

19. Obituary: "Yevgeny Primakov: Steel and Shadows," *The Economist*, July 18, 2015, https://www.economist.com/obituary/2015/07/16/steel-and-shadows.

20. Robert O. Freedman, "Russian Policy toward the Middle East: The Yeltsin Legacy and the Putin Challenge," *Middle East Journal. Middle East Institute* 55, no. 1 (Winter 2001): 58–90.

21. Ilia Rozhdestvenskii, Polina Rusiaeva, and Anton Baev, "Operatsia V Sirii," *RBK Daily*, August 25, 2016.

22. Они сражались за Пальмиру (They Fought for Palmyra), March 29, 2016, https://www.fontanka.ru/2016/03/28/171/.

23. BBC, "MH17 Disaster: Dutch Take Russia to European Rights Court," July 10, 2020, https://www.bbc.com/news/world-europe-53367425.

24. Aljazeera, "Syria: NGOs File Landmark Case against Russian Wagner Group," March 15, 2021, https://www.aljazeera.com/news/2021/3/15/ngos-file-landmark-syria-case-against-russian-wagner-fighters.

Chapter Three

1. Andreas Krieg, interview by Alessandro Arduino, *Boots Off the Ground: Security in Transition in the Middle East and Beyond*, podcast episode 15, "Surrogate Warfare," Middle East Institute at the National University of Singapore, June 17, 2021, https://mei.nus.edu.sg/event/boots-off-the-ground-security-in-transition-in-the-middle-east-and-beyond-episode-15-surrogate-warfare-the-transformation-of-war-in-the-21st-century/.

2. Candace Rondeaux, interview by Alessandro Arduino, *Boots Off the Ground: Security in Transition in the Middle East and Beyond*, podcast episode 10, "Decoding the Russian Private Military Security Companies," Middle East Institute at the National University of Singapore, January 6, 2021, https://mei.nus.edu.sg/event/boots-off-the-ground-security-in-transition-in-the-middle-east-and-beyond-episode-10-decoding-russian-private-military-security-companies/.

3. Thomas Gibbons-Neff, "How a 4-Hour Battle Between Russian Mercenaries and U.S. Commandos Unfolded in Syria," *New York Times*, May 24, 2018, https://www.nytimes.com/2018/05/24/world/middleeast/american-commandos-russian-mercenaries-syria.html.

4. Gibbons-Neff, "How a 4-Hour Battle Between Russian Mercenaries and U.S. Commandos Unfolded in Syria."

5. UN News, "Mercenaries 'Impede' Peace, Must Leave Libya to Allow Elections," July 7, 2021, https://news.un.org/en/story/2021/07/1096752.

6. Niccolò Machiavelli, *The Prince*, translated by W. K. Marriott, Project Gutenberg ebook, July 1, 2022, https://www.gutenberg.org/files/1232/1232-h/1232-h.htm.

7. Tim Lister and Sebastian Shukla, "Arrival of Russian Wagner Mercenaries in Mali Condemned by European Governments," CNN, December 24, 2021, https://edition.cnn.com/2021/12/24/africa/russia-mercenaries-mali-intl/index.html.

8. "Kadyrov Joked About Cash from the FBI for Information about Prigozhin," March 4, 2021, https://www.tellerreport.com/news/2021-03-04-%0A---kadyrov-joked-about-cash-from-the-fbi-for-information-about-prigozhin%0A---.BJGbjpxRfO.html.

9. Kimberly Marten, "Russia's Use of Semi-State Security Forces: The Case of the Wagner Group," *Post-Soviet Affairs* 35, no. 3 (February 2019): 181–204, DOI: 10.1080/1060586X.2019.1591142.

10. Africa Times Editor, "Lavrov Defends Russia's Role in Sahel, Confirms Wagner Plans," September 26, 2021, https://africatimes.com/2021/09/26/lavrov-defends-russias-role-in-sahel-confirms-wagner-plans/.

11. Alessandro Arduino, interview with Russian PMSC director, Moscow, Singapore, January 25, 2022.

12. Declaration of the First Russia-Africa Summit, Sochi, October 24, 2019, https://summitafrica.ru/en/about-summit/declaration/.

13. Sergey Sukhankin, interview by Alessandro Arduino, *Boots Off the Ground: Security in Transition in the Middle East and Beyond*, podcast episode 20, "The Evolution of Russian Private Military Companies from Syria to Mali," Middle East Institute at the National University of Singapore, November 22, 2021, https://mei.nus.edu.sg/event

/boots-off-the-ground-security-in-transition-in-the-middle-east-and-beyond-episode-20-the-evolution-of-russian-private-military-companies-from-syria-to-mali/.

14. James K. Wither, "Making Sense of Hybrid Warfare," *Connections* 15, no. 2 (2016): 73–87.

15. "'Little Green Men': A Primer on Modern Russian Unconventional Warfare, Ukraine 2013–2014," unclassified version of the original document, Johns Hopkins University Applied Physics Laboratory by the National Security Analysis Department, a nongovernmental agency operating under the supervision of the USASOC Sensitive Activities Division, Department of the Army, The United States Army Special Operations Command Fort Bragg, North Carolina, 2014, https://www.jhuapl.edu/Content/documents/ARIS_LittleGreenMen.pdf.

16. Joseph Trevithick, "Russian Mercenaries Take the Lead in Attacks on US and Allied Forces in Syria," February 15, 2018, https://www.thedrive.com/the-war-zone/18533/russian-mercenaries-take-a-lead-in-attacks-on-us-and-allied-forces-in-syria.

17. R. Y. Pelton, *Licensed to Kill: Hired Guns in the War on Terror* (New York: Crown, 2006).

18. Meduza, "'Guys, you're destined for war': Combatant from the Russian Mercenary Group Tied to 'Putin's Chef' Grants Meduza the First Interview of Its Kind," December 3, 2020, https://meduza.io/en/feature/2020/12/03/guys-you-re-destined-for-war.

19. Reuters, "Russian Troops Ill-Prepared for Ukraine War, Says Ex-Kremlin Mercenary," May 12, 2022, https://www.reuters.com/world/us/russian-troops-ill-prepared-ukraine-war-says-ex-kremlin-mercenary-2022-05-10/.

20. Mick Sturdee, "The Wagner Group Files," September 27, 2021, https://newlines-mag.com/reportage/the-wagner-group-files/.

21. Samy Magdy, "UN: 20,000 Foreign Fighters in Libya Are a 'Serious Crisis,'" *Associated Press*, December 3, 2020, https://apnews.com/article/africa-libya-elections-north-africa-united-nations-faa14b50c17d2a462e755bd6e31f0709.

22. Christian Lowe, "Russia Gives Gazprom Right to Form Armed Units," Reuters, July 4, 2017, https://www.reuters.com/article/uk-russia-energy-arms-idUKL0411305020070704.

23. Åse Gilje Østensen and Tor Bukkvoll, "Private Military Companies—Russian Great Power Politics on the Cheap?" *Small Wars & Insurgencies* 33, nos. 1–2 (2021): 130–51, DOI: 10.1080/09592318.2021.1984709.

24. Tor Bukkvoll, interview by Alessandro Arduino, *Boots Off the Ground: Security in Transition in the Middle East and Beyond*, podcast episode 23, "Russian Power Projection on the Cheap? Russian Private Military Companies' Implications for Global Security," Middle East Institute at the National University of Singapore, March 7, 2022, https://mei.nus.edu.sg/event/boots-off-the-ground-security-in-transition-in-the-middle-east-and-beyond-episode-23-russian-power-projection-on-the-cheap-russian-private-military-companies-implications-for-global-security/

25. Joseph Trevithick, "Russia Is Extending One of the Runways at Its Syrian Airbase," The War Zone, February 5, 2021, https://www.thedrive.com/the-war-zone/39113/what-does-russia-have-planned-for-its-lengthened-runway-at-its-air-base-in-syria.

26. Sergey Sukhankin, interview by Alessandro Arduino, "The Evolution of Russian Private Military Companies from Syria to Mali."

27. Andrew Lebovich, *After Barkhane: What France's Military Drawdown Means for the Sahel*, European Council on Foreign Relations, July 2, 2021, https://ecfr.eu/article /after-barkhane-what-frances-military-drawdown-means-for-the-sahel/.

28. Moses Rono, "Mali's Plan for Russia Mercenaries to Replace French Troops Unsettles Sahel," BBC, October 2, 2021, https://www.bbc.com/news/world-africa-58751423.

29. Rono, "Mali's Plan for Russia Mercenaries to Replace French Troops Unsettles Sahel."

30. Aaron Ross, "Factbox: Recent Coups in West and Central Africa," Reuters, January 21, 2022, https://www.reuters.com/world/africa/recent-coups-west-central-africa-2022-01-24/.

31. Alessandro Arduino, "Future of Warfare Determined in Syria," *The Arab Weekly*, September 30, 2018, https://thearabweekly.com/future-warfare-determined-syria.

32. U.S. Department of State, "Potential Deployment of the Wagner Group in Mali," December 15, 2021, https://www.state.gov/potential-deployment-of-the-wagner-group-in-mali/.

33. "Mali: face à Wagner, Jean-Yves Le Drian reste prudent sur l'avenir de la force Takuba," TV5 Monde, January 29, 2022, https://information.tv5monde.com /afrique/mali-face-wagner-jean-yves-le-drian-reste-prudent-sur-l-avenir-de-la-force-takuba-442636.

34. "Mali: face à Wagner, Jean-Yves Le Drian reste prudent sur l'avenir de la force Takuba."

35. United Nations Multidimensional Integrated Stabilization Mission in Mali, Human Rights and Protection Division, "Note on Trends of Human Rights Violations and Abuses in Mali 1 April–30 June 2020," August 2020, https://minusma.unmissions.org/sites/default/files/quarterly_note_on_human_rights_trends_april-june_2020_english_version_final.pdf.

36. UN Working Group on Mercenaries Report, "CAR: Experts Alarmed by Government's Use of 'Russian Trainers,' Close Contacts with UN Peacekeepers," March 31, 2021, https://www.ohchr.org/SP/NewsEvents/Pages/DisplayNews.aspx?NewsID=26961&LangID=E.

37. Candace Rondeaux, interview by Alessandro Arduino, "Decoding the Russian Private Military Security Companies."

38. Ruslan Leviev, "Туран—новая частная военная компания в Сирии или хорошо придуманный миф?" (Turan—A New Private Military Company in Syria or a Well-Made Myth?), June 1, 2018, https://citeam.org/pmc-turan-syria/.

39. Bellingcat, "The Data and the Dossier: Validating the 'Wagnergate' Operation," November 17, 2021, https://www.bellingcat.com/resources/2021/11/17/the -data-and-the-dossier-validating-the-wagnergate-operation/.

40. Belta, "Под Минском задержаны 32 боевика иностранной частной военной компании" (32 Militants of a Foreign Private Military Company Detained Near Minsk), July 29, 2020, https://www.belta.by/incident/view/pod-minskom-zaderzhany-32-boevika-inostrannoj-chastnoj-voennoj-kompanii-400470-2020/.

41. Eliot Higgins, interview by Alessandro Arduino, *Boots Off the Ground: Security in Transition in the Middle East and Beyond*, podcast episode 21, "Bellingcat and Open

Source Intelligence," Middle East Institute at the National University of Singapore, December 18, 2021, https://mei.nus.edu.sg/event/boots-off-the-ground-security-in -transition-in-the-middle-east-and-beyond-episode-21-bellingcat-and-open-source-in- telligence/.

42. Maria Tsvetkova, "Exclusive: Russian Losses in Syria Jump in 2017, Reuters Estimates Show," Reuters, August 2, 2017, https://www.reuters.com/article/us -mideast-crisis-syria-russia-casualtie-idUSKBN1AI0HG.

43. "Список Вагнера" (Wagner List), Fontanka, August 21, 2017, https://www.fon- tanka.ru/2017/08/18/075/.

44. "Four Years After Indian Academic Brahma Chellaney First Introduced the Con- cept of Chinese 'Debt-Trap Diplomacy,' the Now Widely-Debunked Theory Appears to Be Flaming Out. But It Had Quite a Run," Eric Olander, RIP "Chinese Debt Trap Diplomacy" (2017–2021), The China Africa Project, March 1, 2021, https://chinaaf- ricaproject.com/analysis/rip-chinese-debt-trap-diplomacy-2017-2021/.

45. Michael Hastings, "The Runaway General: The Profile That Brought Down McChrystal," Rolling Stone, June 22, 2021, https://www.rollingstone.com/politics/poli- tics-news/the-runaway-general-the-profile-that-brought-down-mcchrystal-192609/.

46. Bellingcat, "The Data and the Dossier."

47. Sergey Sukhankin, interview by Alessandro Arduino, "The Evolution of Russian Private Military Companies from Syria to Mali."

CHAPTER FOUR

1. BBC News, "What Is Russia's Wagner Group of Mercenaries in Ukraine?" April 5, 2022, https://www.bbc.com/news/world-60947877.

2. Ben Hubbard, Hwaida Saad, and Asmaa al-Omar, "Syrian Mercenaries Deploy to Russia en Route to Ukrainian Battlefields," New York Times, March 31, 2022, https:// www.nytimes.com/2022/03/31/world/middleeast/syrian-mercenaries-ukraine-russia. html.

3. BBC News, "Ukraine War: Putin Seeks Foreign Volunteers to Fight in Ukraine," March 11, 2022, https://www.bbc.com/news/world-europe-60705486.

4. David Malet, "The Risky Status of Ukraine's Foreign Fighters," Foreign Policy, March 15, 2022, https://foreignpolicy.com/2022/03/15/ukraine-war-foreign-fighters -legion-volunteers-legal-status/.

5. The Times of Israel, "Ukrainian Forces Destroy Convoy of 56 Chechen Tanks, Kill General Near Kyiv," report, February 27, 2022, https://www.timesofisrael.com/ukrainian -forces-destroy-convoy-of-56-chechen-tanks-kill-general-near-kyiv-report/.

6. Aurélie Campana, "Chechens Fighting in Ukraine: Putin's Psychological Weapon Could Backfire," The Conversation, March 18, 2022, https://theconversation.com/chech- ens-fighting-in-ukraine-putins-psychological-weapon-could-backfire-179447.

7. The Azov Regiment, https://www.globalsecurity.org/military/world/ukraine/ azov-bn.htm, last accessed May 21, 2021.

8. Bellingcat, "The Data and the Dossier: Validating the 'Wagnergate' Opera- tion," November 17, 2021, https://www.bellingcat.com/resources/2021/11/17/the-da- ta-and-the-dossier-validating-the-wagnergate-operation/.

9. "'Wagnerists' are already dying on the territory of Ukraine," The Main Directorate of Intelligence of the Ministry of Defense of Ukraine, Facebook page, March 8, 2022,

https://www.facebook.com/DefenceIntelligenceofUkraine/posts/266634715647956?
__cft__[0]=AZVxEXa5IQhfXv174oZFpohtHvzqFc8ujKiQNz-G-l1Br4bDkkAPtcHs
gehzXrb1pDAWcTogFnx70_J45CVPZMtgraFxcviK0GWFvCVQFjjcbDhTxEyo
JsvKQPFHO0-o4Oh0kXQTCgzfrFymy05GlepC&__tn__=%2CO%2CP
-R, last accessed May 21, 2022.

10. Sean McFate, "The Mercenaries Behind the Bucha Massacre," *Wall Street Journal*, April 12, 2022, https://www.wsj.com/articles/mercenaries-behind-bucha-massacre-russia-ukraine-putin-attack-terror-brutality-wagner-group-moscow-geneva-convention-war-crimes-atrocities-11649797041.

11. Alessandro Arduino, "Kazakhstan's Unrest Adds to China's Growing List of Woes in Central and South Asia," *South China Morning Post*, January 8, 2022, https://www.scmp.com/week-asia/opinion/article/3162585/kazakhstans-unrest-adds-chinas-growing-list-woes-central-and.

12. Uwe Parpart and Andrew Salmon, "China, Russia, Lead US in 'Gray-Zone' Warfare: Erik Prince," *Asia Times*, December 30, 2021, https://asiatimes.com/2021/12/russia-china-beating-us-in-gray-zone-warfare/.

13. Åse Gilje Østensen and Tor Bukkvoll, "Private Military Companies—Russian Great Power Politics on the Cheap? *Small Wars & Insurgencies* 33, nos. 1–2 (2021): 130–51, DOI: 10.1080/09592318.2021.1984709.

Chapter Five

1. Alessandro Arduino, *China's Private Army: Protecting the New Silk Road* (Singapore: Palgrave, 2018).

2. Aaron Klein, "China's Digital Payments Revolution," *Brookings*, April 2020, https://www.brookings.edu/wpcontent/uploads/2020/04/FP_20200427_china_digital_payments_klein.pdf.

3. Edward Schwarck, "Intelligence and Informatization: The Rise of the Ministry of Public Security in Intelligence Work in China," *The China Journal*, no. 80 (March 28, 2018), 1324-9347/2018/8001-0001.

4. Hong Yu, "Motivation behind China's 'One Belt, One Road' Initiatives and Establishment of the Asian Infrastructure Investment Bank," *Journal of Contemporary China* 26, no. 105 (2017): 353–68, DOI: 10.1080/10670564.2016.1245894.

5. China Global Investment Tracker, https://www.aei.org/china-global-investment-tracker/, last accessed May, 15 2022.

6. Zheng Chen, "China Debates the Non-Interference Principle," *The Chinese Journal of International Politics* 9, no. 3 (September 1, 2016): 349, DOI: 10.1093/cjip/pow010.

7. Alessandro Arduino and Xue Gong, *Securing the Belt and Road Initiative: Risk Assessment, Private Security and Special Insurances Along the New Wave of Chinese Outbound Investments* (Singapore: Palgrave, 2018).

8. Chen Qingqing and Hu Yuwei, "Unprecedented China-Russia Ties to Start a New Era of International Relations Not Defined by US," *Global Times*, February 5, 2022, https://www.globaltimes.cn/page/202202/1251416.shtml

9. 关于提醒中国公民注意社会治安风险的通知 驻乌克兰大使馆 中国驻乌克兰大使馆 (Notice on Reminding Chinese Citizens to Pay Attention to Social Security

Risks. Chinese Embassy in Ukraine), February 26, 2022, https://mp.weixin.qq.com/s/dDFf11edzKHksx6GDlebkQ.

10. Nancy Agutu, "Threat to Security? Five Chinese Nationals Arrested in Lavington," The Start, October 5, 2018, https://www.the-star.co.ke/news/2018-10-05-threat-to-security-five-chinese-nationals-arrested-in-lavington/.

11. Nigel Inkster, *China's Cyber Power* (London: IISS Adelphi Book by Routledge, 2016).

12. Arduino, *China's Private Army*.

13. Kerry Brown, "Chinese Storytelling in the Xi Jinping Era," *The Hague Journal of Diplomacy* 16, no. 2–3 (2020): 323–33, doi:10.1163/1871191X-BJA10054.

14. Peng Wang and Xia Ya, "Bureaucratic Slack in China: The Anti-corruption Campaign and the Decline of Patronage Networks in Developing Local Economies," *The China Quarterly* 243 (September 2020): 611–34.

15. Alessandro Arduino's interviews with Chinese PSCs' managers and CEO from June 2017 to January 2022.

16. Alessandro Arduino's interviews with Chinese PSCs' managers and CEO from June 2017 to January 2022.

17. Alessandro Arduino's interview with a manager from a top-tier Chinese PSC, online, January 25, 2022.

18. Anthony H. Cordesman and Grace Hwang, *"China's View of Military-Civil Fusion (MCF)." Chinese Military Dynamics and Evolving Strategy: Graphic Net Assessment*, Center for Strategic and International Studies (CSIS), 2021, http://www.jstor.org/stable/resrep36977.5.

19. Richard A. Bitzinger and James Char, eds., *Reshaping the Chinese Military: The PLA's Roles and Missions in the Xi Jinping Era* (London: Routledge, 2019).

20. Raffaello Pantucci, "How China Became Jihadis' New Target," *Foreign Policy*, November 22, 2021, https://foreignpolicy.com/2021/11/22/china-jihadi-islamist-terrorism-taliban-uyghurs-afghanistan-militant-groups/.

21. Eric Olander, "Q&A: Growing Demand in Africa for China's Private Security Contractors," The China Africa Project, December 3, 2019, https://chinaafricaproject.com/analysis/qa-growing-demand-in-africa-for-chinas-private-security-contractors/, last accessed December 2019.

22. Jane Flanagan and Tom Parfitt, "Russian Mercenaries 'Beheaded' by Mozambique Islamists," *The Sunday Times*, November 1, 2019, https://www.thetimes.co.uk/article/russian-mercenaries-beheaded-by-mozambique-islamists-9jp8w206, last accessed December 2019.

23. Hua Xin Zhong An (Beijing) Security Services 华信中安（北京）保安服务有限公司. With more than twenty thousand security officers, the company passed several quality management system certifications with special regard to the ISO 28000 that certifies the private marine security company risk management system. It is also the Chinese member of the International Code of Conduct for Private Security Provider's Association (ICoCA), official website www.hxza.com.

24. Liu Qing, interview by Alessandro Arduino, *Boots Off the Ground: Security in Transition in the Middle East and Beyond*, podcast episode 5, "China's Private Security and Anti-Piracy," Middle East Institute, National University of Singapore, August 19,

2020, https://mei.nus.edu.sg/event/boots-off-the-ground-security-in-transition-in-the-middle-east-and-beyond-episode-5-chinas-private-security-and-anti-piracy/.

25. HaiweiDui 海卫队, official website http://www.osgjh.com/about/1.html. Overseas Security Guardians was established by ZhongJun JunHong Group (https://www.zjjhgroup.com/Home/Company/index). OSG has earned ISO-9001 (Quality Management), ISO-14001 (Environment Management), OHSAS-18001 (Occupational Health & Safety Assessment), and ISO28007 (Ships and Marine Technology). It is also the Chinese member of International Code of Conduct for Private Security Provider's Association (ICoCA).

26. Alessandro Arduino's survey administered during the research for the book *China's Private Army*.

27. FSG official website, September 7, 2021, http://fsgroup.com/en/news/show-676.html.

28. Matthew Cole and Jeremy Scahill, "Erik Prince in the Hot Seat," *The Intercept*, March 24, 2016, https://theintercept.com/2016/03/24/blackwater-founder-erik-prince-under-federal-investigation/.

29. "Erik Prince, Trump Ally, Violated Libya Arms Embargo, U.N. Report Says," *New York Times*, February 19, 2021, https://www.nytimes.com/2021/02/19/world/middleeast/erik-prince-libya-embargo.html.

30. Market Screener, "Frontier Services: Resignation of Executive Director and Deputy Chairman," April 4, 2021, https://www.marketscreener.com/quote/stock/FRONTIER-SERVICES-GROUP-L-6165919/news/Frontier-Services-RESIGNATION-OF-EXECUTIVE-DIRECTOR-AND-DEPUTY-CHAIRMAN-32967589/.

31. On September 23, 2021, Frontier Services Group entered into an acquisition agreement with Mr. Li Xiaopeng, the founder of DeWe International Security Group. FSG has agreed to acquire the entire issued share capital of DeWe Security Limited wholly owned by Mr. Li at the initial consideration of HK$200 million in cash. Consideration shares of maximum HK$300 million will be issued as deferred consideration in the following three years based on the operation performance after the completion of the acquisition. Source: FSG website http://fsgroup.com/en/news/show-683.html.

32. Katrina Northrop, "Security Clearance. The Private Security Companies Protecting China's Interests Abroad," *The Wire China*, March 13, 2022, https://www.thewirechina.com/2022/03/13/security-clearance/.

33. FSG 2021 Interim Report, https://www1.hkexnews.hk/listedco/listconews/sehk/2021/0916/2021091601564.pdf.

Chapter Six

1. "Private Military Contractors Appear to Be Active in Mozambique," Defence Web, April 15, 2020, https://www.defenceweb.co.za/featured/private-military-contractors-appear-to-be-active-in-mozambique/.

2. Alessandro Arduino, "A Quick Look at the Footprint of Chinese Private Security Companies (PSC) in Africa," China Africa Research Initiative (CARI) blog, December 3, 2019, http://www.chinaafricarealstory.com; Xinhua, "China-Africa Defense, Security Forum Opens in Beijing," June 26, 2018, http://www.xinhuanet.com/english/2018-06/26/c_137282618.htm.

3. Alessandro Arduino, *The Footprint of Chinese Private Security Companies in Africa*, Working Paper No. 2020/35, China Africa Research Initiative, School of Advanced International Studies, Johns Hopkins University, Washington, DC, 2020, http://www.sais-cari.org/publications.

4. Reuters, "Five Chinese Nationals Kidnapped in DR Congo After Attack Near Mine," November 21, 2002, https://www.reuters.com/world/africa/five-chinese-nationals-kidnapped-dr-congo-after-attack-near-mine-2021-11-21/.

5. Alessandro Arduino, "China in the Middle East: From Balanced Vagueness to Selective Engagement," Al Sharq Strategic Research, May 4, 2021, https://research.sharqforum.org/2021/05/04/china-in-the-middle-east-from-balanced-vagueness-to-selective-engagement/.

6. AFP, "9 Chinese among 74 Killed in Ethiopia," Dawn, April 25, 2017, https://www.dawn.com/news/244004/9-chinese-among-74-killed-in-ethiopia.

7. "Chinese Oil Workers Kidnapped, Released After Assurances in East Darfur," Dabanga, August 13, 2014, https://www.dabangasudan.org/en/all-news/article/chinese-oil-workers-kidnapped-released-after-assurances-in-east-darfur.

8. Peter Shadbolt, "Kidnapped Chinese Workers Released in Sudan," CNN, February 7, 2012, https://edition.cnn.com/2012/02/07/world/africa/sudan-hostages/.

9. FSG, "FSG Conducts Security Training for Chinese Companies in DRC," January 4, 2022, http://www.fsgroup.com/en/news/show-706.html.

10. Alessandro Arduino, "Sudan Conflict: China and Russia Have Different Interests," Think China, April 18, 2023, https://www.thinkchina.sg/sudan-conflict-china-and-russia-have-different-interests.

11. Arduino, *The Footprint of Chinese Private Security Companies in Africa*.

12. Sergio Chichava, Shubo Li, and Michael G. Sambo, *The Blind Spot: International Mining in Angoche and Larde, Mozambique*, Working Paper No. 2019/28, China Africa Research Initiative, School of Advanced International Studies, Johns Hopkins University, Washington, DC, 2019, http://www. sais-cari.org/publications.

13. Andrea Ghiselli, *Protecting China's Interests Overseas* (Oxford: Oxford University Press, 2021).

14. Degang Sun and Yahia H. Zoubir, "Securing China's 'Latent Power': The Dragon's Anchorage in Djibouti," *Journal of Contemporary China* 30, no. 130 (2021): 677–92, DOI: 10.1080/10670564.2020.1852734.

15. Lusaka Times, "6 Illegal Miners Shot After Breaking into a Chinese Owned Mine," December 25, 2017, https://www.lusakatimes.com/2017/12/25/6-illegal-miners-shot-breaking-chinese-owned-mine/.

16. Arduino, "China in the Middle East."

17. Arduino, "China in the Middle East."

18. Gordon Lubold and Warren P. Strobel, "Secret Chinese Port Project in Persian Gulf Rattles U.S. Relations With U.A.E.," *Wall Street Journal*, November 19, 2021, https://www.wsj.com/articles/us-china-uae-military-11637274224.

19. Li Weihai, "中国保安企业开展海外业务 Zhongguo baoan qiye kaizhan haiwai yewu de falu yu jianguan yanjiu" [Legal and Regulatory Research on Chinese Security Enterprises' Overseas Business] (Beijing: Law Press China, 2015).

20. Degang Sun, "China's Approach to the Middle East: Development Before Democracy," in *China's Great Game in the Middle East*, ECFR, October 21, 2019, https://www.ecfr.eu/publications/summary/china_great_game_middle_east, last accessed August 24, 2020.

21. Debora Avant, *The Market for Force: The Consequences of Privatizing Security* (London: Cambridge University Press, 2005). See also Simon Chesterman and Chia Lehnardt, *Mercenaries to Market: The Rise and Regulation of Private Military Companies* (Oxford: Oxford University Press, 2007).

22. Alessandro Arduino, "Chinese Private Security Companies in the Middle East," in Jonathan Fulton, *Routledge Handbook on China–Middle East Relations*, December 31, 2021.

23. State Council of the People's Republic of China, *China's Arab Policy Paper*, January 2016, http://english.www.gov.cn/archive/publications/2016/01/13/content_281475271412746.htm, last accessed August 24, 2020.

24. Pieter D. Wezeman et al., "Trends in International Arms Transfers, 2019," SIPRI Fact Sheet, March 2020, https://www.sipri.org/sites/default/files/2020-03/fs_2003_at_2019.pdf.

25. Zhen Xin, "China's Oil Giants Spin Off Pipeline Assets," *China Daily*, July 25, 2020, http://www.chinadaily.com.cn/a/202007/25/WS5f1b8f8ba31083481725bffc.html.

26. Alessandro Arduino, *China's Private Army: Protecting the New Silk Road* (Singapore: Palgrave, 2018).

27. Tom Hussein, "Pakistan Condemns 'Act of Terrorism' After Blast Kills Confucius Institute Official, 3 Others in Karachi," *South China Morning Post*, April 26, 2022, https://www.scmp.com/week-asia/politics/article/3175585/pakistan-university-blast-kills-chinese-confucius-institute.

28. Interview with the author, Shanghai, online, April 28, 2022.

29. Interview with the author, Shanghai, online, April 28, 2022.

30. Niva Yau, interview by Alessandro Arduino, *Boots Off the Ground: Security in Transition in the Middle East and Beyond*, podcast episode 11, "Future of Chinese Private Security Companies in Central Asia," Middle East Institute, National University of Singapore, February 11, 2021, https://mei.nus.edu.sg/event/boots-off-the-ground-security-in-transition-in-the-middle-east-and-beyond-episode-11-future-of-chinese-private-security-companies-in-central-asia/.

31. Niva Yau and Dirk Van Der Kley, "The Growth, Adaptation and Limitations of Chinese Private Security Companies in Central Asia," Oxus Society for Central Asian Affairs, October 2020, https://oxussociety.org/wp-content/uploads/2020/10/the-growth-adaptation-and-limitations-of-chinese-private-security-companies-in-central-asia.pdf.

32. Niva Yau, interview by Alessandro Arduino, "Future of Chinese Private Security Companies in Central Asia."

33. 2021 Corruption Perception Index, https://www.transparency.org/en/press/2021-corruption-perceptions-index-press-release-regional-eastern-europe-central-asia.

34. Niva Yau, interview by Alessandro Arduino, "Future of Chinese Private Security Companies in Central Asia."

35. Alessandro Arduino, "Kazakhstan's Unrest Adds to China's Growing List of Woes in Central and South Asia," *South China Morning Post*, January 8, 2022, https://www.scmp.com/week-asia/opinion/article/3162585/kazakhstans-unrest-adds-chinas-growing-list-woes-central-and.

CHAPTER SEVEN

1. Pei Yan and Wang Wenzhu, "一带一路倡议下中国保安服务业开展海外利益保护的思路与途径" (Thoughts and Paths for Chinese Private Security Companies' Participation in Overseas Interests Protection in Belt and Road Initiative), *Journal of People's Public Security University of China* (Social Sciences Edition), no. 2 (2020), https://kns.cnki.net/kcms/detail/detail.aspx?dbcode=CJFD&dbname=CJFDLAST2020&filename=GADX202002016&v=tlhXMR3qfZqU%25mmd2FlP94x3YWnriV6UpXB-2jcSvenET2giHoDCK8qObA%25mmd2BAr6aLs87byL.

2. Zhou Zhanggui, interview by Alessandro Arduino, *Boots Off the Ground: Security in Transition in the Middle East and Beyond*, podcast episode 24, "Walking on Thin Ice—Chinese Private Security Sector in Complex Environments," Middle East Institute, National University of Singapore, April 6, 2022, https://mei.nus.edu.sg/event/boots-off-the-ground-security-in-transition-in-the-middle-east-and-beyond-episode-24-walking-on-thin-ice-chinese-private-security-sector-in-complex-environments/.

3. Liu Zhongqi, Sheng Ziming, and Liang Xiubo, "一带一路背景下我国民营安保企业走出去研究" (A Study on the Go Out of Chinese Security Companies in Belt and Road), *Journal of Fujian Police College* 166, no. 6 (2018), https://kns.cnki.net/kcms/detail/detail.aspx?dbcode=CJFD&dbname=CJFDLAST2019&filename=FJGA201806005&v=0xzPgf1AgXkMgTFZrsXwVRFmGmlP79liusQBg-ZHAGWQIesecZawueLsC6hXcI0Ov.

4. Wang Panting, 中国海外公民安全保护的私营安保模式 (The Private Security Model of Chinese Overseas Citizens' Security Protection), master's thesis, China Foreign Affairs University, June 2018.

5. Wang Panting, 中国海外公民安全保护的私营安保模式.

6. Cui Shouju and Zhang Zhen, "海外华侨华人社团与一带一路安保体系建构" (Overseas Chinese Communities and the Construction of the Belt and Road Security System), *Journal of International Security Studies* 3 (May 2018), https://kns.cnki.net/kcms/detail/detail.aspx?dbcode=CJFD&dbname=CJFDLAST2018&filename=GGXB201803008&v=yKssbcqpPfHW5yk4AcqWi39VzNms2ZdKOkqnP3OsAFqqnE0%25mmd2Fc9nhOcCUzVltiyAO.

7. FBI website, "The China Threat," https://www.fbi.gov/investigate/counterintelligence/the-china-threat.

8. Liu Yanfeng and Xing Ruili, "私人安保公司：东南亚海上安全治理的新主体" (Private Security Companies: New Actors in Maritime Security Governance in Southeast Asia), *Journal of International Security Studies* 3 (May 2018), https://kns.cnki.net/kcms/detail/detail.aspx?dbcode=CJFD&filename=GGXB201803009&dbname=CJFDLAST2018&uid=WEEvREcwSlJHSldSdmVqM1BLVW9SOERqaTdERXl3bHh6WWpSREhxOHRLOD0%3D%249A4hF_YAuvQ5obgVAqnKPCYcEjKensW4IQMovwHtwkF4VYPoHbKxJw!!

9. "Italy in Compensation Deal with India Fishermen Families," *BBC News*, April 24, 2012, https://www.bbc.com/news/world-asia-india-17825300.

10. Yan Su, "国际法视野下的私营军事安保公司：模式、争论及中国应对" (Private Military and Security Companies from the Perspective of International Law: Patterns, Debates, and China's Measures), *Journal of International Law*, no. 1 (2021), https://kns.cnki.net/kcms/detail/detail.aspx?dbcode=CJFD&dbname=CJFDLAST2020&filename=G-JFX202001006&v=sRh1tlBIpenhIyzTlCkI%25mmd2FRrNGbdzgwm5%25mmd2B9ncu-Zo6eLDDjGcq%25mmd2B1O%25mmd2Fb8mjtWekdLh7.

11. Yan Su, "国际法视野下的私营军事安保公司：模式、争论及中国应对."

12. Liu Bo and Yang Tianna, 私营军事公司及其对国际安全的影响 (Private Military Companies and Their Impact on International Security), *Journal of International Affairs*, no. 9 (2015), https://max.book118.com/html/2018/1105/8142140131001131.shtm.

13. Andrea Ghiselli, *Protecting China's Interests Overseas* (Oxford: Oxford University Press, 2021).

14. Li Xiuna, "我国私营安全公司域外服务的法律困境及其突破" (The Legal Dilemma and Its Breakthrough of Chinese Private Security Companies' Overseas Service), *Contemporary Law*, no. 1 (2021), https://kns.cnki.net/kcms/detail/detail.aspx?dbcode=CJF-D&dbname=CJFDLAST2021&filename=DDFX202101013&v=VPgWrL1W4vViez3m-jwBrx4mehYup8j2lqrJZKS26vT5h%25mmd2BuOURzzfI%25mmd2BNjw1yUaoeA.

15. Liu Zhongqi, Sheng Ziming, and Liang Xiubo, "一带一路背景下我国民营安保企业走出去研究."

16. Zhou Zhanggui, interview by Alessandro Arduino, "Walking on Thin Ice—Chinese Private Security Sector in Complex Environments."

CHAPTER EIGHT

1. Liu Qing, interview by Alessandro Arduino, *Boots Off the Ground: Security in Transition in the Middle East and Beyond*, podcast episode 5, "China's Private Security and Anti-Piracy," Middle East Institute, National University of Singapore, August 19, 2020, https://mei.nus.edu.sg/event/boots-off-the-ground-security-in-transition-in-the-middle-east-and-beyond-episode-5-chinas-private-security-and-anti-piracy/.

2. Liu Qing, interview by Alessandro Arduino, "China's Private Security and Anti-Piracy."

3. Alessandro Arduino, "China in the Middle East: From Balanced Vagueness to Selective Engagement," Expert Brief, *AlSharq Strategic Research*, May 4, 2021, https://research.sharqforum.org/2021/05/04/china-in-the-middle-east/.

4. Zhang Yan and Xin Dingding, "No Hiding Place Overseas for Fugitive Officials," *China Daily*, April 29, 2015, http://www.chinadaily.com.cn/kindle/2015-04/29/content_20575527.htm.

5. Thomas Heberer, "China in 2014: Creating a New Power and Security Architecture in Domestic and Foreign Policies," *Asian Survey* 55, no. 1 (2015): 82–102, https://doi.org/10.1525/as.2015.55.1.82.

6. China File, "Visualizing China's Anti-Corruption Campaign," August 15, 2018, https://www.chinafile.com/infographics/visualizing-chinas-anti-corruption-campaign.

7. Jonas Parello-Plesner and Mathieu Duchâtel, *China's Strong Arm Protecting Citizens and Assets Abroad* (London: Routledge, 2015).

8. Author's interview with Israeli security expert based in Shanghai, January 10, 2022.

CHAPTER NINE

1. Igor Zevelev, *Russian National Identity and Foreign Policy* (Center for Strategic and International Studies [CSIS], 2016).

2. Alexandr G. Dugin, *The Foundations of Geopolitics: The Geopolitical Future of Russia* (Moscow: Arktogeja, 1999).

3. Ömer Taspinar, *Turkey's Middle East Policies: Between Neo-Ottomanism and Kemalism* (Whashington, DC: Carnegie Endowment for International Peace, 2008).

4. Asli Aydıntaşbaş, *A New Gaza: Turkey's Border Policy in Northern Syria*, European Council on Foreign Relations, Policy Brief, 2020, https://ecfr.eu/publication/a_new_gaza_turkeys_border_policy_in_northern_syria/.

5. James Dorsey, "Ignoring the Middle East at One's Peril: Turkey Plays Games in NATO," May 15, 2022, https://jamesmdorsey.substack.com/p/ignoring-the-middle-east-at-ones?.

6. Mesut Uyar and Edward Erickson, *A Military History of the Ottomans: From Osman to Atatürk* (Santa Barbara, CA: Praeger Security International, 2009).

7. Ryan Kelty and Alex Bierman, "Ambivalence on the Front Lines: Perceptions of Contractors in Iraq and Afghanistan," *Armed Forces & Society* 39, no. 1 (2013): 5–27.

8. Uyar and Erickson, *A Military History of the Ottomans.*

9. Uyar and Erickson, *A Military History of the Ottomans.*

10. U.S. Government Accountability Office, "Afghanistan Reconstruction: GAO Work since 2002 Shows Systemic Internal Control Weaknesses that Increased the Risk of Waste, Fraud, and Abuse," January 27, 2021, https://www.gao.gov/products/gao-21-32r.

11. Uyar and Erickson, *A Military History of the Ottomans.*

12. Hay Eytan Cohen Yanarocakand Jonathan Spyer, "Turkish Militias and Proxies," January 27, 2021, https://jiss.org.il/en/yanarocak-spyer-turkish-militias-and-proxies/.

13. Mathieu Duchâtel, Cristina Garafola, Marc Julienne, Jérôme Doyon, and Alexandre Sheldon-Duplaix, *Xi's Army: Reform and Loyalty in the PLA* (European Council on Foreign Relations, 2016).

14. Patrick Savage, "The Russian National Guard: An Asset for Putin at Home and Abroad," American Security Project, 2017.

15. Metin Gurcan, "How Post-Coup Purges Depleted Turkey's Military," *Al Monitor*, September 16, 2016, https://www.al-monitor.com/originals/2016/09/turkey-military-needs-two-year-fill-ranks-emptied-by-purge.html#ixzz7MYFkXPR0.

16. Suat Cubukcu, "The Rise of Paramilitary Groups in Turkey," *Small Wars Journal*, March 3, 2018, https://smallwarsjournal.com/jrnl/art/rise-paramilitary-groups-turkey.

17. Yanarocak and Spyer, "Turkish Militias and Proxies."

18. SADAT Defense official website, https://SADAT.com.tr/en/.

19. Matt Powers, "Making Sense of SADAT, Turkey's Private Military Company," War on the Rocks, October 8, 2021, https://warontherocks.com/2021/10/making-sense-of-SADAT-turkeys-private-military-company/.

20. Confederation of European Security Services, *Private Security in Europe: CoESS Facts & Figures 2008* (Brussels: CoESS, 2008).

21. Powers, "Making Sense of SADAT, Turkey's Private Military Company."

22. Jeremy Binnie, "AFRICOM Says 7,000 Syrian Fighters in Libya," *Janes*, September 3, 2020, https://www.janes.com/defence-news/news-detail/africom-says-7000-syrian-fighters-in-libya.

23. Al Jazeera, "Azerbaijan Denies Turkey Sent It Fighters from Syria," September 28, 2020, https://www.aljazeera.com/news/2020/9/28/azerbaijan-denies-turkey-sent-it-fighters-from-syria.

24. "Syria/Libya: Complaint to the UN Working Group on the Use of Mercenaries: Syrian Organizations Address the Grave Consequences Mercenarism Has for the Families of Recruits, Particularly the Practice's Adverse Impact on Women and Children," March 2022, https://stj-sy.org/wp-content/uploads/2022/03/Complaint-to-the-UN-Working-Group-on-the-Use-of-Mercenaries.pdf.

25. "Syria/Libya."

26. SADAT website, Interview with Agence France-Presse, October 25, 2021, https://www.sadat.com.tr/en/about-us/news.html.

27. Dmitry Zaks, "Turkey's Islamic Defense Consultancy Takes on West," *Jordan News*, October 28, 2021, https://www.jordannews.jo/Section-36/Opinion/Turkey-s-Islamic-defense-consultancy-takes-on-West-8898.

28. Zaks, "Turkey's Islamic Defense Consultancy Takes on West."

29. Jonathan Spyer, "Erdogan's Shadow Army: The Influence of 'SADAT,' Turkey's Private Defense Group," *The Jerusalem Post*, April 16, 2018, https://www.jpost.com/Opinion/Erdogans-shadow-army-The-influence-of-Turkeys-private-defense-group-549698.

30. Ali Coşar, "A New Case in Cooperation in Islamic Countries: Private Military Companies as a Component of Defense Industry Service Industry," ASSAM, March 22, 2022, https://www.assam.org.tr/index.php/en/regions/islam-ulkeleri/central-asia/t%C3%BCrkiye/i%CC%87slam-ulkeleri-i%CC%87sbirliginde-yeni-bir-olgu-savunma-sanayi-hizmet-endustrisi-nin-bir-unsuru-olarak-ozel-askeri-sirketler-en.html.

31. Coşar, "A New Case in Cooperation in Islamic Countries."

32. Intelligence Online, "Akademi Sancak, Ankara's Secret Move to Support Doha," January 17, 2018, https://www.intelligenceonline.com/international-dealmaking/2018/01/17/akademi-sancak-ankara-s-secret-move-to-support-doha,108289891-art.

33. Intelligence Online, "Akademi Sancak, Ankara's Secret Move to Support Doha."

34. Harun Karčić, "Ankara First: How Turkey Is Balancing Between Russia and Ukraine," The National Interest, May 14, 2022, https://nationalinterest.org/feature/ankara-first-how-turkey-balancing-between-russia-and-ukraine-202335.

CHAPTER TEN

1. Grégoire Chamayou, *A Theory of the Drone* (New York: The New Press, 2015).

2. Alessandro Arduino, "The Evolution of Drones for Targeted Killings after 9/11," 9/11 Legacies, September 8, 2021, http://911legacies.com/The%20Evolution%20of%20Armed%20Drones%20for%20Targeted%20Killing%20after%209-11.htm.

3. Author's interview with Chinese PSC manager based in the MENA region, December 10, 2021.

4. Author's interview with Chinese PSC manager based in the MENA region, December 10, 2021.

5. Arduino, "The Evolution of Drones for Targeted Killings after 9/11."

6. T. S. Allen, Kyle Brown, and Jonathan Askonas, "How the Army Out-Innovated the Islamic State's Drones," War on the Rocks, December 21, 2020, https://warontherocks.com/2020/12/how-the-army-out-innovated-the-islamic-states-drones/.

7. Alessandro Arduino, "Increasing Reliance on Drones Raises Critical Questions about War-Time Ethics," The Arab Weekly, August 31, 2019, https://thearabweekly.com/increasing-reliance-drones-raises-critical-questions-about-war-time-ethics.

8. Aaron Stein, "From Ankara with Implications: Turkish Drones and Alliance Entrapment," War on the Rocks, December 15, 2021, https://warontherocks.com/2021/12/from-ankara-with-implications-turkish-drones-and-alliance-entrapment/.

9. Bruce Einhorn, "Combat Drones Made in China Are Coming to a Conflict Near You," Bloomberg, March 18, 2021, https://www.bloomberg.com/news/articles/2021-03-17/china-s-combat-drones-push-could-spark-a-global-arms-race.

10. Cem Cetinguc, "Turkey Expands Combat Drone Sales to Africa," P.A. Turkey, October 15, 2021, https://www.paturkey.com/news/turkey-expands-combat-drone-sales-to-africa/2021/.

11. Reuters, "Factbox: Turkey's Bayraktar TB2 Combat Drones Sales," November 11, 2021, https://www.reuters.com/world/middle-east/turkeys-bayraktar-tb2-combat-drones-sales-2021-11-10/.

12. Official MTCR website, https://mtcr.info/.

13. Official U.S. Air Force website, https://www.af.mil/About-Us/Fact-Sheets/Display/Article/104470/mq-9-reaper/.

14. Stephen Chen, "China Unveils Its Answer to US Reaper Drone—How Does It Compare?" South China Morning Post, July 17, 2017, https://www.scmp.com/news/china/diplomacy-defence/article/2103005/new-chinese-drone-overseas-buyers-rival-us-reaper.

15. James Marson and Brett Forrest, "Armed Low-Cost Drones, Made by Turkey, Reshape Battlefields and Geopolitics," Wall Street Journal, June 3, 2021, https://www.wsj.com/articles/armed-low-cost-drones-made-by-turkey-reshape-battlefields-and-geopolitics-11622727370.

16. Office of the Under Secretary of Defense (Comptroller)/Chief Financial Officer, February 2020, https://comptroller.defense.gov/Portals/45/Documents/defbudget/fy2021/fy2021_Weapons.pdf.

17. Alessandro Arduino, "In Nagorno-Karabakh, Drones Rain Death but Won't Bring Quick End to War," South China Morning Post, October 23, 2020, https://www.scmp.com/week-asia/politics/article/3106807/nagorno-karabakh-drones-rain-death-wont-bring-quick-end-war.

18. "Pakistan Acquires Rights to Anka Drone from Turkey," Joint Production & Technology Transfer, August 22, 2021, https://pakstrategic.com/2021/08/22/pakistan-acquires-rights-to-anka-drone-from-turkey-joint-production-technology-transfer/.

19. Arms Control Association, "Israel Halts Chinese Phalcon Deal," https://www
.armscontrol.org/act/2000-09/press-releases/israel-halts-chinese-phalcon-deal.

20. James Marson and Giovanni Legorano, "China Bought Italian Military-Drone
Maker Without Authorities' Knowledge," *Wall Street Journal*, November 15, 2021, https://
www.wsj.com/articles/china-bought-italian-military-drone-maker-without-authorities
-knowledge-11636972513.

21. Government of Canada, "Final Report: Review of Export Permits to Turkey,"
https://www.international.gc.ca/trade-commerce/controls-controles/reports-rapports
/exp-permits-turkey-licences-turquie.aspx?lang=eng.

22. James Mulvenon and Chenny Zhang, "Targeting Defense Technologies," in
China's Quest for Foreign Technology Beyond Espionage, ed. William C. Hannas and Didi
Kirsten Tatlow (New York: Routledge, 2020).

23. Mike Stone, "U.S. to Sell 34 Surveillance Drones to Allies in South China Sea
Region," Reuters, June 4, 2019, https://www.reuters.com/article/us-usa-defense-drones
-idUSKCN1T42ST.

24. Minnie Chan, "Chinese Drone Factory in Saudi Arabia First in Middle
East," *South China Morning Post*, March 26, 2017, https://www.scmp.com/news/china
diplomacy-defence/article/2081869/chinese-drone-factory-saudi-arabia-first-middle
-east.

25. Isabel Debre, "Who Showed Up for the In-Person UAE Weapons Show?"
Defense News, February 23, 2021, https://www.defensenews.com/digital-show-dailies
/idex/2021/02/22/who-showed-up-for-the-in-person-uae-weapons-show/.

26. International Human Rights and Conflict Resolution Clinic at Stanford Law
School and Global Justice Clinic at NYU School of Law, "Living Under Drones: Death,
Injury, and Trauma to Civilians from US Drone Practices in Pakistan," 2012, https://
www-cdn.law.stanford.edu/wp-content/uploads/2015/07/Stanford-NYU-LIVING
-UNDER-DRONES.pdf.

27. Council on Foreign Relations Global Conflict Tracker, "War in Yemen," https://
www.cfr.org/global-conflict-tracker/conflict/war-yemen, last accessed February 18, 2021.

28. Council on Foreign Relations Global Conflict Tracker, "War in Yemen."

29. Alessandro Arduino, "Houthi Attacks Signal New Chapter in Drone Warfare,"
The Arab Weekly, May 26, 2019, https://thearabweekly.com/houthi-attacks-signal-new
-chapter-drone-warfare.

30. Aaron Stein, "Low-Tech High-Reward: The Houthi Drone Attack," Foreign
Policy Research Institute, January 11, 2019, https://www.fpri.org/article/2019/01/low
-tech-high-reward-the-houthi-drone-attack/.

31. Alessandro Arduino, "Attack on Saudi Oil Facilities Demonstrates Drone Threat,"
The Arab Weekly, September 28, 2019, https://thearabweekly.com/attack-saudi-oil-facili-
ties-demonstrates-drone-threat.

32. Arduino, "Attack on Saudi Oil Facilities Demonstrates Drone Threat."

33. Alessandro Arduino, "Drone Strikes Leave the UAE Between a Rock and a
Hard Place," Insights Middle East Institute, National University of Singapore, January
19, 2022, https://mei.nus.edu.sg/think_in/drone-strikes-leave-the-uae-between-a-rock
-and-a-hard-place/.

CHAPTER ELEVEN

1. Samira Shackle, "The Mystery of the Gatwick Drone," *The Guardian*, December 1, 2020.
2. W. Chappelle, T. Goodman, L. Reardon, and W. Thompson, "An Analysis of Post-Traumatic Stress Symptoms in United States Air Force Drone Operators," *J Anxiety Disord*. 28, no. 5 (June 2014), https://pubmed.ncbi.nlm.nih.gov/24907535/.
3. Alessandro Arduino, "Nagorno-Karabakh Conflict Offers Insight into the New Art of War," *South China Morning Post*, October 4, 2020, https://www.scmp.com/weekasia /opinion/article/3104068/nagorno-karabakh-conflict-offers-insight-new-art-war.
4. Jacob Parakilas, "Tanks vs. Drones Isn't Rock, Paper, Scissors," *The Diplomat*, October 7, 2020, https://thediplomat.com/2020/10/tanks-vs-drones-isnt-rock-paper -scissors/.
5. The Bureau of Investigative Journalism, "Drone War," https://www.thebureauinves- tigates.com/projects/drone-war.
6. Sebastien Roblin, "The Navy's Underwater Drone Is the Future of Submarine War- fare," The National Interest, November 6, 2020, https://nationalinterest.org/blog/reboot/ navys-underwater-drone-future-submarine-warfare-172169.
7. Department of Commerce Bureau of Industry and Security, 15 CFR Part 744 [Docket No. 201215-0347] RIN 0694-AI37, December 18, 2020, https://publicinspec- tion.federalregister.gov/2020-28031.pdf.
8. Joint Statement by Microsoft & AnyVision, AnyVision Audit, March 27, 2020, https://m12.vc/news/joint-statement-by-microsoft-anyvision-anyvision-audit/.
9. Alessandro Arduino, "Middle East Offers Singapore Some Lessons on Countering Rogue Drones," *Today Online*, July 20, 2020, https://www.todayonline.com/commentary/ middle-east-offers-singapore-some-lessons-countering-rogue-drones.

CHAPTER TWELVE

1. Qiao Liang and Wang Xiangsui, *Unrestricted Warfare* (Beijing: PLA Literature and Arts Publishing House, 1999).
2. Campaign to Stop Killer Robots official website, https://www.stopkillerrobots .org/about/.
3. Zachary Kallenborn, "A Partial Ban on Autonomous Weapons Would Make Everyone Safer," *Foreign Policy*, October 14, 2020, https://foreignpolicy .com/2020/10/14/ai-drones-swarms-killer-robots-partial-ban-on-autonomous -weapons-would-make-everyone-safer/.
4. Guillaume Lavallée, "Flying High: Military Prowess Helps Israel Become Global Force in Drone Industry," The Times of Israel, November 28, 2019, https://www. timesofisrael.com/flying-high-military-prowess-helps-israel-become-global-force-in- drone-industry/.
5. "U.S. Imposes CAATSA Sanctions on Turkey for S-400 Purchase," The Hindu, December 15, 2020, https://www.thehindu.com/news/international/us-imposes-caat- sa-sanctions-on-turkey-for-s-400-purchase/article33333317.ece, and "U.S. Sanctions Turkey Over Purchase of Russian S-400 Missile System," CNBC, December 14, 2020, https://www.cnbc.com/2020/12/14/us-sanctions-turkey-over-russian-s400.html.

6. Alessandro Arduino and Asif Shujia, "Russia's Scalable Soft Power: Leveraging Defense Diplomacy through the Transfer of S-400 Triumph," *Defense & Security Analysis* 37, no. 4 (November 7, 2021), https://www.tandfonline.com/doi/citedby/10.1080/14751798.2021.1995963?scroll=top&needAccess=true.

7. Grégoire Chamayou, *A Theory of the Drone* (New York: The New Press, 2015).

8. Rachel Cohen, "Design Gets Underway on DARPA's 'LongShot' Drone," *Airforce Magazine*, February 8, 2021, https://www.airforcemag.com/design-gets-underway-on-darpas-longshot-drone/.

9. Mark Episkopos, "How Russia's Okhotnik-B Stealth Drone and Su-57 Stealth Fighter Are Joining Forces," *The National Interest*, February 22, 2021, https://nationalinterest.org/blog/buzz/how-russia%E2%80%99s-okhotnik-b-stealth-drone-and-su-57-stealth-fighter-are-joining-forces-178639.

10. Carl Von Clausewitz, *On War*, trans. Michael Howard and Peter Paret (Princeton, NJ: Princeton University Press, 1976/1984).

CHAPTER THIRTEEN

1. Neal Stephenson, *Snow Crash* (New York: Bantam Books, 1992).

2. Frank Hoffman, "You May Not Be Interested in Cyber War, But It's Interested in You," *War on the Rocks*, August 7, 2013, https://warontherocks.com/2013/08/you-may-not-be-interested-in-cyber-war-but-its-interested-in-you/.

3. "Exclusive: China Captures Powerful US NSA Cyberspy Tool," *Global Times*, March 14, 2022, https://www.globaltimes.cn/page/202203/1254856.shtml.

4. Mark Galeotti, "The Cyber Menace," *The World Today* 68, no. 7 (2012): 32–35.

5. Shane Harris, *@War: The Rise of the Military-Internet Complex* (Boston: Mariner Books, 2015).

6. Report of the Working Group on the Use of Mercenaries as a Means of Violating Human Rights and Impeding the Exercise of the Right of Peoples to Self-Determination, "The Human Rights Impacts of Mercenaries, Mercenary-Related Actors and Private Military and Security Companies Engaging in Cyberactivities," A76/151, July 15, 2021, https://documents-dds-ny.un.org/doc/UNDOC/GEN/N21/192/08/PDF/N2119208.pdf?OpenElement.

7. Report of the Working Group, "The Human Rights Impacts of Mercenaries."

8. Charlie Osborne, "NotPetya an 'Act of War,' Cyber Insurance Firm Taken to Task for Refusing to Pay Out," January 11, 2019, https://www.zdnet.com/article/notpetya-an-act-of-war-cyber-insurance-firm-taken-to-task-for-refusing-to-pay-out/.

9. Securelist by Kaspersky, "Schroedinger's Pet(ya)," June 27, 2017, https://securelist.com/schroedingers-petya/78870/.

10. Alessandro Arduino, "From the Middle East to China, Pegasus Spyware Revelations Show the Spread of Hacking as a Service," *South China Morning Post*, July 31, 2021, https://www.scmp.com/week-asia/politics/article/3143251/middle-east-china-pegasus-spyware-revelations-show-spread.

11. Arduino "From the Middle East to China."

12. "EU Restrictive Measures Against Cyber-Attacks," 2019, https://eur-lex.europa.eu/legal-content/EN/TXT/HTML/?uri=LEGISSUM:4399784.

13. William Ralston, "The Untold Story of a Cyberattack, a Hospital and a Dying Woman," *Wired*, November 11, 2020, https://www.wired.co.uk/article/ransomware -hospital-death-germany.

14. UN, "Group of Governmental Experts on Advancing Responsible State Behaviour in Cyberspace in the Context of International Security (GGE)," in Michael Smith, *"The Sixth United Nations GGE and International Law in Cyberspace,"* Just Security, June 10, 2021, https://www.justsecurity.org/76864/the-sixth-united-nations-gge-and -international-law-in-cyberspace/.

15. Tim Maurer, *Cyber Mercenaries: The State, Hackers, and Power* (Cambridge: Cambridge University Press, 2018).

16. Charles W. Mahoney, "Corporate Hackers: Outsourcing US Cyber Capabilities," *Strategic Studies Quarterly* 15, no. 1 (Spring 2021): 61–89.

17. Josef Federman, "NSO Turns to US Supreme Court for Immunity in WhatsApp Suit," ABC News, April 14, 2022, https://abcnews.go.com/International/wireStory/nso-turns-us-supreme-court-immunity-whatsapp-suit-84015049.

18. Federman, "NSO Turns to US Supreme Court for Immunity in WhatsApp Suit."

19. Christopher Bing and Joel Schectman, "Mercenaries. Ex-NSA Operatives Reveal How They Helped Spy on Targets for the Arab Monarchy—Dissidents, Rival Leaders and Journalists," Reuters, January 30, 2019, https://www.reuters.com/investigates/special-report/usa-spying-raven/.

20. "International Humanitarian Law and Cyber Operations during Armed Conflicts: ICRC Position Paper Submitted to the Open-Ended Working Group on Developments in the Field of Information and Telecommunications in the Context of International Security and the Group of Governmental Experts on Advancing Responsible State Behaviour in Cyberspace in the Context of International Security," *International Review of the Red Cross* 102, no. 913 (2020): 481–92, doi:10.1017/S1816383120000478.

21. Bing and Schectman, "Mercenaries."

22. Michael Schmitt, *Tallinn Manual 2.0 on the International Law Applicable to Cyber Operations*, second edition (Cambridge: Cambridge University Press, 2017).

23. NATO Cooperative Cyber Defence Centre of Excellence (CCDCOE), https:// ccdcoe.org/research/tallinn-manual/.

24. Eric Talbot Jensen, "The Tallinn Manual 2.0: Highlights and Insights," *Georgetown Journal of International Law* 735 (March 13, 2017), BYU Law Research Paper No. 17-10, https://ssrn.com/abstract=2932110.

25. Jensen, "The Tallinn Manual 2.0."

26. Maurer, *Cyber Mercenaries*.

CHAPTER FOURTEEN

1. James Miller, *Swords for Hire: The Scottish Mercenary* (Edinburgh: Birlinn Limited, 2007).

2. Joshua Reno, *Military Waste: The Unexpected Consequences of Permanent War Readiness* (Oakland, CA: University of California Press, 2020).

3. Joshua Reno, interview by Alessandro Arduino, *Boots Off the Ground: Security in Transition in the Middle East and Beyond*, podcast episode 14, "Rethinking Military Waste," Middle East Institute National University of Singapore, May 13, 2021, https://

mei.nus.edu.sg/event/boots-off-the-ground-security-in-transition-in-the-middle-east-and-beyond-episode-14-rethinking-military-waste/.

4. Joshua Reno, interview by Alessandro Arduino.

5. Noah Coburn, *Under Contract: The Invisible Workers of America's Global War* (Redwood, CA: Stanford University Press, 2018).

6. Noah Coburn, interview by Alessandro Arduino, *Boots Off the Ground: Security in Transition in the Middle East and Beyond*, podcast episode 16, "The Invisible Nepali Labour of US War in Afghanistan," Middle East Institute National University of Singapore, August 5, 2021, https://mei.nus.edu.sg/event/boots-off-the-ground-security-in-transition-in-the-middle-east-and-beyond-episode-16-the-invisible-nepali-labour-of-us-war-in-afghanistan/.

7. Noah Coburn, interview by Alessandro Arduino.

8. Author's interview with Chinese PSC manager in Shanghai, for *China's Private Army* book (2017).

9. Author's interview with Chinese PSC manager in Beijing, January 10, 2020.

10. Adam Moore, *Empire's Labor: The Global Army That Supports U.S. Wars* (Ithaca, NY: Cornell University Press, 2019).

11. Adam Moore, interview by Alessandro Arduino, *Boots Off the Ground: Security in Transition in the Middle East and Beyond*, podcast episode 17, "America's Global Military-Labour Infrastructure," Middle East Institute, National University of Singapore, August 19, 2021, https://mei.nus.edu.sg/event/boots-off-the-ground-security-in-transition-in-the-middle-east-and-beyond-episode-16-the-invisible-nepali-labour-of-us-war-in-afghanistan/.

12. Adam Moore, interview by Alessandro Arduino.

13. *13 Hours*, 2016, https://www.imdb.com/title/tt4172430/.

14. Candace Rondeaux, interview by Alessandro Arduino, *Boots Off the Ground: Security in Transition in the Middle East and Beyond*, podcast episode 10, "Decoding Russian Private Military Security Companies," Middle East Institute, National University of Singapore, January 13, 2021, https://mei.nus.edu.sg/event/boots-off-the-ground-security-in-transition-in-the-middle-east-and-beyond-episode-10-decoding-russian-private-military-security-companies/.

15. *Granit*, 2021, https://www.imdb.com/title/tt17352384/.

16. Luke Harding and Jason Burke, "Russian Mercenaries behind Human Rights Abuses in CAR, Say UN Experts," *The Guardian*, March 30, 2021, https://www.theguardian.com/world/2021/mar/30/russian-mercenaries-accused-of-human-rights-abuses-in-car-un-group-experts-wagner-group-violence-election.

17. Neil Munshi, "In 'Touriste,' Heroic Russians Save the Central African Republic. The Truth Is Even Stranger," *Financial Times*, January 14, 2022.

18. U.S. Department of the Treasury, "Treasury Escalates Sanctions Against the Russian Government's Attempts to Influence U.S. Elections," April 15, 2021, https://home.treasury.gov/news/press-releases/jy0126.

19. Statista, "How Africa Voted in the UN Resolution Condemning the Russia-Ukraine War," March 2, 2022, https://www.statista.com/statistics/1294260/africa-voting-on-un-resolution-condemning-russia-invasion-of-ukraine/.

20. Patrick Frater, "Chinese Blockbuster 'Wolf Warrior 2' Impacts Careers, Especially Star Celina Jade," *Variety*, December 7, 2017, https://variety.com/2017/film/asia/celina-jade-wolf-warrior-2-china-wu-jing-1202631942/#!.

21. Patrick Brzeski, "'Wolf Warrior II' Star Frank Grillo on How China's $780M Blockbuster Was Made (Q&A)," *The Hollywood Reporter*, August 22, 2017, https://www.hollywoodreporter.com/news/general-news/wolf-warrior-2-star-frank-grillo-how-chinas-780m-blockbuster-was-made-1031929/.

22. Patrick J. McDonnell, "Haiti President's Assassination Exposes Shady World of Colombian Mercenaries," *Los Angeles Times*, July 18, 2021.

23. McDonnell, "Haiti President's Assassination Exposes Shady World of Colombian Mercenaries."

24. Dearbail Jordan and Simon Jack, "Ex-Nissan Boss Carlos Ghosn: How I Escaped Japan in a Box," *BBC News*, July 13, 2021, https://www.bbc.com/news/business-57760993.

25. BBC, "Carlos Ghosn: US Father and Son Extradited to Japan," *BBC News*, March 2, 2021, https://www.bbc.com/news/business-56248558.

26. Joshua Goodman, "Sources: US Investigating Ex-Green Beret for Venezuela Raid," AP News, May 7, 2020, https://apnews.com/article/miami-us-news-ap-top-news-venezuela-virus-outbreak-038e966350a9d7e8ec7a38341f0efeac.

27. Andrew Roth, "Russian Mercenaries Reportedly in Venezuela to Protect Maduro," *The Guardian*, January 25, 2019, https://www.theguardian.com/world/2019/jan/25/venezuela-maduro-russia-private-security-contractors.

28. Alessandro Arduino and Nodirbek Soliev, "Malhama Tactical—The Evolving Role of Jihadist Mercenaries in the Syrian Conflict," Insight 262, Middle East Institute, National University of Singapore, June 22, 2021, https://mei.nus.edu.sg/publication/insight-262-malhama-tactical-the-evolving-role-of-jihadist-mercenaries-in-the-syrian-conflict/.

29. "Head of Jihadist Training Outfit Malhama Tactical Reportedly Killed in Syria," BBC Monitoring, September 5, 2019.

30. Neil Hauer, "Chechens Fighting Chechens in Ukraine," *New Lines Magazine*, March 3, 2022, https://newlinesmag.com/reportage/chechens-fighting-chechens-in-ukraine/.

31. "Leader of Jihadi Military Contractor Malhama Tactical (MT) Killed in Syria," Freerepublic.com, August 20, 2019, available via Memri, https://www.freerepublic.com/focus/f-news/3773228/posts.

32. Joanna Paraszczuk's interview with Chechen Tactical, "Chechen Mujahid with Liwa Muhajireen wal Ansar," interviewer's personal blog *From Chechnya to Syria*, June 3, 2020, http://www.chechensinsyria.com/?p=26387.

33. Arduino and Soliev, "Malhama Tactical."

CHAPTER FIFTEEN

1. "Russia Drafts Up to 40,000 Syrians for Ukraine War: Monitor." The Syrian Observer, March 16, 2022, https://syrianobserver.com/news/74194/russia-drafts-up-to-40000-syrians-for-ukraine-war-monitor.html.

2. Molly Dunigan, interview by Alessandro Arduino, *Boots Off the Ground: Security in Transition in the Middle East and Beyond*, podcast episode 25, "Russian Mercenaries a Weak Link in Great-Power Competition," Middle East Institute, National University of Singapore, May 25, 2022, https://mei.nus.edu.sg/event/boots-off-the-ground-security-in-transition-in-the-middle-east-and-beyond-episode-25-russian-mercenaries-a-weak-link-in-great-power-competition/.

3. Alexandra Marksteiner et al., "The SIPRI Top 100 Arms-Producing and Military Services Companies," 2020, https://sipri.org/sites/default/files/2021-12/fs_2112_top_100_2020_1.pdf.

4. Molly Dunigan, interview by Alessandro Arduino.

5. Chinese president Xi Jinping's keynote speech at the opening ceremony of BFA annual conference 2022, BaoAo Forum, April 23, 2022, https://english.boaoforum.org/newsDetial.html?navId=3&itemId=0&permissionId=114&detialId=16834.

6. Neil Walker, "Border Management and Human Rights," Border Security Report, February 11, 2022, https://border-security-report.com/border-management-and-human-rights/.

7. UN Security Council (UNSC) Resolution 2396 (2017) imposes legal obligations on states to establish systems for the collection, processing, and analysis of large amounts of personal data to detect terrorist travel and identify terrorists.

Bibliography

Arduino, Alessandro. *China's Private Army: Protecting the New Silk Road.* Singapore: Palgrave, 2018.

Arduino, Alessandro. *The Footprint of Chinese Private Security Companies in Africa.* Working Paper No. 2020/35. China Africa Research Initiative, School of Advanced International Studies, Johns Hopkins University, Washington, DC, 2020. http:// www.sais-cari.org/publications.

Arduino, Alessandro, and Gong Xue. *Securing the Belt and Road Initiative: Risk Assessment, Private Security and Special Insurances Along the New Wave of Chinese Outbound Investments.* Singapore: Palgrave, 2018.

Asli, Aydıntaşbaş. *A New Gaza: Turkey's Border Policy in Northern Syria.* European Council on Foreign Relations, Policy Brief, 2020. https://ecfr.eu/publication/a_new_gaza_ turkeys_border_policy_in_northern_syria/.

Avant, Deborah. *The Market for Force: The Consequences of Privatizing Security.* London: Cambridge University Press, 2005.

Bellingcat. "The Data and the Dossier: Validating the 'Wagnergate' Operation." November 17, 2021. https://www.bellingcat.com/resources/2021/11/17/the-data -and-the-dossier-validating-the-wagnergate-operation/.

Bilban, Christoph, and Hanna Grininger. "Labelling Hybrid Warfare: The 'Gerasimov Doctrine.'" Think Tank Discourse, November 2, 2020. https://www.academia. edu/44424163/Labelling_Hybrid_Warfare_The_Gerasimov_Doctrine_in_Think _Tank_Discourse.

Bitzinger, Richard, and James Char, eds. *Reshaping the Chinese Military: The PLA's Roles and Missions in the Xi Jinping Era.* London: Routledge, 2019.

Brown, Kerry. "Chinese Storytelling in the Xi Jinping Era." *The Hague Journal of Diplomacy* 16, no. 2–3 (2020): 323–33. doi:10.1163/1871191X-BJA10054.

Chamayou, Grégoire. *A Theory of the Drone.* New York: The New Press, 2015.

Chappelle, W., T. Goodman, L. Reardon, and W. Thompson. "An Analysis of Post-Traumatic Stress Symptoms in United States Air Force Drone Operators." *J Anxiety Disord.* 28, no. 5 (June 2014). https://pubmed.ncbi.nlm.nih.gov/24907535/.

Chen Zheng. "China Debates the Non-Interference Principle." *The Chinese Journal of International Politics* 9, no. 3 (September 1, 2016): 349. DOI: 10.1093/cjip/pow010.

Chesterman, Simon, and Chia Lehnardt. *From Mercenaries to Market: The Rise and Regulation of Private Military Companies.* Oxford: Oxford University Press, 2007.

Chichava, Sergio, Shubo Li, and Michael G. Sambo. *The Blind Spot: International Mining in Angoche and Larde, Mozambique.* Working Paper No. 2019/28. China Africa Research Initiative, School of Advanced International Studies, Johns Hopkins University, Washington, DC, 2019. http://www. sais-cari.org/publications.

Coburn, Noah. *Under Contract: The Invisible Workers of America's Global War.* Redwood, CA: Stanford University Press, 2018.

Connable, Ben, and Molly Dunigan. "Russian Mercenaries in Great-Power Competition: Strategic Supermen or Weak Link?" The RAND Blog, March 9, 2021. https://www.rand.org/blog/2021/03/russian-mercenaries-in-great-power-competition-strategic.html.

Connable, Ben, et al. *Russia's Limit of Advance.* RAND Report, May 27, 2022. https://www.rand.org/pubs/research_reports/RR2563.html.

Cordesman, Anthony H., and Grace Hwang. *"China's View of Military-Civil Fusion (MCF)."*

Chinese Military Dynamics and Evolving Strategy: Graphic Net Assessment. Center for Strategic and International Studies (CSIS), 2021. http://www.jstor.org/stable/resrep36977.5.

Cubukcu, Suat. "The Rise of Paramilitary Groups in Turkey." *Small Wars Journal,* March 3, 2018. https://smallwarsjournal.com/jrnl/art/rise-paramilitary-groups-turkey.

Cui Shouju and Zhang Zhen. "海外华侨华人社团与一带一路安保体系建构" (Overseas Chinese Communities and the Construction of the Belt and Road Security System). *Journal of International Security Studies* 3 (May 2018). https://kns.cnki.net/kcms/detail/detail.aspx?dbcode=CJFD&dbname=CJFDLAST2018&filename=GGXB201803008&v=yKssbcqpPfHW5yk4AcqWi39VzNms2ZdKOkqn-P3OsAFqqnE0%25mmd2Fc9nhOcCUzVltiyAO.

De Haas, M., E. Gaberščik, T. Jenkins, and A. Kumar. "Russia's Military Action in Syria Driven by Military Reforms." *The Journal of Slavic Military Studies* 33, no. 2 (2020): 292–99. DOI: 10.1080/13518046.2020.1756705.

Dorsey, James. "Ignoring the Middle East at One's Peril: Turkey Plays Games in NATO." May 15, 2022. https://jamesmdorsey.substack.com/p/ignoring-the-middle-east-at-ones?.

Duchâtel, Mathieu, Cristina Garafola, Marc Julienne, Jérôme Doyon, and Alexandre Sheldon-Duplaix. *Xi's Army: Reform and Loyalty in the PLA.* European Council on Foreign Relations, 2016.

Duchâtel, Mathieu, and Jonas Parello-Plesner. *China's Strong Arm Protecting Citizens and Assets Abroad.* London: Routledge, 2015.

Dugin, Alexandr. *The Foundations of Geopolitics: The Geopolitical Future of Russia.* Moscow, Arktogeja, 1999.

Erickson, Edward, and Uyar Mesut. *A Military History of the Ottomans: From Osman to Atatürk.* Santa Barbara, CA: Praeger Security International, 2009.

Freedman, Robert. "Russian Policy toward the Middle East: The Yeltsin Legacy and the Putin Challenge." *Middle East Journal. Middle East Institute* 55, no. 1 (Winter 2001): 58–90.

Fulton, Jonathan. *Routledge Handbook on China–Middle East Relations*. New York: Routledge, 2021.

Ghiselli, Andrea. *Protecting China's Interests Overseas*. Oxford: Oxford University Press, 2021.

Government of Canada. *Final Report: Review of Export Permits to Turkey*. https://www.international.gc.ca/trade-commerce/controls-controles/reports-rapports/exp-permits-turkey-licences-turquie.aspx?lang=eng.

Harris, Shane. *@War: The Rise of the Military-Internet Complex*. Boston: Mariner Books, 2015.

Heberer, Thomas. "China in 2014: Creating a New Power and Security Architecture in Domestic and Foreign Policies." *Asian Survey* 55, no. 1 (2015): 82–102. https://doi.org/10.1525/as.2015.55.1.82.

Inkster, Nigel. *China's Cyber Power*. London: IISS Adelphi Book by Routledge, 2016.

Jensen, Eric Talbot. "The Tallinn Manual 2.0: Highlights and Insights." *Georgetown Journal of International Law* 735 (March 13, 2017). BYU Law Research Paper No. 17-10. https://ssrn.com/abstract=2932110.

Jones, Seth. *Three Dangerous Men: Russia, China, Iran, and the Rise of Irregular Warfare*. New York: W. W. Norton Company, 2021.

Kelty, Ryan, and Alex Bierman. "Ambivalence on the Front Lines: Perceptions of Contractors in Iraq and Afghanistan." *Armed Forces & Society* 39, no. 1 (2013): 5–27.

Lanigan, Kevin. "US Military Court-Martialling Civilian Contractor Ali While DOJ Slumbers." *Jurist*, May 19, 2008. https://www.jurist.org/commentary/2008/05/us-military-to-court-martial-ali-while.

Le Huérou, Anne, and Elisabeth Sieca-Kozlowski. "A 'Chechen Syndrome'? Russian Veterans of the Chechen War and the Transposition of War Violence to Society." In *War Veterans in Postwar Situations: Chechnya, Serbia, Turkey, Peru, and Côte d'Ivoire*, edited by Nathalie Duclos. New York: Palgrave Macmillan, 2012.

Lebovich, Andrew. *After Barkhane: What France's Military Drawdown Means for the Sahel*. European Council on Foreign Relations, July 2, 2021. https://ecfr.eu/article/after-barkhane-what-frances-military-drawdown-means-for-the-sahel/.

Li Weihai. 中国保安企业开展海外业务 Zhongguo baoan qiye kaizhan haiwai yewu de falu yu jianguan yanjiu [Legal and Regulatory Research on Chinese Security Enterprises' Overseas Business]. Beijing: Law Press China, 2015.

Li Xiuna. "我国私营安全公司域外服务的法律困境及其突破" (The Legal Dilemma and Its Breakthrough of Chinese Private Security Companies' Overseas Service). *Contemporary Law*, no. 1 (2021). https://kns.cnki.net/kcms/detail/detail.aspx?dbcode=CJFD&dbname=CJFDLAST2021&filename=DDFX202101013&v=VPgWrL1W4vViez3mjwBrx4mehYup8j2lqr-JZKS26vT5h%25mmd2BuOURzzfI%25mmd2BNjw1yUaoeA.

Liu Yanfeng and Xing Ruili. "私人安保公司：东南亚海上安全治理的新主体" (Private Security Companies: New Actors in Maritime Security Governance in Southeast Asia). *Journal of International Security Studies* 3 (May 2018). https://kns.cnki.net/kcms/detail/detail.aspx?dbcode=CJFD&filename=GGXB201803009&dbname=CJFDLAST2018&uid=WEEvRECwSlJHSldSdmVqM1BLVW9SOER-

qaTdERXl3bHh6WWpSREhxOHRLOD0%3D%249A4hF_YAuvQ5obgVA-
qNKPCYcEjKensW4IQMovwHtwkF4VYPoHbKxJw!!.

Liu Zhongqi, Sheng Ziming, and Liang Xiubo. "一带一路背景下我国民营安保企业
走出去研究" (A Study on the Go Out of Chinese Security Companies in Belt
and Road). *Journal of Fujian Police College* 166, no. 6 (2018). https://kns.cnki.
net/kcms/detail/detail.aspx?dbcode=CJFD&dbname=CJFDLAST2019&file-
name=FJGA201806005&v=0xzPgf1AgXkMgTFZrsXwVRFmGmlP79liusQBg-
ZHAGWQIesecZawueLsC6hXcI0Ov.

Mahoney, Charles. "Corporate Hackers: Outsourcing US Cyber Capabilities." *Strategic
Studies Quarterly* 15, no. 2 (Spring 2021): 61–89.

Marten, Kimberly. "Russia's Use of Semi-State Security Forces: The Case of the
Wagner Group." *Post-Soviet Affairs* 35, no. 3 (February 2019): 181–204. DOI:
10.1080/1060586X.2019.1591142.

Maurer, Tim. *Cyber Mercenaries: The State, Hackers, and Power.* Cambridge: Cambridge
University Press, 2018.

McFate, Sean. *The Modern Mercenary: Private Armies and What They Mean for World Order.*
Oxford: Oxford University Press, 2014.

McFate, Sean. *The New Rules of War: Victory in the Age of Durable Disorder.* New York:
William Morrow, 2019.

Miller, James. *Swords for Hire: The Scottish Mercenary.* Edinburgh: Birlinn Limited, 2007.

Moore, Adam. *Empire's Labor: The Global Army That Supports U.S. Wars.* Ithaca, NY: Cornell University Press, 2019.

Mulvenon, James, and Zhang Chenny. "Targeting Defense Technologies." In *China's
Quest for Foreign Technology Beyond Espionage*, edited by William C. Hannas and
Didi Kirsten Tatlow. New York: Routledge, 2020.

Østensen, Åse Gilje, and Tor Bukkvoll. "Private Military Companies—Russian Great
Power Politics on the Cheap?" *Small Wars & Insurgencies* 33, nos. 1–2 (2021):
130–51. DOI:10.1080/09592318.2021.1984709.

Pei Yan and Wang Wenzhu. "一带一路倡议下中国保安服务业开展海外利益保护的思
路与途径" (Thoughts and Paths for Chinese Private Security Companies' Participation in Overseas Interests Protection in Belt and Road Initiative). *Journal of People's
Public Security University of China* (Social Sciences Edition), no. 2 (2020). https://kns.
cnki.net/kcms/detail/detail.aspx?dbcode=CJFD&dbname=CJFDLAST2020&-
filename=GADX202002016&v=tlhXMR3qfZqU%25mmd2FlP94x3YWnriV6U-
pXB2jcSvenET2giHoDCK8qObA%25mmd2BAr6aLs87byL.

Pelton, R. Y. *Licensed to Kill: Hired Guns in the War on Terror.* New York: Crown, 2006.

Peng Wang and Xia Ya. "Bureaucratic Slack in China: The Anti-Corruption Campaign
and the Decline of Patronage Networks in Developing Local Economies." *The
China Quarterly* 243 (September 2020): 611–34.

Percy, Sarah. *Mercenaries. The History of a Norm in International Relations.* Oxford: Oxford
University Press, 2017.

Qiao Liang and Wang Xiangsui. *Unrestricted Warfare.* Beijing: PLA Literature and Arts
Publishing House, 1999.

Reno, Joshua. *Military Waste: The Unexpected Consequences of Permanent War Readiness.* Oakland, CA: University of California Press, 2020.

Rondeaux, Candace. "Decoding the Wagner Group: Analyzing the Role of Private Military Security Contractors in Russian Proxy Warfare." New America/Arizona State University Future of War Project, 2019. https://www.newamerica.org/international-security/reports/decoding-wagner-group-analyzing-role-private-military-security-contractors-russian-proxy-warfare/.

Rumer, Eugene. "The Primakov (Not Gerasimov) Doctrine in Action." Carnegie, June 5, 2019. https://carnegieendowment.org/2019/06/05/primakov-not-gerasimov-doctrine-in-action-pub-79254.

Savage, Patrick. "The Russian National Guard: An Asset for Putin at Home and Abroad." American Security Project, 2017.

Scahill, Jeremy. *Blackwater, The Rise of the World's Most Powerful Mercenary Army.* New York: Nation Books, 2007.

Schmitt, Michael. *Tallinn Manual 2.0 on the International Law Applicable to Cyber Operations.* Second edition. Cambridge: Cambridge University Press, 2017.

Schwarck, Edward. "Intelligence and Informatization: The Rise of the Ministry of Public Security in Intelligence Work in China." *The China Journal,* no. 80 (March 28, 2018). 1324-9347/2018/8001-0001.

Shambaugh, David. "The Illusion of Chinese Power." *The National Interest,* no. 132 (2014): 39–48.

Shamiev, Kirill. *Understanding Senior Leadership Dynamics within the Russian Military.* Center for Strategic and International Studies (CSIS), July 20, 2021. https://www.csis.org/analysis/understanding-senior-leadership-dynamics-within-russian-military.

Singer, P. W. *Corporate Warriors: The Rise of the Private Military Industry.* Ithaca, NY: Cornell University Press, 2003.

Spearin, Christopher. "Private, Armed and Humanitarian? States, NGOs, International Private Security Companies and Shifting Humanitarianism." *Security Dialogue* 39, no. 4 (2008): 363–82. Classical Library Vol. III. Harvard University Press.

Stein, Aaron. "Low-Tech High-Reward: The Houthi Drone Attack." *Foreign Policy Research Institute,* January 11, 2019. https://www.fpri.org/article/2019/01/low-tech-high-reward-the-houthi-drone-attack/.

Stephenson, Svetlana. "It Takes Two to Tango: The State and Organized Crime in Russia." *Current Sociology* 65, no. 3 (May 2017): 411–26. https://doi.org/10.1177/0011392116681384.

Sukhankin, Sergey. *From "Volunteers" to Quasi-PMCs: Retracing the Footprints of Russian Irregulars in the Yugoslav Wars and Post-Soviet Conflicts.* Global Research & Analysis. Jamestown Foundation, June 25, 2019. https://jamestown.org/program/from-volunteers-to-quasi-pmcs-retracing-the-footprints-of-russian-irregulars-in-the-yugoslav-wars-and-post-soviet-conflicts/.

Sun, Degang, and Yahia H. Zoubir. "Securing China's 'Latent Power': The Dragon's Anchorage in Djibouti." *Journal of Contemporary China* 30, no. 130 (2021): 677–92. DOI: 10.1080/10670564.2020.1852734.

Taspinar, Ömer. *Turkey's Middle East Policies: Between Neo-Ottomanism and Kemalism.* Carnegie Endowment for International Peace, 2008.

United Nations. "Group of Governmental Experts on Advancing Responsible State Behaviour in Cyberspace in the Context of International Security." In Michael Smith, "The Sixth United Nations GGE and International Law in Cyberspace." *Just Security.* June 10, 2021. https://www.justsecurity.org/76864/the-sixth-united-nations-gge-and-international-law-in-cyberspace/.

Urban, William. *Medieval Mercenaries: The Business of War.* London: Green Hill Book, 2005.

U.S. Government Accountability Office. "Afghanistan Reconstruction: GAO Work Since 2002 Shows Systemic Internal Control Weaknesses That Increased the Risk of Waste, Fraud, and Abuse." January 27, 2021. https://www.gao.gov/products/gao-21-32r.

Wang Panting. 中国海外公民安全保护的私营安保模式 (The Private Security Model of Chinese Overseas Citizens' Security Protection). Master's thesis, China Foreign Affairs University, June 2018.

Wither, James K. "Making Sense of Hybrid Warfare." *Connections* 15, no. 2 (2016): 73–87.

Yan Su. "国际法视野下的私营军事安保公司：模式、争论及中国应对" (Private Military and Security Companies from the Perspective of International Law: Patterns, Debates, and China's Measures). *Journal of International Law,* no. 1 (2021). https://kns.cnki.net/kcms/detail/detail.aspx?dbcode=CJFD&dbname=C-JFDLAST2020&filename=GJFX202001006&v=sRh1tlBIpenhIyzTlCkI%25m-md2FRrNGbdzgwm5%25mmd2B9ncuZo6eLDDjGcq%25mmd2B1O%25mmd-2Fb8mjtWekdLh7.

Yanarocak, Hay Eytan Cohen, and Spyer Jonathan. "Turkish Militias and Proxies." January 27, 2021. https://jiss.org.il/en/yanarocak-spyer-turkish-militias-and-proxies/.

Yau, Niva, and Dirk Van Der Kley. "The Growth, Adaptation and Limitations of Chinese Private Security Companies in Central Asia." Oxus Society for Central Asian Affairs, October 2020. https://oxussociety.org/wp-content/uploads/2020/10/the-growth-adaptation-and-limitations-of-chinese-private-security-companies-in-central-asia.pdf.

Yu, Hong. "Motivation behind China's 'One Belt, One Road' Initiatives and Establishment of the Asian Infrastructure Investment Bank." *Journal of Contemporary China* 26, no. 105 (2016): 353–68. DOI: 10.1080/10670564.2016.1245894.

Yudina, Natalia, and Alexander Verkhovsky. "Russian Nationalist Veterans of the Donbas War." *Nationalities Papers; Abingdon* 47, no. 5 (September 2019): 734–49. DOI:10.1017/nps.2018.63.

Zevelev, Igor. *Russian National Identity and Foreign Policy.* Center for Strategic and International Studies (CSIS), 2016.